WORK AND PLAY

WORK AND PLAY

WORK AND PLAY

Ideas and experience of working life
before and after industrialization

Alasdair Clayre

Weidenfeld and Nicolson
London

© 1974 Alasdair Clayre

Weidenfeld and Nicolson
11 St John's Hill, London SW11

ISBN 0 297 767585
Printed by Willmer Brothers Limited
Birkenhead

for Davina Lloyd

It is work alone that ennobles man; all work, no matter what its nature

Carlyle

Along the country roads alas but waggoners few are seen
The world is topsy-turvey turned and all things go by steam
And all the past is passed away like to a moving dream

Ballad

Coming out of the building trade I felt like a bird in a cage what's been used to wild life, and it wants some sticking, the machinery

Motor assembly worker, Cowley

Contents

Acknowledgements

Certain people have been kind enough to read through part or all of this book: Asa Briggs, Christopher Harvie, James Curran, Maurice Freedman, John H. Goldthorpe, Annabel Jones, A. L. Lloyd, Max Hartwell, Kate Mortimer, Angus MacIntyre, Peter Matthias, John Plamenatz, Phillip Rieff, Leslie Russon, Keith Thomas, Dorothy Thompson and E. P. Thompson. The book draws on a number of specialist disciplines; and the generous suggestions of people working within each have been of great value.

For earlier introductions to the history of ideas, to traditional songs and to the use of actuality tape-recordings I am grateful to Isaiah Berlin and Stuart Hampshire; to Isla Cameron, Peggy Seeger, Ewan MacColl and Maurice Bowra; and to Charles Parker and David Kennard. The BBC, by commissioning a number of programmes based on actuality tape recordings, greatly helped the understanding of the subject of this book. The part of the study done in the London Docks benefitted from generosity on the part of Jacob Rothschild. Finally, the entire book was assisted by a non-academic prize fellowship of All Souls College, Oxford, to whose Warden and Fellows I am very grateful.

I should also like to thank Mrs V. Iliffe for typing the book.

Acknowledgements

Certain people have been kind enough to read through part or all
of the book: Asa Briggs, Christopher Harvie, James Curran,
Maurice Freedman, John H. Goldthorpe, Aubdul Jones, A.L.
Lloyd, Max Hartwell, Karl Miller, Angus MacIntyre, Peter
Marnon, John Plamenatz, Philip Rieff, Leslie Russon, Keith
Thomas, Dorothy Thompson and E.P. Thompson. The book
draws on a number of specialist disciplines, and the general
suggestions of people working within each have been of great
value.

For earlier introductions to the history of ideas, to medieval
history and to the use of actuality tape-recordings I am grateful to
Enish Heffer and Stuart Hampshire; to Iain Cameron, Peggy
Seeger, Ewan MacColl and Maurice Bowra; and to Charles
Parker and David Kennard. The BBC, by commissioning a
number of programmes based on actuality tape-recordings,
greatly helped the understanding of the subject of this book. The
experience on the study done in the London Docks benefited from
experience on the part of Jacob Rothschild. Finally, the entire
book was assisted by a non-academic prize fellowship of All Souls
College, Oxford, to whose Warden and Fellows I am very
grateful.

I should also like to thank Mrs V. Hine for typing the book.

Introduction

A tradition has been developing for two hundred years: that work, for every one, is potentially of the greatest significance, and should be the central interest of every life. Simone Weil, for example, wrote shortly before her death in 1943:

> Our age has its own particular mission, or vocation – the creation of a civilization founded upon the spiritual nature of work. The thoughts relating to a presentiment of this vocation, and which are scattered about in Rousseau, George Sand, Tolstoy, Proudhon and Marx, in papal encyclicals and elsewhere, are the only original thoughts of our time, the only ones we haven't borrowed from the Greeks.[1]

Despairing of the possibility of such work being created for any but a small minority, Herbert Marcuse has written from California of the 'hell of the affluent society', and has urged people to withdraw from a cycle of ever-increasing production and obedient consumption, to rediscover the primacy of sex, freedom and the enjoyment of nature.[2] Not work but play is the area where significance and happiness are to be found.

Between these two philosophies, the compromise commonly found in our society is an attitude sometimes said to be a product of industrialization – the idea that work has got to be done, but is of interest only insofar as it provides money for spending outside work. These three philosophies – and the part they have played in the ideas of writers and the experience of working people – will be the central themes of this book.

Anyone interested in the possibility of improving the work that

goes on in modern mass production – in trying to bring about jobs
that are more interesting, less repetitive, less noisy, less dangerous,
and that leave people less tired and restricted at the end of the
day – is likely to find at least an ancestry, and often a body of still
applicable ideas, in the thought of writers such as Marx, Ruskin
or Morris, who attacked the deprivations of industrial labour in
their own time. Their ideas, which played so great a part in the
revolutionary and reforming politics of fifty and a hundred years
ago – in the formation of communism on the one hand and of the
Labour Party or the ideas of Gandhi on the other – have been
widely revived in the second half of the twentieth century by both
radicals and conservatives; and many contemporary critiques of
industrial labour have begun to draw again in particular on the
ideas of Marx, especially the early Marx, for their terminology
and their central concepts.

Yet the picture of human nature implied in these writers of the
nineteenth century does not seem quite to fit with what people
working in factories tend to say about themselves.

Leisure seems to be of far greater significance to many people
in the accounts they give of their work than their actual occupation; not necessarily to craftsmen and to people in small workshops, but to many in mass production. Furthermore, even at
work, social life is frequently much more prominent in people's
descriptions of what goes on than the experience of work itself.
Work and a concern for the quality of work, far from being the
essential element and centre of all life, as in Carlyle, Marx,
Ruskin or Morris, frequently seems subordinated to the simple
earning of money; leisure, which to the nineteenth-century
theorists was an area for further creative activity, is to many
people a space for freedom, enjoyment and playing with their
children.

It is of course possible to explain this – as some people do – by
saying that the economic system has 'distorted' the original nature
of contemporary working people into a forgetfulness of the essential role that work should play in their lives; by saying that they
are 'alienated' or 'self-estranged' and – victims of 'false consciousness' – do not even know it.

For a number of reasons this book looks beyond such explanations and examines the tradition of philosophical ideas about industrialization more carefully, to see, first, when it arose and from what origins; then, whether the gap that seems to exist today between the ideas of critics of industrialization and those of many people working with their hands (a gap which could still be weakening the chances of some possible improvements in working life) could be traced to the nineteenth century, or even further back still.

This study, then, contrasts the thought of certain writers from the eighteenth and nineteenth centuries, especially those who emphasized the central significance of work in human life, with the recorded words – and in some cases the songs – of their contemporaries, and ours, who have worked with their hands. Certain modern theories about work, leisure and happiness are then examined in the light of these experiences, and provisional conclusions drawn – conclusions which another book will test in greater detail in the modern world.

Part I

Theories of work, leisure and happiness

I

Rousseau

'Men move mountains, break rocks, scoop out lakes, put up vast buildings',[1] says Rouseau in the *Discourse on the Origins of Inequality Among Men*; and yet, with all this, only increase their miseries out of a mad pride.

Men 'fell' from a golden age when they realized that they could get advantage from the work of others[2]. Out of property came the enslavement of one man by another, and the perpetual discontnet of competition.[3] The development of civilization led men to hate each other; private interests conflicted with those of society, and each man found profit in the misfortune of others.

> Perhaps there is . . . not one ship at sea whose wreck would not be good news for some trader . . . not one people that does not rejoice at the disasters of its neighbours. . . .[4]

Men long for public calamities; they weep at plentiful harvests; they make their fortune out of great fires. The appearance of benevolence is only on the surface of society: men are 'forced mutually to caress and destroy each other'. And the idea that men gain by serving each other is itself superficial; each man gains more by harming others. In society criminal ways work best.

By contrast, *l'homme sauvage* does not scheme against his neighbours and would gain nothing from any vice. Rousseau imagined that he lives in solitude, does not recognize the faces of his fellows, and so does not involve his pride in conflicts with them. If two primitive men fight over food, the loser moves on to another place and forgets.

But civilized men are instatiable. First they must have what is necessary, then what is unnecessary, then luxuries, then immense riches, then subjects, then slaves, and as their desires lose touch with nature they grow in force; men become more equipped with means of satisfying them, the more unnatural their wishes grow. In secret every civilized man always wants the world at the expense of others.

Civilized men live in crowds, unhealthily, in great cities; their wars and their maladministration destroy them in vast numbers. They produce fewer children as they become more civilized. Unhealthy trades – mining, metal- and mineral-work – multiply, shortening men's lives; dangerous trades – those of tin-workers, tilers, carpenters, masons, quarrymen – kill men. Luxury degrades crowds of men into valets, and ruins the peasant and the citizen.

The useless arts attract higher prices to their products because they are sold to the rich; agricultural prices remain at the subsistence level of the poor. Therefore men neglect the useful arts and flock to cities, leaving the farms where they were taxed to support luxury. Peasants, lost in the cities, end broken on the wheel or lying on a dungheap. Thus great states sap their inner strength and become victims of their poorer neighbours, who, invading and despoiling them, are ruined in their turn.

Eight years after the *Discourse* Rousseau published two books: *Du Contrat Social* (1762), which concerns the political conditions that would allow men to associate while remaining free; and *Émile, ou De l'Education*, which shows how an individual boy can be brought up freely and naturally and how he should choose his work.

Before the coming of industrialization *Émile* provides a study of different forms of manual work, with distinctions between the crafts and trades in terms of how they affect the men who practise them; it contains – again before industrialization – an account of trades that brutalize by their monotony, by the restricted nature of the movements they demand, by their routine, and by the subjection of those who practise them to the commands of others; and – perhaps for the first time in modern Europe – it puts forward craftsmanship as the best of all ways of life. It is thus at the head of the long line of critical work that passes through Ruskin and Morris to our modern world. The praise of craftsman-like labour, the idea that demand should be limited to what is 'natural' and 'needed', and the belief that civilization and urban life entail some form of 'self-estrangement' can all be traced back to Rousseau. These central and recurrent ideas in the critical theory of industrial society are already present before industrialization itself can properly be said to have begun in the country where they were first enunciated.

In the *Discourse on Inequality*, work has no redemptive role. The primitive man, like 'man in the state of nature', works as little as possible. He is idle and happy, and Rousseau contrasts his condition with that of the busy, self-divided minister in a modern state, whose work and whose frantic life would shock the savage.

But in *Émile* Rousseau takes a different position; Émile must not be 'aussi fainéant qu'un sauvage' Here Rousseau suggests that work is a duty in society, and not for the poor alone, but for everybody.[5]

> Outside society, man lives alone and, owing nothing to anyone, has the right to live as he likes; but in society, where he inevitably lives at the expense of others, he owes them in work the price of his maintenance. . . . Work is therefore an indispensible duty for man in society.

In a boy brought up naturally there is a spontaneous desire to work, which will not have been stifled but encouraged by his freedom to wander round the fields and watch grown men working. Rousseau argues that work and creativity are natural in man, especially in childhood, when they are associated with the imitation of adults.

> Living in the country the child will have gained some idea of country work. It is characteristic of every age, and especially of his own, to want to create, to imitate, to produce, to give signs of power and activity. As soon as he has once or twice watched

a garden being dug ... he will want to be a gardener in his turn.[6]

The boy whose education Rousseau deals with has been kept from the schoolroom, and taught by speech and action rather than by books. He has already learnt, in an exchange with the gardener whose plants he has unwittingly destroyed, that 'everyone should respect other people's work, so that his own may be safe'.[7] He has also learnt to rank occupations in a hierarchy of value: a hierarchy very different from that with which the world judges:

> In his eyes, iron is bound to have a greater value than gold, and glass than diamond. In the same way he honours a shoemaker or a mason much more than a l'Empereur, a Le Blanc or any of the Jewellers of Europe.[8]

Substances are of value insofar as they are useful to men, and satisfy needs that spring from nature rather than from the suggestions of fashion. And the trades and occupations are ranked in order of their independence of other trades; again in contrast to the world's judgement. Men tend to rank the finisher of a product – a jeweller or painter of porcelain – higher than the prime producer; Rousseau inverts the world's order in the name of elementary needs as the sole criteria of true value.

Again, in selecting work for Émile, Rousseau considers trades from the point of view of their effect on the life of the workman, not from that of their status in the world, nor from that of their likely profitability. He has already said elsewhere that *L'homme qui médite est un monstre*, and he has explicitly rejected the writing of books as a valuable activity: 'I would rather he were a shoemaker than a poet; I would prefer him to pave the main roads than to paint porcelain flowers.'[9] Men think too much; what Émile needs is 'a trade, a real trade, a purely mechanical skill where the hands work more than the head, and which does not lead to a fortune, but on which one can manage to live.'[10]

Rousseau chooses craftsmanship not because of its social standing or its pay, but because of its closeness to the independence of nature: because of its lack of excessive mental activity, and because the conditions in which it was exercised in France seemed to him the freest open to anyone.[11]

The trade that of all possible ones Rousseau himself would prefer for the boy is that of carpenter. It is independent, it allows a man to work indoors, and there is some scope for skill in it. But Rousseau says the choice of the boy's tutor would not be given special prominence; he would, above all, consult the boy's own inclination.

He would not forbid any heavy work, or even dangerous work if the boy chose it. He is, however, severely critical of trades involving monotony :

> I would not in fact like those stupid occupations whose work-men, without industry and almost automata, exercise their hands in one task alone. Weavers, stocking-makers, stone-cutters; what is the use of employing a man of intelligence in these trades? It is one machine working another.[12]

Monotony did not need the invention of powered machinery to produce its effects. Furthermore, it is not only modern factories that have created rigid disciplines and stupefying routine :

> There are two kinds of men whose bodies are continually exer-cised and who certainly think equally little about cultivating their minds : peasants, and primitive men. The former are dull, coarse and clumsy; the latter, noted for their sense, are still more remarkable for the subtlety of their minds. Generally there is nothing clumsier than a peasant, nothing finer than a primitive man. What is the source of this difference? It is because the peasant, always doing what he is told to do or what he has seen his father do or what he has done himself since his youth, never acts except by routine, and in his almost automatic life, ceaselessly busy at the same tasks, habit and obedience take for him the place of reason.[13]

Rousseau sees in the primitive man, as in the child, a spontaneity which civilized life, the life of the rich world, destroys. Freud also noted how the intelligence of children contrasted with the stupid-ity of most adults, and asked how this change came about.

Rousseau's own answers – compulsion, routine, the loss of simplicity and of the 'self' in the complexity of dividing desires – could
all equally apply to modern industrial work – and to the schooling that is in many respects a preparation for it.

> A child of ten or twelve: I see him bubbling with life,
> animated, without gnawing care, completely in his present
> existence, and enjoying a fullness of life that seems to want to
> burst out beyond him. The clock strikes. What a transforma-
> tion! On the instant his eye goes dull, his gaiety disappears,
> goodbye, to joy, goodbye fantastic games! A severe and irritable
> man takes him by the hand, says to him gravely 'Come along
> then, sir' and leads him away.[14]

The disciplines of modern factory and office life were already
present in the schooling of children before industrialization. By
contrast Émile, brought up 'naturally', will have no such discipline to fear:

> He does not know what routine, custom and habit are; what he
> did yesterday has no influence on what he does today; he never
> follows a formula, never yields to authority and example.[15]

Rousseau thus prepares in advance a criticism of factory discipline. He also prefigures the hatred of machinery: 'I do not want
us to go into a laboratory of experimental physics. I don't like all
that apparatus of instruments and machines. The scientific
atmosphere kills science.'[16]

An industrial world, in his theory, can only be a gigantic superfluity, corrupting in its products and destructive in its productive
methods. His attitude to large towns and to their standardization
is one of loathing: 'Men are not made to be piled up in ant heaps,
but spread out over the earth which they cultivate. The more they
are together the more they become corrupt.'[17]

All the main aspects of industrial society thus stood condemned
by the most eloquent philosopher of the eighteenth century before
machines had begun thoroughly to transform his own world. And
any instrumental justification of industrialization in terms of its
products would have been attacked by Rousseau unhesitatingly.

To take on a routine job for the sake of money – or to industrialize an agricultural society for the sake of greater riches – would be the greatest of crimes. The very expansion of desires promoted by industry, through advertising and the cultivation of consumption, was the prime target of Rousseau's attack.

When Rousseau writes in a famous passage : 'Man is born free, and everywhere he is in chains', his notion of freedom means, for each man, independence of all others for the satisfaction of his wishes; and this entails complete independence of human command and of inner craving and desire – not only of the command of others from above, but of the act of commanding others, and of all desires for what is outside a man's immediate power.

For all these are equally forms of slavery. The man who commands depends on another man for the satisfaction of his wishes, and is as enslaved as his servant. True freedom means the reduction of our wishes to the point where we can gratify them ourselves with the minimum of dependence on other people; it is therefore a freeing from the inner tyranny of 'artificially stimulated' civilized desires, as much as from the outer bonds of obedience to other men.

> There are two sorts of dependence; on things and nature and on men and society. Dependence on things does not harm liberty or engender vices; dependence on men, being disordered, does engender them, and it is through this that master and slave deprave each other mutually. . . . Keep the child in dependence on things alone. Give nothing to his desires because he asks for it, but only because he needs it. . . . It is our passions that make us weak because to gratify them, it would need more force than nature gave us. So, diminish desires.[18]

Rousseau offers an alternative to the division of labour and of men, and a picture of integrated character based on restrained desires and simple work, that still survives as an ideal today among many people who are sceptical of the values of further industrialization and ever-expanding consumption. He would bring up Émile to 'work like a peasant and think like a philosopher'. He will be *'un sauvage fait pour habiter les villes'*, 'a primitive man made for living in cities' – free in the centre of a corrupt society.

Although Rouseeau's interest in primitive life was never more than one element in his thought, more populat with his followers than one element in his thought, more popular with his followers modern European philosophy the entire value of civilization. He suggests the idea that civilized development must be either controlled, reversed or personally escaped. This is an idea that is being vigorously revived today at our present stage of industrialization. But it was not, in its origins, a response to industrialization: Rousseau propounded it before powered machinery had seriously begun to transform the world he knew.

2

Schiller

Goethe, looking back to his youth in his *Dichtung und Wahrheit* (4 vols, 1811–33), writes of one of his young friends that 'Émile was his cornerstone and foundation', and that 'the book exercised, at the time a general effect over the entire cultivated world'.[1] One of its effects was to enhance – in the Germany of Goethe's generation – the status of everything natural and organic; and to contribute to the idea that the 'artificial' and the 'mechanical' were odious.

Rousseau had complained in his First Discourse that humanity had become fragmented into men of various trades, none of them any longer citizens. Among his successors in late eighteenth-century Germany the criticism of fragmentation developed into a complaint against all specialization as such, for its effect not so much on the social duties of citizenship, as on the wholeness of human nature. What is whole is organic. What is specialized is fragmented and mechanistic.[2]

This was the world in which Schiller grew up, and a quotation from Rousseau appeared in the epigraph to his *Letters on the Aesthetic Education of Man*, when they were first published in the magazine he and Goethe edited – *Horen* – in 1795.

According to his most recent translators, Schiller had an early fondness for mechanistic models of human nature.[3] In the eighteenth century there is a considerable body of writing welcoming the coming of machinery,[4] and Schiller may not have been hostile to it initially. But by the time he wrote the Aesthetic Letters any such enthusiasm he may have had had been reversed. There are a number of machine metaphors in the Aesthetic Letters. When they occur, they are derived from clockwork, and are all hostile. The modern state is based on crude mechanics; it is a piece of ingenious clockwork; it is cold, and alien to man. By contrast the Greek city state is praised because of its cell structure, because it was organic.

In the opening six letters, Schiller's ideas resemble Rousseau's in many respects and derive from many sources among his contemporaries whom Rousseau influenced.[5] Specialization has brought about the ruin of human nature; and specialization was inevitable. It followed from the expansion of knowledge and of art. Contemporary civilization as it is cannot heal these wounds. A new source of healing must be found. The problem Schiller sets himself is to reconcile this civilized development – without repudiating any of the arts and sciences – with men's inner harmony.

If, for Schiller, arts and sciences ruin men, they do not ruin at once; not at the entry into civilization. Schiller's contrast is not with primitive man, or even with a theoretical model of man in a state of nature, but with the civilization of the ancient Greeks; and not with Greek political institutions only, but with the supposedly harmonious development of each individual in the Greek city state, and with the perfectly balanced products of Greek art and philosophy.

> The Greeks put us to shame ... at once full of form and of content, at once philosophizing and shaping, at once gentle and energetic, we see them uniting the youth of imagination with the maturity of reason in a splendid humanity. ... [To the Greeks] unifying nature gave its forms; to [the modern man] intellect, which divides everything.[6]

The modern rational age for Schiller is one of commerce and abstraction.

> Utility is the great idol of the age, which all powers must serve and to which all talents must kneel. In its crude scales the spiritual worth of art has no weight, and, robbed of all encouragement, art vanishes from the howling marketplace of the century. Even the spirit of philosophical enquiry siezes one province after the other from imagination, and the wider

science spreads its bounds, the narrower shrink the frontiers of art.[7]

Inventive spontaneity is lost in the cultivation of an accurate memory, useful for the job. Each man devotes himself, as a duty, to a single talent which brings him praise and pay. Only the exceptional man has time for any activity that he likes, outside his daily work. The job takes all his energy. Consequently he grows in an ever more fragmentary way the more labour is divided.[8]

For Schiller, ancient Greek character was harmonious and undivided; modern man is incomplete, his character formed by the specialized role that he plays in the machinery of society. In the decline from Greece,

> ... enjoyment was separated from labour, means from end, effort from reward. For ever now chained to an individual small fragment of the whole, man himself develops only as a fragment; for ever in his ears now the monotonous sound of the wheel he turns, he never brings out the harmony of his being; and instead of printing on what he touches the humanity in his nature, he becomes a mere impression of his job or of his science.[9]

The centre of criticism has shifted from man's loss of liberty to his loss of harmony; and the direction of change is towards a reconciliation of inner harmony with the full development of the arts, sciences and civilization, not towards the spartan austerities of Rousseau's politics, with their basis in 'diminished desires', nor the 'flight to the woods' that the Second Discourse had earlier presented as the preferable, even if unattainable, ideal.

The way forward for Schiller is still, from one point of view, a return to nature. But, writing in the years of the Terror, he believed that 'nature' needed restraint. Men who do not in any way restrain 'nature' are savages, *Wilder*; as much in need of development as the commercial or philosophical *Barbarer* who despise nature altogether. A savage's passions govern him. And the State of Nature for Schiller would have had none of the splendour of Rousseau's ideal. Indeed he relates it to the Terror. In the political world of his own day he saw revolution as one kind of return to nature, but as a return to chaos rather than a release into natural liberty : 'Unfettered society, instead of hurrying onwards into organic life, is falling back into the primal state.'[10] For men's original nature, left to itself, will not support the demands men make on each other when they live together. Men seek the destruction of society.[11] But Schiller's thought already shows a dialectical pattern. If politically a mere return to nature is to be dreaded, equally no answer is to be found in political repression. On the contrary, the division of labour and of knowledge has been accompanied by an expansion of government to intolerable limits, where all its moral authority is lost and the state becomes merely one more power among other powers.

> This ruin, which art and learning began in the inner man, the new spirit of government makes complete and general. It was certainly not to be expected that the simple organization of the first republics should outlive the simplicity of early morals and relationships; but instead of rising to a higher animal life, it sank to a common and coarse mechanism. That polyp-like nature of the Greek states, where each individual enjoyed an independent life and when necessary could become the whole, now gave place to an ingenious clockwork where, from the piecing together of infiintely many lifeless parts a mechanical life takes shape in the whole.[12]

The idea had been put forward by Rousseau – both in the Second Discourse and in *Du Contrat Social* – that in a divided state individual men could not themselves be at unity. Schiller too sees the organization of society creating or destroying the unity of men's inner life. He says that the modern state 'remains perpetually alien' to its citiezns, who cannot identify with it in feeling. The state resembles the ideal of his own life which a man carries within him. If an individual cannot 'become' the state[13] the state 'annuls' him; just as his own inner ideal oppresses him if he is not able to identify with it.[14]

No abstract ideal of the 'man' each individual is striving to become can possibly be identified with the actual states of Europe in Schiller's day; they have no moral appeal to their subjects, and – in the case of which Schiller himself was most bitterly aware from his own experience of prison – repress their activities brutally.

Schiller is thus led by his need to recreate individual wholeness to require a complete transformation of society and of the state. Like Rousseau, whose individual liberty is possible only in a society made to embody it, Schiller shows the private and the public worlds as inextricably related; and he judges the public world by its capacity for creating individual wholeness. Thus, though Schiller's ideas of change are not intentionally violent, his theories, like Rousseau's, have revolutionary implications; no one can put right his own world without putting right the world as a whole. This is a belief which still inspires those theories today that are couched in terms such as 'alienation'.

But Schiller's ideas are in one respect the reverse of revolutionary. No generation should be expected to sacrifice itself to the possible perfection of a later society :

> In what relationship would we then stand to past and future ages if [the] improvement of human nature required such sacrifice? We would have been the serfs of humanity; we would have done several millenia of slave's work for them and printed the shameful traces of this servile labour on our mutilated nature. . . .
> But can man really be required, for any end whatever, to neglect himself?[15]

'A man is a citizen not only of his country, but of his generation', Schiller wrote. One generation should not be sacrificed for the possible benefit of its successors.

As we have seen, Schiller rejected abandonment to impulse : it could lead to formlessness and chaos. Equally, he distrusted the merely formalizing repression of abstract moralists; this threatened to sever man from his senses. The redeeming impulse he sought had to be neither chaotic nor repressive. The one impulse that satisfied all these demands for him was that of play : detached enjoyment free from any purpose.

The instinct for play in Schiller is derived from a balance of two rival instincts, that of sense and that of form. The liberating impulse must come, not from a repression of either, but from their reconciliation in a third. And this third impulse – the 'instinct of play' – has as its object not mere form, or mere life, but a reconciliation of the two; living form, beauty. The impulse to 'play' with beauty is the criteria of humanity. 'Man is only to play with beauty, and he is to play only with beauty. For . . . man plays only where he is man in the full meaning of the word; and he is wholly man only when he plays.'[16]

The play impulse is shown bringing men into harmony. It gives back to the abstract 'barbarian' the world of sense to which he was a stranger; and tames the wild man who ignored reason.

Schiller believes the instinct of play and the feeling for beauty to be rooted even in animal nature :

When no hunger gnaws the lion and no beast of prey challenges him to battle, his idle strength itself creates an object; with a spirited roar he fills the resounding deserts, and luxuriant power enjoys itself in aimless display. With joyful life the insect revels in the shaft of sunlight; and it is certainly not the cry of desire that we hear in the bird's melodious singing. Undeniably there is freedom in these movements.[17]

And at a certain point in the past this became a dominant impulse in men :

Now the ancient German seeks out more splendid animal skins, more magnificent antlers, more elegant drinking horns, and the Caledonian selects the prettiest shells for his feasts. Even weapons are no longer allowed to be mere objects of terror, but also of delight, and the ingenious ornamental swordbelt will be no less noticed than the sword's deadly edge. Not content with bringing an aesthetic superfluity into what is necessary, as the play impulse becomes freer it at last breaks loose from the fetters of necessity, and the beautiful becomes an object of striving for itself alone. Man adorns himself. Free pleasure becomes numbered among his needs, and the unnecessary is soon the best part of his joys.[18]

Schiller's 'aesthetic man' is visual. He holds back from full enjoyment and from passionate seizing.[19] His reward is a restored harmony, a full humanity, a return to nature in place of both violence and other-worldliness.[20] And beauty creates a kind of equality also among men.[21]

How is play related to work in Schiller's world? Is it to be earned, like the modern 'weekend', by submitting to necessity for the rest of the time and used to decorate the products of necessity. Or is it to be paid for by the many, labouring for the 'play' of the few as in Mandeville's morality? Schiller hints at a much more profound significance for play. Although it may originate in mere decoration, according to his account, its influence may spread into the rest of life. The ancient German who starts by elaborating his scabbard when weary of killing, ends by becoming gentle under the influence of beauty. It civilizes him, since love of beauty calls for love in return, and reciprocity cannot be forced but can only be wooed by gentleness.

The man shown at the start of the Letters giving all his energy to his monotonous job, could, according to Schiller, come to recover the neglected part of his life by developing his impulse for play. Work alone is not a sphere where man's full humanity can be expressed.

The central idea in Schiller's Aesthetic Letters then is that the source of our energy and our wholeness, even in aspects of our life that seem to have no connection with 'play', may lie in an unpossessive relationship to something loved, outside ourselves and – as Kant had suggested – detached from our practical interests. This Schiller called beauty, and the relation of man to beauty, play. A paradigm of play is the making of works of art and the enjoyment of them. For Schiller it is by a continual return to play that a man recovers his humanity and the wholeness of his nature, even if he must then re-enter the more fragmentary activities of everyday working life.

3
Hegel

Hegel read the Aesthetic Letters when they were first published, in the magazine *Horen*, in 1795. He then wrote to his friend Schelling, informing him that the letters were a masterpiece.[1] At the time he was two years out of the Tübingen Theological Seminary and beginning his career as a philosopher. At Tübingen, according to Leutwein his contemporary there, he was always reading Rousseau, who was 'his hero' and whose works he thought 'liberated' him.[2]

So far, then, Hegel seems to be typical of his generation. But he rapidly developed certain elements of its thought to an unprecedented degree. Hegel has above any of his contemporaries the feeling for fluidity, for change, for development. This is partly a matter of personal liking, and can be seen in what his eye caught in a book or in a landscape. His diary of a journey in the Bernese Alps the year after he read the Aesthetic Letters, recording his boredom in front of the 'eternally fixed masses of the mountains', goes on to comment on the effects of water pouring over a fall: it is 'the gracious, unconstrained, free and playful descent' of what he calls the 'water-dust': that move him. It produces for him 'the image of free play'.[3] For Hegel, looking at the waterfall, no static art can be adequate to reality:

> Painting would render only the sameness of the image that it has to present in determinate outlines and parts; the other part of the impression, however, the eternal inexorable alteration of every part, the eternal dissolution of every wave, every foam, which always draws down our eyes with it, which does not

permit us the same directions for our glances for [a moment] : all this power, all this life is wholly lost. . . .[4]

A static picture, showing organic shape frozen at one particular moment, is inadequate; even a series of such pictures, spaced out and compared, would be inadequate. For Hegel, movement itself must be shown. And early in his life he applied such a sensibility – among the first of European philosophers – to the question of work in a commerical and industializing world.

Hegel treats work twice[5] in his early writings : in *Die Phänomenologie des Geistes* (1807) and also in two earlier texts, thought (at least until recently) to be written for lectures in Jena in 1803–4 and 1804–5,[6] and known until now as the *Jenenser Realphilosophie*. They are much clearer at a first reading than the Phenomenology and this has given rise to various speculations. One, for which I believe Nietzsche is responsible, is that Hegel thought clearly at first, and added 'profundity' before publishing, to improve the German reception of his work; or, in a variant,[7] to save revealing views more radical than the authorities permitted. On the alternative and more widely accepted theory, Hegel worked out his thought in these early clear ideas and developed his system out of them; they were necessary first stages to a higher level of abstraction, which was for him a higher level of rationality.

Hegel treats the questions of work and of machinery in detail in both sets of early lecture notes, arriving at the questions in both cases towards the end. In the 1803–4 notes he argues that men need not work merely to satisfy their desires like animals, but to be recognized by other consciousnesses. They need their work to be recognized by other people as work. Men learn work as a set of rules; work is not an instinct but a 'rationality' which confronts each individual as something 'general'. The individual contributes to it by discovery, seeking out new tools in the course of making himself competitively more skilful, tools which other men then learn to use. Tools distance men from the material 'destruction' in their activity; machines allow them to transcend even this activity and let 'activity' work for them. But this is a trick played on nature, and it takes its revenge; the more man subjects nature, the deeper he himself sinks.[8] Machines do not allow him to do less work :

> While he sets many kinds of machines to work on nature, man does not annul the necessity of his labour, but merely defers it, distances it from nature, and no longer confronts nature vitally as a vital being; this negative vitality vanishes, and the labour that remains to him becomes itself *more mechanical*; he reduces it only for the whole, not for the individual, but rather increases it, for the more mechanical work becomes, the less value it has, and the more he must work in this fashion.[9]

As a summary of the immediate effects of the introduction of 'labour-saving' machinery, and of the tendency which this sets up in the whole economy in the absence of other constraints, this is extraordinarily compressed; it looks forward to later nineteenth-century arguments that labour-saving machinery saves not 'labour' but the wages of labour; that it could thus tend to increase the hours of work if – as some nineteenth-century theorists expected – wages were to remain stable around sub-sistence level, though this is not what in fact occurred.

It also shows the value of Hegel's refusal to accept formal barriers between academic subjects, for he combines this economic proposition with a further psychological one, necessarily less exact but perhaps no less significant for those who work at machinery : that when machines come between men and the nature they have been used to working on, vitality is lost. Many subsequent records confirm this from first-hand experience, thought not all treat it as an unmixed evil.

Hegel's ability to break through divisions of thought is shown again when he goes on to speak in detail of the factory from *The Wealth of Nations*.[10] After analyzing it from the point of view of its higher productivity and the lower value it creates for each man's work, he makes three compressed pronouncements on the effects of the division of labour.

The first is an observation familiar from Adam Smith and a certain school of eighteenth-century economists :[11] as work becomes machine work 'the skill of the individual becomes so infinitely more limited, and the consciousness of the factory worker is depressed into the most ultimate stupidity'.

Secondly, each man's work becomes dependent on all other parts of the economy; so a distant operation or invention can render the work of whole classes superfluous.

Finally – most pregnantly perhaps for his modern commentator Marcuse with his expression 'the hell of the affluent society' – the mass of comforts leads to a situation which is itself 'absolutely uncomfortable.'

A whole system of mutual dependence bound together by money, says Hegel, forms in a great people a self-activating life of the dead that lurches here and there in a blind and elementary way. Like a wild beast, it requires taming. A page later Hegel ends the first set of lecture notes;[12] in Marcuse's view as if he were 'terrified' by what his analysis of the commodity-producing society disclosed.[13]

In the second set of writings, provisionally known as Notes for the Lectures of 1804–5, Hegel returns to the question of machinery, once more leading up to this 'monstrous general dependence of one man on the whole', with its chaotic lurchings that can suddenly destroy the livelihood of vast masses of people. Hegel sees men first dividing their labour until it becomes more 'abstract', then, when all they still require is movement, substituting the movement of nature for their own activity, or 'pure movement ... the relationship of abstract forms of space and time – abstract external activity, the *machine*.[14]

But by now he has contracted his ideas more fully into a system; and there is a certain loss. Thus, while he still notes the psychological effects of machinery, he has evolved a formula for describing machine work. *Maschinen-arbeit* is conjoined with the words *geteilt* and *abstrakt* even elsewhere than in the discussion of machinery itself.[15] This tends to place 'machinery' – as if there were only one sort – at the end of a single train of developments necessarily connected with abstraction and division of labour. And it also tends to standardize and render ambiguous the psychological effects which machinery is supposed to have.

As his work is this abstract thing, so he relates himself as an
abstract ego or after this manner of thingness, not as an
embracing circumspect spirit, rich in content, who conquers a
great circumference and is master over it.[16]

The very ambiguity that Hegel uses to make such an intuitive
movement into psychology may, as we shall see, become an
obstacle to truth when it is built into a rigid system.

Towards the end of the 1804–5 *Realphilosophie*, all the previous themes are drawn together. 'The general system is pure
necessity for each individual workman'. 'Society is his nature',
and he depends on its blind, elementary movements. He has his
place in it through pure chance. To the extent that he does
abstract work he overcomes nature; but this victory is reversed by
another form of chance. For the more he works, the less his work
is worth; needs become multiplied, tastes are refined, goods are
worked up and polished; man is formed as a pure enjoying thing.
But 'In the same degree he becomes ... more *mechanical*, more
blunted, more spiritless. Spiritual life, that fulfilled self-scon-
sciousness, becomes empty activity. ...'[17]

Fashion demands constant specialization. Beauty itself is not
subject to fashion; but 'no free beauty occurs here', only forms of
'charm' arranged by others to excite desire. Each man's skill is the
condition of the maintenance of his existence; but it is subjected
to all the complications of the fate of the whole.

Then again comes a terrifying evocation – reminiscent of
Rousseau's *Discourse on Inequality* – of the mass of men condemned to 'stupefying, unhealthy, insecure skill-less work in
factories, workshops and mines'. Whole branches of industry
vanish because of changes in fashion or discoveries in foreign
countries, and masses of men are given over to misery. Riches and
povery jostle each other : the rich get richer; 'to him who has is
given'. Again Hegel breaks out of the merely economic in his
economic descriptions. 'This inequality of riches and poverty', he
says, 'this need and necessity, create the utmost dislocation of the
will, inner rebellion, and hatred.' And yet, 'this necessity, which is
the world of complete chance for individual existence, is at the

same time its supporting substance'. Into this chaos – at the end of these lectures – he brings the stabilizing power of his state.

In *Die Phänomenologie des Geistes,* which was written over the following two years, Hegel introduced the concepts *Entfremdung* and *Entäusserung* – alienation. They have both a general and a particular use in his writings.[18] On the one hand, the whole of consciousness and of history is an estrangement of spirit from itself.[19] Alienation can in fact quite generally be seen as the second stage in any dialectical process in the Phenomenology, and in the sense the whole of human life is a 'second stage' between the undisturbed state of Spirit before history, and the self-consciousness of Spirit that has achieved absolute knowledge through philosophy at the end of history.

On the other hand, alienation is also a particular stage corresponding, in consciousness, to the moment of 'self-consciousness'; and, in history, to the change from the Ancient City to the world of 'culture,' the world of 'spirit estranged from itself' in the Roman Empire; a world which the 'spirit certain of itself' – the world of morality – had brought to an end in Hegel's day in the French revolution.

Hegel's ideas notoriously cannot be summarized into a system. Their concrete examples are as important as their form. But in the Phenomenology the process by which one 'moment' leads to another – by the invocations of its contradictory, and by a third, in which the previous two are superseded (*aufgehoben*) – is seen not as a relation between statements – or not as that only – but as a relationship between states of developing consciousness, which correspond in the second part of the Phenomenology to stages of world history. History is, for Hegel, the progressive development of Spirit through different 'moments' of consciousness which succeed each other in a unique and also a necessary series.

The origin of the development is a struggle to the death between two consciousnesses, each demanding from the other 'recognition'. Every human consciousness, says Hegel, demands that another should 'recognize' it : he makes this the essential fact about human as opposed to animal consciousness. The demand for recognition leads, through a 'struggle to the death', to a relationship between master and slave, in which the loser, to save his life, 'recognizes' the other as master; while the victor, in sparing the loser's life and becoming master, does not return the slaves's recognition, but makes use of the slave's labour to shield himself from what is 'negative' in nature. Thus he enjoys material things only after they have been worked on by the slave; and he is enjoying another's consciousness in doing so.[20]. But the slave, in labouring, transforms both nature and himself and the next development of consciousness arrives through him, not through his master. Whereas the master 'negates' what he enjoys, which vanishes as he enjoys it, the slave creates something permanent outside himself. 'Labour ... is restrained desire, delayed disappearance, or labour forms. The labouring consciousness thus comes to the intuition of independent being. . . .'[21] And this exteriorization of consciousness in labour is what creates the human world.

It was on a critical reading of *Die Phänomenologie des Geistes* that Marx founded his own philosophy. He did not know of Hegel's earlier work directly. And though on several topics he found his own way to ideas similar to those of the early Hegel, he derived them from their more abstract form in the Phenomenology, at the same time combining them with his own experience, with what he knew from contemporary journalism, and from conversations with Engels and the Paris and Brussels revolutionaries. Thus he derives from Hegel not the analysis of the economy, or of machine labour in the early lectures, but the idea of 'alienation' and the redemptive pattern of thought in which it is embedded; the idea of a struggle to the death between master and slave – the assumption that the next development in history comes through the victim of the previous one; and the notion of work as the dynamic element in all human history.

It is also arguable that he inherited much which Hegel had derived from the culture of the late eighteenth century, and that his early notion of an unalienated state of completeness and reconciliation with all that has gone before – an ideal that, however disciplined by economic studies, remains with him even in his late writings, in *Capital* and the *Grundrisse* – derives from the same source as Hegel's : through Schiller from the eighteenth century Rousseau-ist idealization of a lost freedom and harmony to which men will somehow in the future – enriched by all they have experienced in exile – return.

4

Early criticisms of modern society

There is a specialist interest in the first expression of any theory, and the works of the early Marx, as well as of his predecessors in France and Germany, have been drawn on more than once recently by contemporary theorists for insights into our own condition, especially since the apparent failures of 'mature Marxism', or of the political systems set up in its name. For instance, Herbert Marcuse, in his early work *Reason and Revolution*,[1] has called attention to the economic passages in Hegel's *Jenenser Realphilosophie*, in part for their analysis of our own commodity-producing society, and in his *Eros and Civilzation* has drawn on the Aesthetic Letters of Schiller. Rousseau's views about moderation and desire are echoed by many modern ecologists, and also by economists like Galbraith who see over-production and over-stimulated consumption as twin distortions in modern Western economies. Meanwhile much industrial sociology, and many movements of protest, have inspiration and often detailed accounts of industry from Marx's Economic-Philosophic Manuscripts of 1844 which show traces of the thought of these earlier writers. Are there dangers as well as possible benefits in these returns to the first expressions of radical theory?

From Rouseeau's idea of a state of nature and his notion of a fall men still derive the hope of a single total revolutionary solution to all human problems. There is a strong affinity with Rousseau in any pattern of thought that criticizes the present state of man in society by contrast with some better and more natural state which is both buried in the past, latent within men and capable of emerging again given the right conditions in the future; or in any argument which blames society and its 'contradictions' for the self-division of individual men.

These ideas are present in Rousseau in a highly original form. And their importance in 'the critical theory of society', as Marcuse calls it, is by no means yet exhausted. It is possible that this critical theory still embodies not only Rousseau's ideas, but also some of his styles of exposition, or devices of justification; so that along with original insights such as the difference between the effects of monotonous and of craftman-like work, we may still be deriving from Rousseau ideas about 'nature' which he owed not so much to his original observations of reality as to the expository framework within which, in the philosophical world of his time, it was normal to justify any political arguments.

We can no longer believe without question that nature is a source of all goodness and that naturalness is a sufficient criterion of what is right for man. The terms are too uncertain in their meaning. But concepts like 'alienation' and 'self-estrangement' are inexplicably conneced with the idea of a lost and potentially redemptive 'nature'. The fact that such notions are still, two hundred years later, found as a tool of criticism of modern industrial society, suggests either a great power in Rousseau's and Hegel's insights, or possibly a tendency in critical concepts to outlive the cosmology and methods of argument which gave them their original force.

These particular concepts have perhaps survived above all from religions – from Christianity and Judaism. Several critics have pointed to the religious 'sources' of Hegel's early ideas.[2] One writer has drawn an analogy between Marx's own idea of the unalienated state of man in the classless society, and the Hebrew notion of *t'shuvah* – the return to God of the strayed soul.[3]

Perhaps a pattern of fall and redemption is inherent in all close secular derivatives of religious thought in the generations immediately after the lapse of a religion – the echo of a religion where the religion itself has become silent. It is as if men who cease to believe in a Christian or a Hebrew God cannot at first, for a generation or more, grasp the idea that there might not be something similar to take His place; some force – conscious or living if not personal – working out a destiny for man in history, replacing God.

Today, perhaps, the most immediately vital aspects of Rousseau's thought are the ideas of moderation in material things; of freedom from the tyranny of ever-expanding desires. In this part of his work Rousseau re-asserts an idea that Europe had lost but which is present in the classical period of Greek thought. As late as the first century AD, in the pages of Plutarch, wise men like Solon speak about moderation in material things while fools like Midas want everything and think that happiness consists in having enormous riches. Our own society, it could be said, has taken the beliefs of Midas as its central principles of economics, and Rousseau was already challenging it on this in the mid-eighteenth century.

But it may be that in setting his goal as something more austere than moderation – in hoping for the complete independence of each man from all others – Rousseau follows a Calvinistic rather than a classical tradition, making his requirements too absolute to follow. As Kierkegaard remarked, some people think the Christian precepts are intentionally made a little too difficult, as if one were to put the clock forward in order to be punctual; equally, this excessive difficulty may be used in practice as an excuse for ignoring them altogether. In several areas Rousseau's prescriptions are ones he did not follow himself. This is not to make a simple accusation of hypocrisy against him. But perhaps people have a need to speak of 'nature' and 'simplicity' in civilized societies, a need which may grow the more they experience the opposite. Perhaps Rousseau speaks for what is repressed in modern life, in a language which unconsciously we understand better than we can understand it consciously; of a nature from which we have come, spotless, and to which, purging ourselves, we may be able some day to return. This is a language in which it is possible to make eloquent criticism; but a new question arises when a critical theory formed out of such Rousseau-esque concepts is made the basis for a fresh construction of reality. Since Rousseau wrote, a still clearer belief in a fall has come to be widely accepted: the idea of a fall from agriculture into industrialization. We shall have to ask what grounds there are for either belief today. Is the language of nature and of men's fall into the present sufficiently clear – in the daylight of action – to build on? Or is it only, by moonlight, a marvellous alternative to the real?

Rousseau's diagnosis of the ills of modern society and the ideal of what a cure would entail remain persistent in radical thought. Only the means change; from 'play' in Schiller, to political revolution and work in Marx. Schiller seems to have developed from Rousseau and his successors, and handed on to Hegel, many of the ideas that Marx would seek to embody in economic theory – even though Marx is said to have had little feeling for Schiller himself: the idea that society has decayed and that it must be restored to its first harmony, with all the subsequent gains in science, technology and civilization; the idea that human society has as its object the full and harmonious development of all its individuals' powers; and that this is possible only in a new society without contradictions, since social and individual harmony must develop together.

There is throughout the Aesthetic Letters a triple movement of thought, a conception of change through the reconciling of opposites in a higher stage of history or of personal development, which includes all that has gone before. This form of thought was to affect Hegel and Marx in the succeeding century.

By the time the first European countries were beginning to industrialize there were already two traditions of thought about machinery ready to confront it.[4] The enthusiasts for machinery foresaw the expansion of the economies and the lightening of labour. But a hostility to the mechanical already existed in

Europe among certain writers and artists. This was not the reaction to cotton slums and railways trains that occurs in the nineteenth century. The late eighteenth-century horror of the machine is found in countries where powered machinery is still scattered and undeveloped, and before the large-scale industrialization even of England.

Schiller belongs to this tradition. For him Greek life was organic. By contrast, everything about the modern world that is mechanical is remarked on with hostility. Yet Schiller does not single out industry from the other features of his commerical, profit-seeking, utilitarian age, and when he attacks what is mechanical in his society he is not writing about life in a factory. The wheel endlessly droning in the ears of modern man could be the wheel of a clock, or of a treadmill, or of any job in modern bureaucratic society.

It would have been hard for any writer or artist who inherited this pre-industrial attitude to machinery and to machine imagery, from Schiller and from his contemporaries, to have looked at industrialization itself without preconception; and it would need an act of intentional disassociation from this pre-industrial imagery if one looks – with Marcuse[5] – to Schiller's Aesthetic Letters for critical ideas. Some aspects of this eighteenth-century hostility to the mechanical derive from observations of the effects of work – such as Rousseau's comments on the stone-cutters and stocking-workers. They are a reminder that much of the monotony we associate with industrialization and machinery predates it and is part of a wider phenomenon, perhaps what has been called the universal application of technique to all activities in European civiliaztion;[6] or perhaps something inherent in all human labour in varying degrees.

Generally, however, the late eighteenth-century literary feeling for the organic, insofar as it is a reaction, may not be a reaction against forms of work or against powered machinery, so much as against clockwork; and against clockwork primarily as a model and a metaphor for the human. It is arguably a turning away from the Hobbesian and Newtonian imagery that the seventeenth century had used in psychology; a reaction against the following of academic rules in poetry, and of society's rules in life, and also again the cold efficiency of commerce and bureacracy of which the clock, the special plaything of many small German princes,[7] stood as a particularly notable symbol in the Germany of the late eighteenth century. This praise of the organic by contrast with the mechanical, prepared – on the part of certain writers – a literary reception for powered machinery which was not necessarily related to powered machinery itself, and not based on the actual experience of people working at it.

The effect of these ideas on the young Karl Marx shows chiefly in his early writings, which he did not publish. In this century they have been widely revived. But there is another body of thought significantly influenced by them, independent of Marx. Much English criticism of early industrialization was the work of writers who were either influenced by Rousseau – as Wordsworth was – or who read and translated German – Colderidge, Carlyle, J. S. Mill; the German of an age immediately before their own, at an earlier stage of industrialization even in their own time. In this way, eighteenth-century literary preconceptions based on non-powered machinery were even further projected into the thought of the most advanced industrial country of the early nineteenth century. Because pre-industrial literary horror of machinery in some ways parallelled, and could seem to explain, the feelings of people who actually worked at powered machinery, and the people whose jobs were destroyed by it, and because it suggested insights into these feelings which the theories of utilitarian economics failed to provide, it has remained near the centre of critical ideas about industrialization for many scholars, imaginitive writers and artists ever since.

Working people in England have also reacted, sometimes violently, against powered machinery; but they have reacted generally for different reasons from artists and writers, and with different contrasts in mind.[8] If there has been a gulf between their feelings and the ideas of writers and artists of their country and time, two separate inheritances may have to be traced; a literary heritage, to the 'organic' imagery of the late eighteenth century; that of the working people, to their own songs and ballads and to records of what they said in the same period and over the subsequent century. Both will include instances of passionate hostility to machines but the feelings behind them will perhaps turn out to be strikingly different.

Hegel's use of the concept 'machine' in the Jena lectures of 1803–5 is an example of thought affected by a pre-industrial notion of machinery. The first spinning jennies came into Saxony at about the turn of the century, and Hegel may have known about them. He could certainly have known of the water pumps used in silver mines, salt mines and coal mines, the elaborate water-driven hammers traditional in Germany, and the machinery used in paper-making and the minting of coins. Something approaching factory organization already existed in metal-work and in chemical industries.[9] But the main specific illustration of industry in the lectures is based on the account of pin-making in *The Wealth of Nations*[10] which was published in German translation twenty years after it was written,[11] about the same time as Hegel read Schiller's Aesthetic Letters. And it is not what we could recognize as a description of powered machinery at all.

Hegel moved to his account of machinery in the first set of lectures, like Adam Smith himself, directly from the description of divided labour in the pin-making factory. In the second lectures, building his own system, he showed the development of machinery as yet a further step in the direction of 'abstraction', 'division' and 'formality'. And though at the end of this section on 'work', in 1804–5, Hegel used the two distinct words for factories, *Fabrik* and *Manufaktur*, he used them without dwelling on any distinction.

This was usual at the time. In the eighteenth century, *Fabrik* had tended to be used primarily of those workplaces where fire of some kind was an element, and *Manufaktur* of those where there was merely a division of labour. By the turn of the century the uses were interchangeable. Only in the early nineteenth century does a new distinction between the two words begin to be made fairly systematically in official statistics : *Fabrik* being used for a place where a single 'prime mover' was central to a whole factory, driving many machines; while *Manufaktur* referred either to the places where work was merely divided, or to those where many small machines ranged round a workshop played a peripheral role in production.[12] But it is on this distinction that Marx founds much of the argument of his mature works, the *Grundrisse* and *Capital* : for it is the newer form of production in the *Fabrik* that for him creates the material possibility of a practical communist society, while *Manufaktur* represents the technologically backward handwork that he disparaged.

In *Capital*, Marx starts with the same example from Adam Smith as Hegel had cited, that ten men can make 48,000 pins a day by dividing their labour; but where Hegel, like Adam Smith, contrasts this with what one man alone could make, Marx contrasts it with the more than half a million pins a day that one girl could make with machinery in the mid-nineteenth century.[13] Using *Manufaktur* for the merely divided labour of the pre-mechanical factory, Marx argues that in an already industrialized society vestigial hand-labour may involve much worse conditions, worse wages and worse forms of work than machine-labour in factories; while the cottage system of dispersed hand-labour – 'putting-out' – may in an industrialized society generate the worst work of all.

But in Marx's early theories, as in Hegel's, a much simpler unitary concept of 'machinery' is used. Any modern theory based on the early Marxian manuscripts, or on the *Jeneuser Realphilosophie*, risks missing this distinction, which is among the central thoughts of the *Grundrisse* and *Capital*, and which is essential for any understanding of industry in Marx's time, and perhaps still more in ours.

In the treatment of the groups of men who invent and construct machinery, the mature Marx made another development from the simplicity of his early writings, and from Adam Smith. In *The Wealth of Nations* Smith hardly treats the making or design of machinery as a distinct trade; and indeed in 1776 this was not unnatural. He gives the single instance of a small boy tying a string to the valve of a 'fire engine' to open and shut the furnace door, and he suggests only the 'inventive' aspect in the making of a new machine, not the constructive skills; perhaps because he thought of inventions mainly as very simple, like this piece of string. Smith attributed invention either to the workmen of the particular trade on the one hand, or to people whom he calls 'philosophers' – perhaps 'scientists' in today's speech, but nevertheless people outside industry. In his later writings Marx by contrast spoke of men between these two – those who built machinery – who had indeed appeared since Adam Smith wrote. Marx uses the word *halbkünsterisch* – 'almost artistic' – of their activities,[14] and argues that they had to be replaced or reinforced by a new kind of machinery which itself constructed machinery before the pace of industrial change could significantly quicken in the nineteenth century. Since the design of new machinery today is one of the most important areas of contemporary decision, the question of the design of machines – and of their own machine-making machines – is vital. Any theory that returns to the early Marx or to the young Hegel for its account of industry risks missing, also, the identification of this area of work and decision-making, with the multiplier effects on the rest of the society's working life which it must have.

There is a second danger in such a 'return to origins', that one word, 'mechanical', may be used to describe all the activities that surround machinery, from their design and construction, through their operation, repair and demolition, to their use in work and leisure alike. Hegel's use of the words 'machine' and 'mechanical' in the *Jenenser Realphilosophie* obscures the fact that 'mechanical' can be used in totally different ways.

First, 'mechanical' work can mean the *machine-like* work of the man who performs a single repetitive action. Repetitive actions may be called forth by a machine; but they may occur equally in a hand-working factory where the labour is sub-divided. They may also – though to a less extent because of the freer movement of the body – arise in agriculture and other trades that are 'concrete', 'undivided' and pre-industrial, as Rousseau noted when he said that peasants followed stupefying routines and that men sawing stone or making stockings worked mechanically.

Secondly, mechanical work can mean work *at machinery* as an operator; and though some of this is undoubtedly mechanical in the first sense – machine-like – some is not : it depends on the design of the machine. It may be more machine-like to dig a hole without machines, by spade, than to dig it operating one of those huge, manoeuverable scoops which lift the earth accurately into a waiting lorry.

Thirdly, 'mechanical' work can mean 'the work *of a mechanic*'; the work of a man who makes or maintains machinery. He may work, personally, without using machinery – only tools; and he may work without repetition, in a very far from machine-like way.

These possible senses of 'machine work' are quite different. But Hegel has defined machine work as one single thing. Furthermore, he has said one formulatic thing about it : it is 'abstract' and 'divided'. Now it is not quite clear what Hegel meant by calling machine work 'abstract'. But, giving the word any meaning at all, it is not obvious that a man operating a complex power-drill, or a dentist's drill for that matter, is doing work more 'abstract' than that of a shepherd counting sheep. The latter may be in fact more *machine-like*, more mechanical in the first sense. And it is hard to see in what sense it is 'abstract' to confront metal with a hammer or a welding torch, while confronting a ditch with a spade is not. Again, a man sawing stone may do work which is more divided than a man operating a modern numerical control machine-tool. The same difficulty applies when we think of the construction and maintenance of machinery. This may or may not be 'divided'. In one kibbutz in Israel great pride was taken at the lorry-servicing workshop in the fact that each man repaired the whole lorry, from carburettor to rear light. Equally a man servicing television sets does not generally deal with the tube only but with the whole set. Some firms have introduced 'undivided ways' of assembling machinery recently. So work with machinery, servicing and maintaining it, need not be divided. Similarly, there are divided and undivided ways of making machinery.

This is not to accuse Hegel of failing to foresee all the developments of machinery after his death. But it is to note the danger of making general statements about 'machine work' as if this had only one meaning; and of conflating different meanings into words like 'mechanical' with several quite different uses, worlds of experience apart to those who actually labour.

Since such conflations are particularly characteristic of Hegel's *Jenenser Realphilosophie* and of the 1844 Manuscripts the danger is not irrelevant today when these earlier writings are again being drawn on. Plenty of work at modern machinery still is machine-like. But not all is, and it is possible that the use of machinery could develop in many respects in the opposite direction from one which requires machine-like human action.

If the words *geteilt* and *abstrakt*, associated by formula with machine labour, can lead to standardization of the psychological effects attributed to all work connected with machines, Hegel's logical method can itself generate a standardized ambiguity about psychology which we may find taking root in the history of ideas about work.

Consider what Hegel says in the *Realphilosophie* about being related to one's work 'as a thing'. If a man is said to be related to his work as a thing, it may mean either that he feels he is a thing, or that he feels he is being treated as a thing, or that Hegel or some other outside observer thinks he is related to his work as a thing. They are different ideas. If the statement is psychological, it seems question-begging, for we cannot know in advance how people feel about their relation to their work as it becomes more divided; we have to ask them, and ask them individually. If it is a statement about how people treat each other in factories, it could not be necessary truth, since people differ, and may come to differ more, in the way they treat others in industry. And if it is a statement not about people's feelings or treatment in industry at all but about some outside observer's feelings for working people

– if Hegel feels they are like 'things' – this may be due mainly to the writer's unfamiliarity with the people concerned or to his horror of machinery or of labouring people who do not read philosophy.

Again, although in the *Realphilosophie* Hegel discusses machinery in the same context as the 'monstrous system of mutual dependence' in the economy, they are not necessarily connected in reality. The dependence of one man on fluctuations of taste and trade and on new inventions elsewhere is itself largely a matter of commerce and communications; it could, and did, eixst before industrialization. Alternatives for reducing the dependence of each individual on the economy's 'blind movements' – private property, social insurance, government intervention or workers' control of industry – can exist in industrial or non-industrial economies, and in both mechanized and unmechanized work alike. Industrialization and the commercial dependence of the individual on a fluctuating economy, while clearly related in many historical contexts, and to some extent conditions for each other when they first originate, are not necessarily connected : they can be found originating independently of each other, and they can be separated.

Here, as elsewhere, Hegel's fluid method is an instrument for establishing the possibility of connections between areas of experience that men have been holding apart in their minds. But when the lava solidifies – when the relationships he himself established are allowed to set into necessary connections supported only by speculation – then they must be questioned. This is just what is so hard once political parties become involved with their maintenance and solidification.

Schiller considered work less significant than beauty and men's relation to it in play. But before him in Rousseau and among his contemporaries as he wrote, work was becoming increasingly significant in philosophy, as it was becoming in economic life.

Rousseau was among the first to give work a new standing. Himself the son of a craftsman, he was proud of the dignity conferred by work[15] and selected craftsman-like labour as the ideal way of life for his Émile. When his remains were brought to the Pantheon 'the Assembly had representatives of the various trades march in procession carrying a tablet on which was written "To the man who restored the honour of useful industry" '.[16]

European philosophy before Rousseau inherited perhaps two broad traditions about work : a Hebraic one that regarded it as a curse, and a Greek one that saw it as contemptible and deforming. Yet in Christianity the curse was seen as something that could be turned to good by being undertaken in the right spirit; and since Augustine, according to one historian, there was an idea in Christian theology that Adam worked in the Garden of Eden, while 'a long medieval tradition' can be traced 'behind Milton's strongly protestant assertion that Adam's work in paradise "declares his dignity",' that ' "idleness had been worse" '.[17]

The great changes in the respect for work that characterize modern Europe between the sixteenth and eighteenth centuries have been attributed at various times to religious causes, to economic causes, or to the inventions of Renaissance artists, themselves perhaps inspired by a reading or mis-reading of classical texts as praises of artists;[18] or finally to the 'industrial revolution' itself. Labour is increasingly valued by economic writers and by governments from the sixteenth century onwards[19] – a grim indication of this being the number of prohibitions on labourers' suicide that date from that period. Locke in the seventeenth century saw the mixing of men's labour with nature as the source of property : but he included a man's servant's labour with his own, not differentiating between them. It was Adam Smith – whom Marx was to call 'the Luther of Economics'[20] – who reduced the concept of private property to that of work, which is seen as creating all value. In the following century Ricardo argued that capital is nothing but 'accumulated labour' – a view that Marx elaborated and made fundamental to his philosophy.

In the visual arts also in this period there is a fresh concern for industry. Klingender notes the gradual re-emergence of images of labour freed from the sixteenthe century onwards from classical mythology, in the younger Breughal, in the brothers Le Nain, and in Velasquez; and finally in those eighteenth-century painters like Wright of Derby who depicted men at work without disguise.[21]

Everywhere in the generation that succeeded the first steam-powered industry there is a concern with the effect each individual can have on reality, forming it in his own image; a new way of looking at the world, a new interest in history and in change rather than in the static aspects of the world, and a stress in every sphere on men's work.[22] The idea of a 'right to work' became an object of social policy in this period through the writings of Fichte, one of the interpreters of Rousseau's thought to the Germans. It is he to whom Schiller refers in the Letters on the Aesthetic Education of Man as his particular friend. Schiller, from this point of view, is outside the stream in selecting another aspect of human life to praise. After him, the writers we shall consider increasingly assume that the world and each individual life is based on productive work as its essence or centre; until, by the late nineteenth century, even the most popular philosophy could echo a praise of work. As Nietzsche complained.[23]

> Every man is ashamed to be calm; long reflection almost causes pangs of conscience. . . . All clear conscience stands on the side of my work : any disposition towards joy calls itself need for recuperation, and begins to be ashamed of itself. . . . Work has lost its curse ever since the bourgeois Christian world – to use the title of a much read anthology of Carlyle – began to do 'work' in order to avoid 'desperation' and to speak of the 'blessings of work'.

One modern commentator has seen in this glorification of work the seeds of totalitarian militarism;[24] once work is an end in itself only war can occupy a people to the utmost extent; while a military organization, and the use of leisure to increase the productivity of work – *Kraft durch Freude* – are end products of a regimentation of all life in order to produce.[25]

The idea that work is a 'blessing' is more original to the nineteenth century than the notion of work's importance, of which we have seen evidence earlier. It may perhaps be ascribed in part to new conditions of life, in which mechanized ease made many activities and lives potentially formless to an unprepared generality. When travel could be rapid, when choice of occupation could be increasingly free, when neither style nor fashion bound a new rich class to strict formality and ceremony in every action, the spectre of chaos and formlessness must have been increasingly real to the rich and the comparitively rich. Introspection and melancholy are perhaps especially characteristic of much of the literature of this time. From both, work offered release – social acceptance and an identity, inner freedom from formlessness or brooding, a shape, a routine, as well as the more obvious advantages of money, company or power. It may have offered a more necessary release to those who had been educated in religious beliefs about the necessity for right choice, yet who grew up in a world where many questions seemed capable of no answer. Work in the nineteenth century must at least have offered an answer to the question : 'What shall I do' when, perhaps for the first time, many men who did not need to labour had, by past standards, almost no formality and ceremony – no 'games' and 'play' in Huizinga's sense – to shape their time either. Later we shall have see whether such a praise of work – either of its blessings or even or its 'significance' – is to be found in the surviving words of people who at the time had to work, whether they wanted to or not.

5

Marx

In the 1844 Manuscripts Marx attributed his idea of the fundamental significance of work to Hegel's Phenomenology:

> The great thing in Hegel's Phenomenology and its end result – the dialectic of negativity as the moving and productive principle – is simply that Hegel grasps the self-production of man as a process, as objectification and as supersession of this alienation; that he thus grasps the nature of *work* and comprehends objective man, true because the real active relationship of man to himself as a species-essence, as a real i.e. human essence, is only possible so far as he actually brings forth all his *species-power* – which in turn is only possible through the collective operation of mankind, only as the result of history, and relates himself to them as objects, something which immediately again is possible only in the form of estrangement.[1]

Marx himself wrote about work and about the human effects of industrial labour at every stage of his life, but particularly in three places: first in the Paris Notebooks and 1844 Manuscripts; then in the chapter entitled 'Machinery and Large-Scale Industry' in the first book of *Capital*;[2] and in the *Outlines for a Critique of Political Economy, (Draft)*, or *Grundrisse*,[3] which forms a link between the early and later writings, containing both the philosophical concepts of the 1844 Manuscripts and the concern with the possibilities of automatic machinery that characterize *Capital*.

Both the Notebooks and Manuscripts and the *Grundrisse* were left unpublished in Marx's lifetime; but quite possibly for different reasons. Marx subsequently spoke slightingly of his early writings, and of the recurrent use of the concept 'alienation of man' in the German philosophical thought of his time. However important these Notebooks and Manuscripts were in forming his later thought, and however much continuity can be seen between them and the later work, they were regarded by him and Engels as not for publication. But their own order of priorities has been reversed by many modern writers, who see in the early writings more penetrating analyses of industry and society than in the later works.

The *Grundrisse* on the other hand are in that group of Marx's later writings from which *Capital* was mined, the first volume by Marx himself and the second and third, after Marx's death, by Engels. The most recent translator of the *Grundrisse* in English[4] has argued that we have in the whole of *Capital* only the first part of a single massive work, perhaps twelve times as long, of which the *Grundrisse* – itself a thousand pages in the original – is the sketch.

The Notebooks and Manuscripts remained unpublished in German until 1932; the *Grundrisse* until 1953. Thus 'Marxism' both as a political force and as an established set of dogmas was formed in its main outlines before their publication.

The notion of alienation occurs first in Marx's writings in an early essay, *The Critique of Hegel's Philosophy of the State* (1843). Marx there regards 'alienation' as arising out of all political relationships that divide or enslave men.[5] He complains that in his time man is divided into a 'citizen' with private egoistic interests, and a member of society with 'universal' interests : he is two men, not one. This division of man, which Hegel merely presented, Marx attacked as intolerable.

But Marx also picked out of Hegel two other ideas which he subsequently made more fundamental than the theme of political alienation : the dialectical struggle of master and slave, and the idea of work as the prime mover in shaping human history. Both these led him to concentrate, in his own time, on the question of industrial labour and on the condition of labouring people.

Feuerbach had seen religion as man's worship of the divine in himself projected on to an illusory 'God'. For him the task of philosophy was to return to man what man had 'alienated' from himself and allow him to accept the divine within him. For Marx, the alienation of man's essence or 'species-existence' into exchange and money was even more fundamental than religious alienation, and it underlay religious alienation, as he argued in an early essay on *Bruno Bauer*.

Money is the external substance on to which men have projected their humanity, and which they must supersede in order to return to their full humanity. They must get rid of bargaining, of buying and selling. In so doing they will heal a fundamental split between two natures, one actual – their individual sensuous existence – and the other not yet realized – what he calls their species-existence.[6]

Human essence, or species-existence, is productive, conscious and free activity, undertaken for other men. In his notes on James Mill in the Paris Notebooks of the spring of 1844 Marx shows the split between this and men's 'sensuous existence' occurring even earlier than with the invention of money : in the first primitive exchange itself. Instrumentalism – work done not for other men but for the sake of money or for traded goods – is an inversion of means and ends : man's essence or productive species-existence being treated as a means for the sustenance of his individual life.[7]

Instrumentalism can be traced in all human exchange, and from instrumentalism in this sense the evils that Marx was later to deduce from alienated industrial labour could already be derived.

Men learn to communicate with each other through objects. For the earliest men there may have been a time before the existence of trading, and before instrumentalism; and in this condition their relation to each other would have been a human one. But at the first exchange they lost the idea of a 'human language' that was free of any idea of mutual trading and of reference to a world of property.

As soon as exchange occurs ... each of us sees in his product only his own objectified self-interest and in the product of

another person another self-interest which is independent, alien
and objectified. . . . When I produce more than I can consume
I subtly reckon with your need. . . .

We mutually regard out product as the power each one has
over the other and over himself. . . . Our objects in their relation to one another constitute the only intelligible language we
use with one another. We would not understand a human
language, and it would remain without effect.[8]

Thus men's species-character – his 'common life' – has never yet
been expressed in the world in its full powers, freely, and has been
buried successively by the first private property, the first
exchange, the first division of labour and the first wage.

So long as man does not recognize himself as man and does not
organize the world humanly, [this] common life appears in the
form of *estrangement*. Because its *subject*, man, is a being
estranged from itself. . . . His activity, therefore, appears as a
torment, his own creation as a foreign power, his wealth as
poverty, the *essential bond* connecting him with other men as
something inessential, so that separation from other men
appears as his true existence, so that his life appears as the
sacrifice of his life, the realization of his essence as the diminu-
tion of his life, his production as the production of his destruction, his power over the object as the power of the object over
him, so that he, the master of his creation, appears as the slave
of this creation.[9]

By contrast, Marx poses the prelationships that could exist
between men if each produced for the other in accordance with
his 'species-essence' :

Suppose we had produced things as human beings . . . our
productions would be so many mirrors reflecting our
nature. . . . My labour would be a *free manifestation of life* and
an *enjoyment* of *life*. Under the presupposition of private property it is an *alienation of life* because . . . I work *in order to
live* and provide . . . for myself the *means* of living. Working is
not living. . . . Under the presumption of private property my

individuality is alienated to the point where I *hate* this *activity* and where it is a torment for me.[10]

This concept of 'instrumentalism' is re-introduced in the Economic Philosophic Manuscripts of 1844 as one aspect of a more general notion : 'alienated' or 'estranged' wage-labour.

For Marx men begin to define themselves as a species and distinguish themselves from animals when they produce. 'Productive life ... is a species-life. It is life begetting life. In the mode of life activity lies the entire character of a species, its species-character; and free conscious activity is the species-character of man.' Alienated labour is the estrangement of each individual from his human essence which is free, conscious, productive life and the turning of the products of his labour into a world hostile to the producer.

A fourfold loss is entailed in alienated labour. First man loses his relationship to nature – to the product of his work; then he loses his relationship to himself and to his 'life-activity' – the act of production; then his relationship to his species-life – free spontaneous activity; and finally his relationship to other men.[11]

Thus there is no possibility of a man finding a true relation to himself or his work in a society where men's relations to each other are not fundamentally healed. Rousseau's and Schiller's belief that inner integrity is possible only in a re-ordered society, is confirmed by Marx more forcefully. The revolutionary implications of this view become overt. Whereas earlier ideas of man's relation to his self – in Stoicism, or in Christianity – have allowed that a man can find his own true nature in a still corrupt society, Marx has so defined his terms that this is impossible.

The 'mutilated', 'fragmented' worker who tends the machine in Marx's later writings is mutilated not only because of some simple repetitive action he must perform; not only because he is not a 'harmoniously developed individual'; but because the full development of man's species essence, as Marx has defined it, can come about only in a society where all men work for each other. The idea Marx quoted in 1875, that 'the free development of each will be the condition for the free development of all', is not a slogan merely; it is consistent with his whole system, since men are 'free' and 'developed' insofar as they attain their 'species-life', which is for him a certain kind of socially productive relationship to nature, to their work, to each other and thus to themselves, that can be attained not individually but only collectively, through revolution.

Though Marx used the concept of 'alienation' less in *Capital* than in the 1844 Manuscripts, he still continued to use it, and the later theories which centre on the concept of exploitation do not contradict, but develop, the ideas of his earlier writings.

In the later Marx, machinery is frozen exploitation. It is expropriated labour-power built into a solid form. And while the means for the development of production in the modern world could be used to supply the needs of the labourer, they are in fact used for exactly the opposite purpose : to drive down still further the value of the labourer's work, and allow an ever more powerful hostile world to confront him. They thus

> ... mutilate the labourer into a fragment of a man, degrade him to the level of an appendage of the machine, destroy the content of his work with the torment of it, estrange from him the intellectual potentialities of the labour process in the same proportion as science is incorporated into it as an independent power; they distort the conditions under which he works; subject him during the labour process to a despotism the more hateful for its meanness; they transform his life-time into working-time, and let his wife and child fall beneath the juggernaut of capital.[12]

This passage has often been quoted and it can easily lead – out of context – to the idea that Marx 'attacked industrialization' in itself. But a view of Marx as a destructive critic of machinery – like Ruskin – or as a theorist of 'alienation by technology' – as he is sometimes presented today – cannot conveivably be based on his writings.

In the 1844 Manuscripts it was wage labour, not specifically machine labour, that was shown to involve 'alienation'. Work at machinery was dealt with purely as one aspect of modern wage labour; not as the original source of 'alienation'. Again, in *Capital*, Marx explicitly states that he opposes the 'capitalist' use of machinery but not machinery itself.[13] To confuse the two, says Marx, is exactly the reasoning of the celebrated Bill Sykes : 'It is the knife that did the murder, not the murderer.'

Even 'the capitalist use of machinery', for Marx, was not necessarily worse than the capitalist use of human beings in pre-mechanical forms of labour. The treatment of this subject in *Capital* is more detailed than the brief argument in the 1844 Manuscripts. For where in his early writings Marx is hardly emanicpated from an eighteenth-century view of machinery as merely a further intensification of the division of labour – a view similar to that of Hegel in his *Jenenser Realphilosophie* – by the time he wrote *Capital* Marx had begun to pick out quite other elements in it.

Marx distinguished between cottage industry, hard-working 'manufacturies', and factories employing powered machinery, referring to the second type of establishment as a *Manufaktur* and to the third as a *Fabrik* or, collectively, as *Industrie*.

One of the main empirical developments in *Capital* from the 1844 Manuscripts is this singling out of labour with machines as a distinctive activity, different from divided labour by hand in either 'manufacturies' or cottages. Far from displaying hand labour favourably by comparison with machine work, Marx shows it as leading – at least in the world of capitalism and with machinery as a competitor – to worse degradation; and he shows domestic labour or 'outwork' as still more appalling :

> The exploitation of cheap and immature labour is carried out in a more shameless manner in modern Manufacture than in the factory proper. . . . This is because the technical foundation of the factory system, namely the substitution of machines for muscular power, and the light character of the labour, is almost entiely absent in Manufacture, and at the same time women and over-young children are subjected in a most unconscionable way, to the influence of poisonous or injurious substances.

This exploitation, in the so-called domestic industries, is worse than in Manufacture. . . .[14]

But Marx is not a mere idealizer of machinery, any more than he is an opponent of it, and he does not represent the intervention of machinery as a mere advance over forms of work that were always intrinsically worse, for he shows that it is machinery which has degraded the trades which it supplants or which it requires to feed it.[15]

In this, the Marx of *Capital* explains something in the history of working people that other critics of industrialization so far had not explained. He may have been mistaken in believing that factories drew a vast influx of population from the countryside to the towns in the early half of the nineteenth century; but even if, as is now sometimes argued, the population of the factories was supplied largely from the rapidly increasing urban population itself, the individual decisions of millions of men in the nineteenth and twentieth centuries to live in cities and to work in factories have to be accounted for. These may well have been in most cases, as Thomas Hardy said, instances of 'the tendency of water to flow uphill when forced.' Marx, while showing the appalling nature of factory work at its cruellest, recognized the alternatives with which an individual worker in a factory economy might be faced; and in his mature writings he had the same priorities as most working people in their individual choices have shown since.

His contemporary Ruskin and his successor Morris do not always seem to grasp what the choices may have been for individual working people. To the amateur craftsman in a factory economy, hand work may be a pleasure, or a consolation. But it is not likely to be either if it is a man's sole source of livelihood, and if the economy produces substitutes for his product by machines, creating huge fluctuations in the demand for his product and diminishing its price towards zero. And in the main alternative to factory work in the nineteenth century was in any case not craftsmanship; for most people it was either outwork, domestic service, or agricultural labour.

Marx's preference for factory labour over cottage industries, under capitalism at least, may appear inconsistent with an account that is often given of his views about work after 'the revolution'. It has often been argued that he envisaged future society as largely pastoral. The basis for this interpretation is the paragraph in The German Ideology where he says :

> In Communist society, however, where nobody has an exclusive area of activity and each can train himself in any branch he wishes, society regulates the general production, making it possible for me to do one thing today and another tomorrow, to hunt in the morning, fish in the afternoon, breed cattle in the evening, criticize after dinner, just as I like, without ever becoming a hunter, a fisherman, a herdsman or a critic.[16]

This is a perfectly accurate quotation often found isolated in summaries of Marx's thought. But Marx is particularly hard on theories that imply that men should revert to simpler levels of demand, and to pre-industrial or pre-agricultural ways of life.

In The German Ideology Marx has been talking of the division of labour as the 'first example' of alienation. He is writing in terms of origins, and of the first division of labour into material and mental work. '*Jäger, Fischer, Hirt*' is a phrase he uses here and elsewhere to refer to early men, with as unstudied a choice of words as a modern anthropologist talking of a 'hunting and gathering society'. The set phrase appears earlier in the same passage and, for instance, in a similar context in the *Grundrisse*.[17]

At the same time Marx is speaking at this point in The German Ideology not merely of origins, but of 'aspects of social activity', ' "moments" which have existed simultaneously since the dawn of history and the first men and still exist today'. He recognizes – with irony – that this is to state his argument in a specifically German way; the manner of thought common to both Hegel's Phenomenology and to the earlier Aesthetic Letters of Schiller. Speaking in terms that cover the whole of human history, therefore, he refers within the same paragraph to the origins and to the latest stage of the division of labour :

The division of labour offers us the first example of the fact that man's own act becomes an alien power opposed to him. . . . For as soon as labour is distributed each person has a particular exclusive area of activity which is imposed on him and from which he cannot escape. He is a hunter, a fisherman, a herdsman or a critical critic, and he must remain so if he does not want to lose his means of livelihood.

The juxtaposition of three primitive activities with one from his own society and age, and the taking up again of the same phrase in the context of communist society in the next sentence, is thus unstudied and lends no support to the idea that he intended his communist society to have a mainly pastoral future. The shepherd and the critic are merely two extremes, at the beginning and at the end of pre-revolutionary divided labour.

But if Marx did not believe that some re-discovered pastoral world would be the cure of 'alienation', nor that work with machinery was itself its cause, he did believe that work should be re-designed. The idea of work in Marx's later writings is the healing of a threefold division of labour. Work is to be social – without separate owners; freely rotating – without permanent specialization; and both scientific and manual at the same time.

If there is to be undivided work in the future good society, how much of men's time is to be devoted to it? Marx wrestles with the ambivalence of work in the *Grundrisse*. On the one hand, says Marx, Adam Smith had seen only the 'curse' of work. For Adam Smith

> . . . rest appears as the adequate condition, as identical with freedom and happiness. . . . It seems to be far from A. Smith's mind . . . that the individual . . . needs a normal portion of work and of supersession of rest. A. Smith notices just as little that [this] overcoming of obstacles is in itself the practice of freedom . . . and that, furthermore, external purposes take on an appearance stripped of totally external natural necessity, and are determined as purposes which the individual first determines for himself – thus as self-realization, objectification of the subject, hence real freedom, whose action is in fact work.[13]

For Marx, Adam Smith was right in saying that work has always appeared to men as something repulsive, as labour imposed by outside compulsion. Marx makes it clear that this was so even in early human society, but doubly true of work in modern capitalist economies, 'this contradictory labour which has not yet created the subjective and objective conditions (which it lost when it abandoned pastoral conditions), which make it into *travail attractif* and individual self-realization'.

Travail attractif is a – more or less – Fourier-esque phrase. But Fourier is quickly put in his place for offering the hope of an over-simplification, the reverse of Adam Smith's. Fourier has, 'with grisette-like naïveté conceived of work as just fun, just amuse-ment'. This is equally mistaken : 'Really free work, e.g. compos-ing, is precisely at the same time in the most damned earnest, the most intense effort.'[19]

Thus it was an ideal of artistic production that Marx took as the model to which material production should be made to approximate in his future society; but as we shall see, he did not mean either craftsmanship alone, or – as has been argued by one modern commentator – some kind of 'aesthetic' feeling, like the feeling of playing in an orchestra, with which the discipline of an otherwise normal factory or city life was to be experienced. It is not true that Marx, viewing the entire condition of men after the revolution as in some general way harmonious with each other and therefore 'aesthetic', regards this as in itself a solution to problems like those of factory labour.[20]

Marx does develop an aesthetic model of work after the revolu-tion, but not that of an orchestral player : his picture is of the composer at work. Comparing the work of material production to the ideal of 'really free activity, for example composing', he says :

The work of material production can take on this character only insofar as (1) social character is assigned to it, and (2) that it is of scientific character, [and] at the same time is general work, not effort of man as a natural force trained in a definite way, but [of man] appearing as subject in the production process not in mere natural primitive form but as activity regulating all forces of nature.[21]

This redemption of the process of material production by mixing science with labour and varying the labour itself would also bring about a healing of the split between production and consumption. As Marx says in 'The Critique of the Gotha Programme', work itself will become not only a means to life but life's primary want or need. And this makes the exact number of working hours in the future a secondary question for Marx, when he writes in this vein at least: the distinction between work and leisure would be a comparatively thin one.

It is true there are traces of a different model in Marx. The work of material production remains in certain of his writings a 'realm of necessity'. So in a different context he says that hours must be cut drastically, and the measure of civilization in a country is the shortness of its working day. And in the last volume of *Capital* the idea that there is a separate 'realm of necessity', beyond which freedom begins, is repeated in the context of post-revolutionary production.

It appears to have troubled Marx, at least in those writings printed by Engels as the third volume of *Capital*, that even if labour were to be re-organized into an alternation of mental and varied manual work, insofar as it was still the satisfaction of 'needs' it would remain in the 'realm of necessity'; whereas the full development of human potentiality could begin only beyond this realm, in a distinct 'realm of freedom':

> The realm of freedom, in fact, first begins where labour that is determined by need and external expediency, ceases. . . . Beyond it begins human development of powers, which counts as its own end, the true realm of freedom, which, however, can flourish only upon that realm of necessity as its basis. The shortening of the working day is its fundamental condition.[22]

It is reasonable to suppose that Marx had two models of free work, one still showing traces of its ancestry in the Greek conception of necessity that Schiller also followed, one in his own ideal of necessity and freedom reconciled. The distinction is not practically significant if, in the future society, work and leisure cease to be rigidly divided. In fact it can be argued that 'leisure production' is at some moments envisaged by Marx as 'the main productive force of the new society'.[23]

The analysis of the effects of machinery on men in *Capital* is in place empirical and humane. For instance – crediting Engels with the observation – Marx writes :

> At the same time that factory work exhausts the nervous system to the uttermost, it does away with the many-sided play of the muscles, and confiscates every atom of freedom both in bodily and intellectual activity. The lightening of the labour even becomes a sort of torture, since the machine does not free the labourer from work, but deprives the work of all interest.[24]

But while Marx devotes many pages to descriptions of recent machines, such as the Nasmyth steam hammer, in general his accounts of the effects of machinery on the sensibility of workmen are not as detailed or as varied as his descriptions of the machinery itself, or of the economic system which produces the standard results in which he believes. And even where he describes machinery empirically, a quite different *a priori* manner is liable suddenly to show through, when he speaks of their effects on men. A few lines after the vivid quotation from Engels describing the way machinery can rob workmen of the play of their different muscles, Marx continues : 'By means of its conversion into an automaton, the means of labour confronts the labourer, during the labour process, as capital, as dead labour, that dominates, that sucks dry, living labour power. . . .'[25] Maybe some workmen do actually experience their machines as 'dead labour power'. But when someone does not feel this, his feelings may be explained away : his experience is 'ideological'; he has been deluded, lulled into quiescence by propaganda. He is not experiencing the machine as it 'really' confronts him – as 'dead labour power' – but is the victim of 'false consciousness'.

The invitation to dismiss conflicting opinions and feelings as 'false consciousness', and the use of concepts such as 'alienation' and 'self-estrangement' as categories for describing the condition of working people, may make an appeal today to intellectuals similar to its appeal to a Marxist party in power. 'Alienation' is a concept that both seems to explain, and seems to explain away, the troublesomely diverse experience of working people as this changes in changing society. The 1844 Manuscripts are a philosopher's projection of his ways of feeling on to a model of an industrial worker, and to that extent they contain sympathetic insight. But they can also be taken as offering a model of 'man in industrial society' : a single model. By providing a picture of 'man' they can replace the need to listen to real working people. And even when working people are listened to, neo-Marxism can imply a standard of 'correct' experience in the light of which men's actual feelings can be judged, and also a theory of ideology which allows their divergences from this to be dismissed. And this is true of revivals even of early Marxism.

To dismiss the actual wishes of contemporary working people as not 'really' theirs, to ascribe to them a 'false' consciousness – if that is the appropriate translation of *unrichtiges Bewusstsein* – is not the only possible attitude to take to those feelings and beliefs. From another point of view they are the most real things that there can be, the forms in which, for better or worse, men do at the moment experience their work and live their lives.

If Marx's model of the universe is not quite of the geometrical, Pythagorean kind – in which, to understand a man you must, as with a triangle, understand its defining properties; if it is not quite seventeenth-century clockwork, in which – as for Hobbes – there are wheels turning human nature from central 'springs'; if Marx, like many of his immediate predecessors and contemporaries, uses metaphors of growth and plant life rather than of geometry or of clockwork for human nature, he has still not evolved a logic that deals fully with either individual variety or growth in its own terms. He writes of mankind as a single organism that still somehow resembles a watch-hand in being driven by a sole determining force; he still writes of mankind as 'essentially' this or that; of certain elements of men's life as their *Wesen* – their essence.

And this habit of thought has been communicated to a contemporary generation of critics of industrial society; in the last two decades there has been a revival in both East and West of early Marxist criticism of industry and industrial society. Khruschev's denunciation of Stalin in 1956 and his own invasion of Hungary a few months later was followed by a mass exodus from the communist parties of the West. Meanwhile, in the eastern part of Europe, a generation of thinkers trained in Marxism had grown up, determined to bring out what they felt to be its humanist content – its criticisms of all inhumanity, whether capitalist or nominally socialist. Certain young people in the East and West found themselves speaking a common language, and criticizing the monotony, the authoritatian disciplines and the fragmented nature of work in both Russian-style and capitalist factories. Since Marx remained the starting point for many of these writers such criticisms were made in terms of his early writings – only recently become widely available – which, with their passionate denunciation of the conditions of wage labour, seemed to apply with great relevance to work in both East and West in the late 1950s, and had the advantage of being in a theoretical language which students and philosophers could readily understand and develop.

Some of the bolder theorists in the East, such as Leszek Kolakowski, suffered for their writings, and it became more than ever natural to assume that the championship of the early Marx was the cause of justice, liberty, truth and, throughout the world, of 'socialism with a human face'. By contrast, the ideas of the later Marx which – deprived of their central emphasis on the abolition of divided labour – had been used to justify industrialization in Russia by a combination of one – party dictatorship with Taylorism seemed discredited.[26]

This championship of the early writings of Marx led to a widespread use of the term 'alienation', particularly in discussions of work and industry. But over the century since 1844 the concept

had undergone many transformations, having been associated
with different and often loosely conflicting images of human
nature in German sociology after Marx, without ever taking root
as a concept used in the ordinary speech of the majority of
unreflective people; so that neither from disputes in scientific
theory conducted according to any agreed rules, not from the
weathering process that gives a firm shape to the concepts of
ordinary speech, had it acquired any precise meaning.

To some, the jumble of different definitions now associated
with 'alienation' could seem a strength : it might seem a concept
of very general application. To others it appeared more like an
alchemical concept in a late stage of decay, lacking any decision-
procedures for settling disputes between different uses of it, lacking roots in contemporary speech, and rapidly losing any useful-
ness, as a result.

It was perhaps a particularly unfortunate concept for the
representation of working people's feelings since it was one they
seldom used – in England at least – and in theoretical studies it
tended to replace the words they did use. Like a 'puppet government' it claimed to represent people's feelings yet it was used
more easily by people outside than within the form of life that it
was held to represent, and it saved some people outside this form
of life the trouble of finding out about the concepts that really did
represent those feelings.

In studies of modern industry using the term 'alienation', one
finds facts derived from present-day life, and values coming
straight from the facts of the 1840s. Thus a worker who is more
interested in his home than in his job, even when he is at work,
may be defined as 'self-estranged'. His preference is accorded a
'negative value' and classified as an aspect of 'alienation' in just
the same way as with Marx, who believed that productive activity
was men's species-essence, and that home life consisted of 'animal
functions'. However, Marx formed this view at a time when for
most industrial workers their factory life really was their only
possible area of productive activity, since it took simply all their
waking time, and there might be six hours of darkness, a hovel

and subsistence wages available for sleep and the living of home life.

One modern writer who has used the language of the early Marx writes: 'Observation and research have disproved [Marx's] statement that "as soon as no physical or other compulsion exist, labour is shunned like the plague".'[27]

But 'observation and research' about work in the mid-twentieth century cannot have 'disproved' Marx's statement about the shunning of labour 'like the plague' in the mid-nineteenth century. Equally Marx's evaluation of the significance of work in relation to home life cannot be uncritically retained when the proportion of life spent in each has simply been reversed. The revival of Marx's early works in recent years, with some of the same biblical status that communist parties in power have attached to his later writings, seems to have led to their immediate application, without historical reservations, to the industry of the mid-twentieth century, and this has distorted the understanding of factory workers' lives on the part of those who perhaps most wish to improve the possibilities of those lives.

In the early 1840s factory workers did not stay on at work at knocking-off time. After sixteen hours of work a day this is not unnatural. In this historical situation Marx makes an antithesis between an 'essence' of man – productive activity – which is arguably a somewhat schoolmasterly ideal in the first place, and man's 'merely animal functions' – eating, drinking 'procreating'. He calls the use of the former as a means to the sustenance of the latter 'self-estrangement'. And when half a dozen hours a day in a crowded room are allowed for all four 'functions' – eating, drinking, sleeping and 'procreating' – they may well have become a little 'animal', at least in the eyes of a philosopher from outside; and they will probably have included little 'free, conscious activity'. To apply the same concept of 'self-estrangement' to a preference for the three-quarters of the week that include home and leisure life – which may involve much more 'free, conscious' or even 'productive' activity than attendance at a contemporary office or factory – is to make a fundamental mistake, not only about many lives in the present world, but even about Marx's own view of leisure, freedom and the possibility of productive activity away from 'the job'. In the present world, the kind of instrumentalism that subjects leisure and marriage to the demands of advancement in a job can surely be at least as savage as the kind that sacrificed work to the demands of marriage in the past two centuries.

Perhaps the whole period since 1800, at least in Britain, is to be seen as one over which people, in some cases by adopting an instrumental attitude to work, and in other cases by retaining an existing instrumentalism, freed some part of their lives for 'play' – often by a loss of 'play' in their working lives – while at the same time partly liberating their marriages from the dictates of chance and of economics. If there were a form of self-estrangement prevalent today, comparable to Marx's, it could well be exactly the opposite of the one that modern sociologists who merely quote Marx's words assume. 'Free, conscious' or even 'productive' activity may – for any particular man – be found more in the leisure part of the week than in his time 'on the job'. And what is the ultimate reason for calling such activity the 'human essence' – by contrast with play, for instance, or with love, or with whatever a particular man makes the central activity and interest of his life?

The father of a docking family we will listen to later in this book did very much the same kind of labour throughout his working career, but meanwhile moved with his family from one room to a house, then to a house with a garden, and finally on retirement to a house close to the fishing which was his happiest occupation. Through these changes, against odds, against hardship, through slump, war and the devastating reconstruction of his city, he carried a family he loved. It may not seem, contrasted with some lives, a great story; but this is perhaps chiefly a defect in our conception of a great story, one which Flaubert in *Un Coeur Simple* reverses in a single brush-stroke : 'Elle avait eu, comme une autre, son histoire d'amour.' Neither for the scale of its satisfactions, nor for the fact that they are placed outside a job, is such a life to be judged 'negatively', as meaningless' or as 'self-estranged', by some philosophical stranger.

6

William Morris and his English predecessors

In 1883, when he was forty-nine, William Morris turned vigorously to politics;[1] it was then that he read Karl Marx. A year later he was among the small procession that visited Marx's grave on the first anniversary of his death.[2] Already by this time there was a striking similarity on many points between the two men's theories. But the foundations of Morris' social ideas had been laid much earlier, in his undergraduate days; and by his own account they were laid in an English rather than a Continental tradition, and a literary rather than an economic one. According to one of his biographers, Morris 'while capable of severe intellectual discipline, was unfamiliar with the development of European philosophy'.[3] And at the time when he joined the Social Democratic Federation, as he later wrote, 'I had had never so much as opened Adam Smith, or heard of Ricardo or Karl Marx'.[4] But, thirty years earlier, as an undergraduate

> The books of John Ruskin ... were ... a sort of revelation to me; I was also a good deal influenced by the works of Charles Kingsley, and got into my head therefrom some socio-political ideas which would have developed probably but for the attractions of art and poetry.'[5]

Ruskin was perhaps the strongest influence Morris consistently acknowledged, before his fifties; but he saw him in a tradition. In 1886, replying to an editor with a list of books that had most profoundly impressed him in his lifetime, he grouped together the writing of three authors: 'Sir Thomas More's Utopia, Ruskin's works (especially the ethical and politico-economic parts of them) and Thomas Carlyle's works'.[6] And near the end of his life, again, he wrote of the few men who had given him an ideal in his youth, inspiring him to rebel against the conventional thought of his time: 'a few, say two, Carlyle and Ruskin. The latter before my days of practical socialism, was my master towards the ideal aforesaid.'[7]

Morris' intellectual ancestry, then, derives from an English tradition, one which the present study has not stressed particularly until now.[8] Yet, if it was English, it was not an isolated one, cut off from continental ideas. Sir Thomas More could not be called an insular thinker. And Carlyle as much as any English writer of the nineteenth century fed on and contributed to continental European ideas; particularly in his early ideas, which are the ones that influenced Morris.

One modern critic, who describes Carlyle's *Signs of the Times* (1829) as 'a direct response to the England of his day', and 'to industrialism, which he was the first to name', says that the influence of German thought in the preceding forty years is clear ... [of] Goethe, Schiller, Jean Paul and Novalis ...'; while Coleridge, his other significant influence at this time 'had himself gone to many of the same sources'.[9]

The influence is clearly traceable[10] in Carlyle's pronouncements that in 'this age ... the Age of Machinery', while 'the shuttle drops from the fingers of the weaver, and falls into iron fingers that ply it faster' ... 'not the external and physical alone is now managed by machinery, but the internal and spiritual also ... Men are grown mechanical in head and heart, as well as in hand'.[11] It is evident again in the statement, from *Past and Present*, that 'all work, even cotton-spinning, is noble; work alone is noble'; and in the idea that by clearing jungles and deserts, and by building cities the man himself first ceases to be a jungle and foul unwholesome desert ... The man is now a man'; the idea that 'a man perfects himself by working'.[12]

In his turn, Carlyle had a profound effect on his German

contemporaries. Engles in his early writings – his articles for the *Rheinische Zeitung* and *The Condition of the Working Class in England in 1844* – has been described as 'translating Carlyle freely'[13]; while one phrase used strikingly by Marx and Engels in 1848 – the 'cash nexus' – is directly derived from Carlyle's idea that 'cash payment' had become in the nineteenth century 'the sole nexus between man and man'.[14]

Marx's early, though not his later ideas about machinery suggest common sources with Carlyle's; while above all his estimate of work as the essence, the defining property of human nature places him beside Carlyle as an inheritor of the late eighteenth-century philosophical enthusiasm for productive activity over all other activities – and passivities – of men.

Morris' other great early influence, Ruskin, was himself a disciple of Carlyle. His horror of machinery, which he shared with Carlyle, was lifelong. Ruskin hated all machinery, whatever its nature and however burdensome the manual work it relieved. He had no conception of the kind of dispersed small industry that electricity could bring, perhaps reconciling many of his ideas of craftsmanship with machine production; and he does not seem to have understood that some people actually like machinery and enjoy those forms of precision it encourages. Nor did he foresee the kind of sensibility which found expression later in *Deutscher Werkbund*, the Bauhaus and in Le Corbusier's early theories, that would attempt to fuse traditional forms of craftsmanship, and even some of his own and Morris' ideas, with industrial production. He did not apparently envisage any redemption of industrial landscape for the eye by an art that would recreate it in new forms – as landscape itself has arguably been shaped for the eye by the generations of artists who have painted it.

The machinery he knew was coal and gas. He seems to have believed that much machinery was perpetually liable to explode. Asking 'Have the Watts and Stephensons, then, done nothing but harm?' he answered simply, in 1874, 'Nothing'.[15] All steam engines and railroads were to be excluded from the 'small piece of

English ground, beautiful, peaceful and fruitful', where he wrote of establishing his guild of working people.[16]

Ruskin also shared Carlyle's respect for all work – from the most craftsmanlike to the hardest physical labour. Yet he made discriminations between the quality of different forms of work – distinctions on which Morris would found his mature theories.

Ruskin saw hard and burdensome work as something to be shared equally between men, and taken on voluntarily in a greater degree by anyone who claimed leadership a distinction. Thus he himself swept roads and – not always successfully – tried to build them. He also saw labour as valuable in itself : he describes the satisfactions of sweeping a room in Switzerland for the sense of a burden shared and for the clear frame of mind it left him in for painting and writing afterwards. He measured the nobility of men, as he measured that of the kings in *The Iliad* and the heroes of the *Waverley Novels* chiefly by the unequal share they took of the hardest labour.[17]

Speaking thus of the nobility and of the consolations of labour, he wrote in *The Mystery of Life and its Arts* (1868):

Whenever the arts and labours of life are fulfilled in this spirit of striving against misrule, and doing whatever we have to do, honourably and perfectly, they invariably bring happiness, as much as seems possible, to the nature of man. In all other paths by which that happiness is pursued there is disappointment, or destruction : for ambition and for passion there is no rest – no fruition; the fairest pleasures of youth perish in a darkness greater than their past light : and the loftiest and purest love too often does but inflame the cloud of life with endless fire of pain. But, ascending from lowest to highest, through every scale of human industry, that industry worthily followed, gives peace. Ask the labourer in the field, at the forge, or in the mine; ask the patient, delicate-fingered craftsman, or the strong-armed, fiery-hearted worker in bronze, and in marble, and with the colours of light; and not one of these, who are true workmen, will ever tell you that they have found the law of heaven an unkind one – that in the sweat of their face they should eat bread, till they return to the ground; nor that they ever found it an unrewarded obedience, if, indeed it was rendered faithfully to the command – 'Whatsoever they hand findeth to do – do it with thy might'.[18]

But it was less by his general praise of work than by his attacks on the work that most men do in a civcilization based on mass-production, that Ruskin influenced William Morris. Ruskin saw craftsmanship and art, in every sense, as the most valuable forms of work not only for their products but for their effects on those who do them. He argued that such work had once been the lot of most men, and that it had created the background to daily life at least until the Renaissance.[19]

Ruskin's chapter 'The Nature of Gothic', in the second volume of *The Stones of Venice*, which appeared while Morris was at Oxford, sets out these ideas most clearly. It was this chapter which Morris acknowledged as the most lasting influence from his youth, and which in his old age he reprinted at the Kelmscott press.

In *The Stones of Venice* Ruskin reserved his highest praise of Gothic for the demands it made and the effects it had on the working life and imagination of men of moderate talent, whom it enabled to be artists and craftsmen within the limits of their capacities.

> It is, perhaps, the principal admirableness of the Gothic schools of architecture, that they . . . receive the results of the labour of inferior minds; and out of fragments full of imperfection, and betraying that imperfection in every touch, indulgently raise up a stately and unaccusable whole . . .

He believed all the great artists except Leonardo had accepted the imperfection in their own work – 'of human work none but what is bad can be perfect, in its own bad way',[20] but that certain ideas, new in the Rennaissance, had first ruined the arts themselves and then spread further in their influence on life as a whole.

> . . . as we approach the period of the Renaissance . . . the first

cause of the fall of the arts of Europe was a relentless require-
ment of perfection, incapable alike either of being silenced by
veneration for greatness or softened into forgiveness of
simplicity.[21]

Ruskin pointed to a link between this intense drive of modern
civilization for perfection in art, in machinery and in commerce,
and its way of dealing with human beings at work :

> Men were not intended to work with the accuracy of tools, to
> be precise and perfect in all their actions. If you will have that
> precision out of them . . . all the energy of their spirits must be
> given to make cogs and compasses of themselves . . . and the
> whole human being (must) be lost at last . . . On the other
> hand, if you will make a man of the working creature, you
> cannot make a tool. Let him but begin to imagine, to think, to
> try to do anything worth doing; and the engine-turned pre-
> cision is lost at once. Out come all his roughness, all his dull-
> ness, all his incapability; shame upon shame, failure upon
> failure, pause after pause : but out comes the whole majesty of
> him also.[22]

In what he conceived to be the destruction of men's imagination
and power to invent by post-Renaissance art and by industrial
mass production, Ruskin saw the source of class hatred and latent
revolution.

> The foundations of society were never yet shaken as they are at
> this day. It is not that men are ill fed, but that they have no
> pleasure in the work by which they make their bread, and
> therefore look to wealth as the only means of pleasure. It is not
> that men are pained by the scorn of the upper classes, but they
> cannot endure their own; for they feel that the kind of labour
> to which they are condemned is verily a degrading one, and
> makes them less than men.[23]

The way to find work that will satisfy all men is – for Ruskin – to
share the hard manual labour out among everybody and to com-
bine manual labour with intellectual work and design. Indepen-

dently, he had arrived at a similar position to Marx's on this subject :

> It is no less fatal an error to despise (manual labour) when it is regulated by intellect than to value it for its own sake ...
> The workman ought often to be thinking, and the thinker often to be working ... The mass of society is made up of morbid thinkers, and miserable workers. Now it is only by labour that thought can be made healthy, and only by thought that labour can be made unhappy, and the two cannot be separated with impunity.[24]

Ruskin himself remained a practising artist; some of his strongest aesthetic and moral convictions were based on the experiences he had as he drew, studying and coming to love the forms of nature.[25] Thus, up to a point, he put into practice in his own life the theories he advanced.

But Morris practised them wholesale. One of Morris' contemporaries at Oxford wrote of him 'It was when Burne Jones and he got at Ruskin, that strong direction was given to a true vocation.[26] At first this Ruskinian 'vocation' for the arts led him towards architecture; and also further into his own poetry; then, under the influence of a visit to Northern France in 1854, and a meeting in 1856 with Dante Gabriel Rossetti, Morris decided to become a painter.

But from his quite early days he branched out into other arts and into crafts: into tapestry, dyeing, carpet-making, the illumination of manuscripts and the making of fabrics, wallpapers and stained glass. These not only gave him first-hand experience of manual labour and craftsmanship; they also brought him into day-to-day contact with a number of working people, labourers and craftsmen. And they forced him to reflect on the changes in history which had destroyed those medieval arts he loved so much, making it impossible to 'restore' ancient buildings without ruining them – an activity he opposed vigorously in lectures and pamphlets from the 1870s onwards, founding and becoming the first secretary of the Society for the Protection of Ancient Buildings.

What his handwork did not give him was any experience of the life of a craftsman who is dependent on his work for his living. Left a fortune by his father when he was thirteen, Morris was a rich man all his life. Thus there always was a gulf between his experience and that of the majority of the craftsmen about whom he thought and wrote.

But if his practice, and many of his early theories, were in strong sympathy with those of Ruskin, Morris's ideas changed as he grew older. E. P. Thompson has pointed to the influence of the Icelandic sagas in the 1860's, and of his journeys to Iceland in 1871 and 1873, as that of a rougher world outside the canons of Ruskinian taste and feeling. The other shaping force was political experience.

Morris became more active politically as the 1870s advanced. The first cause that absorbed him was the agitation of 1876 against war over the 'Eastern Question'. The Eastern Question Association brought him into close contact with working men, with a delegation of whom he visited Gladstone and attempted to arrange a mass meeting. When he issued an anti-war manifesto in May 1877 it was to the working men of England that he addressed it. According to Burne Jones, opposition to the persecution of Jews and intellectuals in Russia moved him closer still to active politics. Finally, he read Mill's arguments against socialism, so fairly did Mill put both sides of the case that they convinced him he should formally become a socialist; and in 1883 he joined the Social Democratic Federation, led by Hyndman.[27]

It was to meet arguments that Burne Jones suggests he set about reading Marx, and he did so in the same year. A note of Morris's written in 1883 quotes Marx:[28] 'It is not only the labour that is divided, sub-divided and portioned out between divers men: it is the man himself who is cut up, and metamorphised into the automatic spring of an exclusive operation.'

Through his reading of Carlyle and Ruskin, Morris had

already met such ideas in his youth. But other new influences now were to draw him away from his Ruskinian inheritance. He wrote a year later that though he had 'a great respect for Ruskin, and his works (beside personal friendship)' he could not regard him as a practical socialist, or concerned with any real fundamental change in society.[29] Change, in Morris' view, could come about only by revolution.

For some years before he formally became a socialist, Morris had been saying in letters that only some great cataclysm would ever change English society for the better. Morris believed that the classes in power would be likely to resist change.[30] The need for a time of violence, he thought, might come, and then . . . 'We must not say "we must drop our purpose rather than carry it across the river of violence". To say that means casting the whole thing into the hands of chance, and we can't do that.'[31]

Morris had experience in his own life of agitation, of the violence of mobs and of clashes with the police. The events of Bloody Sunday, 1887, in particular, strenghtened his belief in organization against attacks which he thought would be forthcoming in any socialist movements.[32] Nevertheless his expectations and approval of violence were strictly limited. First he opposed the 'swaggering' references to violence that he thought characteristic of Hyndman.[33] From all nationalistic belligerence and war-making he had as strong a revulsion as Ruskin.[34] Morris speaks in 1878 of 'the war fever raging in England', and of people going about 'in a Rule Brittania style that turns one's stomach'; and again – despite his earlier respect for Gladstone – he writes contemptuously of the liberal leader's 'damned little wars' and his 'market wars which bring forth murders great and grim'.[35] In the context of revolution he did not approve of the use of violence by a minority to impose revolutionary views on a majority; nor of any revolution by a force other than a 'due effective majority' of the people.

Thus the role of education in his ideas is essential; it is a prerequisite of revolution, not something to be imposed after it. And this is a crucial difference between his ideas and the practice of, say, Lenin and Stalin. Morris frequently said that men whose lives and imaginations had been formed by the present system of society would need a great change in their circumstances and in their minds before they could see the value of a new society; and that education was thus the first and indispensible means towards the revolution he desired.[36]

He supported any improvement that could be secured, for the present, in the condition of working people – for instance, shorter working hours. 'Starvelings can only riot' he wrote : the more that could be done to improve working conditions, and housing before a revolution, the better. Morris did not belong to the school of revolutionaries who hold that all such 'palliatives are dangerous in that they postpone revolution; though he did not in fact expect that many would be obtained without one.[37]

Morris was ready to consider that men might make a revolution in a way quite different from his ideas.[38] He was also prepared to entertain the possibility that he might be wrong, or that at least he might be premature, and not proposing a society men generally wanted Finally he hated what he called Bismarckian State Socialism.[39] He accepted however, like other optimistic nineteenth-century figures, that it would be 'passed through' in the course of a revolution without becoming permanent. His ideas of the organization of society after a revolution were – on the large scale – generally somewhat vague, and genially optimistic : the means of production and exchange would be in the hands of 'the whole people duly organized'; society would be 'a great organic mass of well-regulated forces used for the bringing about of a happy life for all;[40] men would be 'all friends and good fellows – united in that communion of happy, reasonable, honoured labour which alone can produce genuine art or the pleasure of life'.[41]

But if in these phrases – two of which, it must be remembered, are from letters written unreflectively – there is enough vagueness to cover a permanent dictatorship, Morris was much more clear over the reorganization of life at an individual level, and about the arrangements of a small community; and he remained clear even when he expounded his views for large audiences in simplified ways in the course of his political career.

Happiness meant to him 'the pleasurable exercise of our energies'. By itself, this recalls Carlyle. But it is right to speak of Morris' breaking sharply with Carlyle's doctrine that 'all labour is noble'.[42] Morris followed Ruskin, and went further than him, in distinguishing between work that is satisfying on the one hand, and, on the other, repetitive, mechanical or hurried work done for commercial reasons, or in conditions of competition, overwork and anxiety. Such labour he believed can never be satisfying :

> It seems to me that the real way to enjoy life is to accept all its necessary ordinary details and turn them into pleasures by taking interest in them : whereas modern civilization huddles them out of the way, has them done in a venal and slovenly manner till they become real drudgery which people can't help trying to avoid.[43]

Thus, far from attempting to enlist men in more enthusiasm for their existing jobs – as if all work could rightly be made the 'essence' or centre of a life – he put as the first task of reform, before even the provision of good housing, a shortening of the working day. Like Marx in a similar context, he expected that the 'leisure' so created would be used by most people in voluntary activity, involving one or more of the arts, once they had been set free from 'overwork and anxiety', the two main obstacles, in his view, to men's recovery of their sense of the possibilities of life, which years of competition, mass-production, long hours of work and an environment of 'shoddy' goods had all but extinguished in the majority.

Art, which might well 'go under' in his day, would thus be created again. In certain of his lectures and essays – for instance *The Lesser Arts, Useful Work Versus Useless Toil* and *A Factory As It Might Be*[44] – Morris suggests a practising artist's answers to the questions that have been explored here. Some of the narratives also – such as *A King's Story* – show that in an imaginative setting Morris sometimes expressed his ideas equally precisely.

He brings a new approach to the criticism of nineteenth-century society in three ways. Where Marx writes about beauty from a distance, as someone who has lost immediate contact with art, but remembers that it was important, in Morris' writings beauty is seen always as one of the human needs : both its making and its enjoyment.

Then Morris advances familiar ideas – about an ending of the division of labour, for example, so that the same men would design, think and work with their hands – without the meta-physical justifications and philosophical system-building that survive even in the works of the later Marx.

Thirdly, Morris believes in persuasion. He was a rough per-suader, even in his youth : there was a boisterous jostling quality in many of his personal contacts, and in his political writings and demonstrations, as has been noted, he did not soak much of peace. He wrote in 1884 :

> We are at war, class against class, and man against man; all our time is taken up with that; we are forced to busy ourselves not with the arts of peace, but with the arts of war, which are, briefly, trickery and oppression . . . This is the system which we seek to overthrow and supplant by one in which labour will no longer be a burden.[45]

But his struggle was to be waged first by argument, by demonstra-tion, by art and by invention. Its end was to persuade the majority to believe in a new way of life, one without capitalist owners, without long hours of drudgery, and with love and care in the making of objects.

Morris' mature ideas about machinery and industry can per-haps be best seen in his essay of 1884, '*A Factory As It Might Be*'. The abolition of competition and the profit motive, together with the expropriation of capitalists who live on the work of others, will release enough constructive energy and material wealth to make possible a complete transformation of the factory system, and will also set free a suppressed desire for beauty.

There will simply be enough. Thus, whenever the objection 'impossible' is raised against a factory garden, or a beautiful building, Morris replies that every factory does sustain such a garden or such a building already; but it is the owner's, somewhere else. Why not a building or a garden for the workpeople, at their work?

But beautiful surroundings are not enough. Good conditions of work 'can be only realized naturally and without affectation by the work which is to be done in them being in all ways reasonable and fit for human beings.'[46]

Such work must have two qualities. First it must be useful. It will be useful in his society because, with no profit motive 'there will be no rich men . . . contriving snares for cash in the shape of trumpery which they themselves heartily despise. Nor will the work turn out trash; there will be no millions of poor to make a market for (it).'[47]

It will also be beautiful, once the burdens of stultifying routine and long hours have been lifted. And these will be removed, for the later Morris as for Marx, by machinery.

There is so widespread a picture of Morris as a persistent opponent of machinery – a picture to which some of his own earlier writings have contributed – that it is worth noting that this factory is itself quite functional and contains up-to-date machines.

Not that Morris ever becomes an enthusiast for machinery in itself. In 'The Aims of Art' he picks out a danger in nineteenth-century machinery that might still be identified today. 'I am thinking of the modern machine, which is as it were alive, and to which the man is auxiliary, and not of the old machine, the improved tool, which is auxiliary to the man, and only works as long as his hand is thinking.'[48]

But even allowing for the danger that machinery may replace the 'hand thinking', Morris goes on : '. . . machines of the most ingenious and best-approved kinds will be used when necessary, but will be used simply to save human labour.'[49]

In Morris' ideal world machinery would lead to a more flexible factory system : first in the matter of hours

The machines being now used only for saving human labour, it follows that much less labour will be necessary for each work-man; . . . so that the working time of each member of our factory will be very short, say, to be much within the mark, four hours a day.[50]

Even if the machine-kinding were still irksome, there would be beside it 'some attractive work . . . which was pleasant in itself to do'; and, as in Marx's theory, men would alternate between jobs : 'whatever is burdensome about the factory would be taken turn and turn about, and so distributed, would cease to be a burden – would be, in fact, a kind of rest from the more exciting or artistic work.'[51]

Finally, some aspects of working life would be enjoyed for their own sake, and 'The organization of such a factory, that is to say of a group of people working in harmonious co-operation towards a useful end, would of itself afford opportunities for increasing the pleasure of life.'[52]

Morris says what he thinks about the ambiguous experience of 'joy' in work more fully in another essay :

> Let us grant, first, that the race of man must either labour or perish . . . It is of the nature of man, when it is not diseased, to take pleasure in his work under certain conditions. And, yet, we must say in the teeth of the hypocritical praise of all labour, whatsoever it may be . . . that there is some labour which is so far from being a blessing that is a curse . . . What is the difference between them, then? This : one has hope in it, the other has not . . . hope of rest, hope of product, hope of pleasure in the work itself . . . I have put the hope of rest first because it is the simplest and most natural part of our hope. Whatever pleasure there is in some work, there is certainly some pain in all work, the beast-like pain of stirring up our slumbering energies to action, the beast-like dread of change when things are pretty well with us; and the compensation for this animal pain in animals is rest . . . As to the hope of pro-duct, I have said that Nature compels us to work for that . . . The hope of pleasure in the work itself; how strange that hope must seem to some of my readers – to most of them ! Yet I think that to all living things there is a pleasure in the exercise of their energies, and that even beasts rejoice in being lithe and

swift and strong. But a man at work, making something which he feels will exist, because he is working at it and wills it, is exercising the energies of his mind and soul as well as of his body. Memory and imagination help him as he works. Not only his own thought, but the thought of the men of past ages guide his hands; and, as a part of the human race, he creates.[53]

Morris sees his 'factory as it might be', as a centre of education. The educational ideas of Rousseau emerge again, though this time side by side with a respect for 'book-learning' : the child would be eager 'to be allowed to work at turning out real, useful wares', and to 'handle shuttle, hammer or whatnot for the first time as a real workman'. The 'bent of each child' would have been considered in choosing its occupation, and education would continue throughout life.

Then Morris' factory would have buildings that were 'beautiful with their own beauty of simplicity of workshops', and other buildings besides its workshops – dining-hall, library, school, places for study of various kinds'; these might carry ornament further. It goes without saying that 'the factory must make no sordid litter, befoul the water, nor poison the air with smoke.'[54]

Since there would be no competition, each factory would also tell anyone who enquired the details of new technical developments, and there would be research into the principles of the different crafts. There would be no severance, therefore, between technical, intellectual and artistic development; such a factory would breed new art. Since few hours would be needed for labour, some men

> – and I think most – would find themselves impelled towards the creation of beauty, and would find their opportunities for this under their hands as they worked out their due quota of necessary work for the common good; these would amuse themselves by ornamenting the wares they made, and would only be limited in the quantity and quality of such work by artistic consideration ... Our workers will be thoroughly educated as workers and will know well what good work and

true finish (not trade finish) means, and ... the public duty to add beauty to their necessary daily work will furnish outlet for the artistic aspirations of most men.[55]

To sum up, in place of the present system, Morris states that he wants 'Art made by the people and for the people, a joy to the maker and to the user'. And art meanwhile has another function beyond itself: it is a means of presenting the future state of fullness and equality to men who have been cut off by modern industrialization from the imagination of a better world.

It must be remembered that civilization has reduced the workman to such a skinny and pitiful existence, that he scarcely knows how to frame a desire for any life much better than that which he now endures perforce. It is the province of art to set the true ideal of a full and reasonable life before him, a life to which the perception and creation of beauty, the enjoyment of real pleasure that is, shall be felt to be as necessary to man as his daily bread.[56]

7
Idealization and reality

We have looked at a series of assessments of work in the European societies that emerged in the eighteenth and nineteenth centuries. Though Rousseau expresses his ideas through a language of nature and virtue, Marx in terms of unalienated productive activity, and Ruskin and Morris through the evocation of forms of work that involve art, they have a strikingly similar idea of the human future. It will centre on work – but work set free from monotony and compulsion. Relying on some sense of 'enough' in human nature, Rousseau held that men could do without many of the products of civilization for whose sake they labour. Ruskin said that every man should learn to live on as little as he could. 'And then from simplicity of life' wrote Morris 'would rise up the longing for beauty, which cannot yet be dead in men's souls, and we know that nothing can satisfy that demand but Intelligent work rising gradually into Imaginitive work : which will turn all 'operatives' into workmen, into artists, into men.'[1] Marx, whose notion of human desire was perhaps less fixed, believed that powered machinery could be developed to produce what men need without long hours of regular divided work.

'Enough' might mean to all of them more than the peasants or urban poor had in their day – to Marx, much more; but once the burden of work was shared in some measure among all, once there were no idle and oppressive rich to consume without producing and to force productions into wasteful or harmful channels, all these writers assumed that it would be comparatively easy to provide plenty for everyone.

Rousseau, who wrote before the coming of powered machinery

to his world, had already left a hostile account of the effects of monotonous labour on a workman : *c'est une machine qui en mène une autre.* He also left a passionate defence of the simplicity that would enable men to dispense with affluence; a vision of the equality that would require any such burdens to be shared; and finally an account of craftsmanship as a training and occupation for a growing child brought up naturally in the recreated world. In more than one way, before the coming of powered machinery, he had established the most persuasive criticisms that would confront it.

His successors who write in the time of the factory system – Marx, Ruskin and Morris, and even, in the economic passages of his early writings, Hegel – single out factory labour as an extraordinarily severe kind of labour. All see the future of mankind as a form of emancipation, in particular from urban factory life as they knew it. Rousseau said that men should not live in anthills but spaced out across the earth. Ruskin and Morris complained of the hideousness of contemporary cities : they believed that to make beauty is an inherent disposition in men, and that beauty will be the natural expression of men set free from monotonous labour. Less forcefully, but in scattered places throughout his work, Marx expresses a similar view.

The question must now be asked bluntly : why in the century after their writings have neither the East nor the West produced societies, or even political parties, that embody these images of the future of mankind except as vague aspirations to which lip-service is occasionally and perfunctorily to be paid?

It seems that in public discourse and public affairs, in both East and West, men are universally assumed to seek economic gain at the expense of all other ends, and countries to pursue a higher national product no matter what its composition. The 'gross' national product[2] – aptly named perhaps – is a figure in which it is possible to discriminate between work that people have enjoyed and work they have hated; between work that has produced something beautiful and useful, and something ugly and sold only by persuasion. Thus in a country where the majority of people dislike their work, if everyone is persuaded to work longer hours at a constant hourly output, the gross national product has gone up, and this is so even if they are deceived or disappointed and find they disliked their work more than they enjoyed the extra goods and services produced in that time. Again, the figure goes up if people destroy the countryside to build factories to produce things they dislike producing, and if they spend further money on persuading people to buy these things, and yet further money escaping from the results. The gross national products of two countries go up if each produces napalm and nuclear missiles to bomb the other, and again if each produces anti-ballistic missiles to defend themselves against the other's threat.

Not only employers and governments, but those institutions that in Britain officially represent working people have for a long time appeared to speak mainly in the language of productivity and income statistics in their official pronouncements. Trade Unions, though they continue to confront employers on many ranges of issues unconnected with the money wages of their members, have nevertheless seemed, at least until recently, to conduct their best publicized battles – as reported by the mass media – in just that area from which the nineteenth-century critics were most concerned to deflect people's attention as a source of only illusory satisfaction, namely money.

Is there a systematic gap between the language of the nineteenth-century critics of society, and that of men who have subsequently worked at machines, a gap so great that ideas on the one hand and experience on the other have not been mutually understood, And if so, is this one source of failure of these ideas to enter into the reality of contemporary life? Or does the gap lie between those who work at machinery and the men and institutions who manage and represent them? Does the misunderstanding occur because the nineteenth-century critics' ideas do in fact represent deep wishes of people at work but have not yet found the institutions to express or to understand them, perhaps because it is particularly hard to organize an institution around qualitative criticism as opposed to quantitative economics, or perhaps because the nineteenth-century critics have simply not yet been fully understood?

It is impossible to be certain how significant is the issue of higher wages compared with the quality of work, to people who work in industry today. To answer the question, it would be necessary to look at evidence of individual working people's feelings independently of the behaviour of the institutions which manage and represent them. For existing expressions of feeling may be restricted by what is considered reasonable or seems attainable. It can be argued that very different feelings will be found if opportunities and institutions exist to express other wishes.

Thus, however much even a large number of people wanted to vary the speeds at which they worked in mass production, it might be a matter on which employers were unwilling to negotiate with them and unions unready to bargain for them. They might thus have no opportunity to express this wish. Meanwhile, institutions already in existence, left over from previous struggles whose frontiers were hours and pay, might remain ready and willing to negotiate with, and to bargain for, any wish they had for more pay. Even if this ceased to be the strongest feeling or the deepest need people had in their work, it might remain the one that could find active expression through an institution and so influence the behaviour of the economy or of the political system immediately. Observers from a distance might even believe that it was the only feeling men had about their work in that society.

A parallel might be sought with the perpetuation of trench warfare in the First World War – or indeed with the perpetuation of war itself since – by the power of institutions on different sides set up to wage it and not subsequently dismantled. The poems of the First World War, as it developed, make it clear that a desire to advance several yeards into no-man's-land was not the strongest wish of many men in the trenches. But it was frequently the only one that the situation allowed to be expressed.

This is not necessarily an appropriate parallel; but it is a possible one. Other feelings about work than are readily expressible in terms of economic concepts of profit maximization and wage-gains could be concealed within our system by an absence of institutions for their expression; and this could be true, even of quite large majorities, without daily overt evidence.

But even if large majorities of individual working people did not agree with them, the nineteenth-century critics of industrial society would not need at once to withdraw their argument; all based their case largely on what they believed to be human needs rather than already existing conscious human wishes.

Men can need what they do not consciously want or wish for at any particular moment. They may not have the concepts to formulate a wish for something that they need; or they may not know they need it. And this is particularly likely to be so when a traditional way of life, which has harmonized wishes with needs stably over a long period of settled conditions, is disturbed by violent changes which destroy the old conditions, creating new dangers like pollution and fatigue, new diseases as well as new pleasures, while leaving people to face these with ideas formed haphazardly out of the experience of the previous settled period, and desires stimulated by the new one.

There is an example of this in the case of fatigue through monotony. In farming life, speaking very generally, men get tired as they work long hours. In the industrial revolution, although factory work was often much lighter physically than alternatives such as mining or agriculture, people complained bitterly of fatigue. They complained not only after the longest hours; Fielden talks of appalling fatigue after days little longer than men now work. Other observers note the listnessness and aimlessness on Sundays of people who have been working all the week. Meanwhile fewer people seem to have complained directly of the monotony of factory life than of this fatigue and listlessness.

But a modern writer like Georges Friedmann in his *Industrial Society* can connect the listlessness and the fatigue specifically with monotony, by referring to studies of the chemical changes that occur in the body after the continuous exercise of a single set of muscles.[3] Careful observers made similar connections even in their own time; and Fielden, in his descriptions of children playing, as well as Engels and Marx quoting him, suggest something in a similar direction. But under the stress of the situation itself, if a man at work feels fatigued, he is much more likely to want lighter work, or shorter work; it takes a step beyond common sense to see that he might need radically different work, with more complexity and – paradoxically – more play for his muscles and more demands made on his brain, rather than simply shorter hours and less work.

Ideals of variety in work like Ruskin's, Marx's and Morris's need not be irrelevant, then, even at a time when they make little appeal to majorities of working people.

But however right a critic of industrialization may be, unless at some point he can persuade people that what he suggests is desirable, arguments from needs or from 'latent' or 'supposed' wishes can be dangerous. They can be held to justify a scientifically arranged beehive of self-styled good being done to people who never want it and are never asked about; and the critic may all the time have been wholly mistaken. Men must choose for themselves. Freedom even from officious 'good' is also a human need. Thus arguments from needs cannot replace a man's free decision when he has all the information the critic has and the leisure and freedom to consider it. The study of industrialization and of ideas about it – however far it leads into questions of objective good and objective need – must end as well as begin with what people freely choose for themselves and actually experience in their lives at work and after work.

All the writers we have been considering – while they were concerned mainly with the future of men at work and with the evils of their own generations – made their criticism of the state of contemporary life not on the basis of a future only; they also – each in his different way – contrasted what they saw with a better past. Rousseau admired the simple life of peasants, and – though less than his followers – primitive life also; Schiller, ancient Greece; Morris, the agricultural England he knew in his youth and more profoundly, like Ruskin, the Middle Ages; while the young Marx – though less simply an idealizer of the past – believed that the state of men at work in the industry of the 1840's was more unbearable than at any previous time, and contrasted it – in one sense – with the whole range of human history;

while in his account of the development of instrumentalism he recalled a 'fully human' time before the first exchange. His concept of alienation implies a human nature whose embryonic expression is buried somewhere in the past, although its full development has never yet been known.

Such beliefs gave much of the credibility to these writers' hopes for a better future. In particular, the possibilities of changing the industrial and political system so that men's normal activity – their work and their greatly increased leisure – would be immediately satisfying to them, was supported by the belief that before industrialization, or before the coming of capitalism, or in certain ages of the more remote past – perhaps in the very earliest human dealings with nature – this had been the normal condition of most men.

Even today, the belief that technological change will by itself change people's feelings about their work may be based on the premise that a painful experience of work, and an instrumental attitude to work, are of comparatively recent origin in human history, and were brought about, or greatly intensified by industrialization – by 'factory technology, increasing division of labour and capitalist property institutions in the industrial revolution'.[4]

If men really have come to dislike their work thoroughly only since the advent of capitalism, or even since industrialization, if it is only recently that they have begun to do their work for reward and to lose some original intrinsic meaning that it had for them, then it should not be impossible to reverse these changes by changing the technology; and in less developed countries to avert them altogether by rejecting capitalism, industrialization or even civilization itself – whichever is seen to be the prime cause of the change.

But how far have all these ideals of better work in the past – in very early human life, in the life of primitive tribes, in ancient Greece, in the Middle Ages, and in pre-industrial craftsmanship and agricultural labour – been idealizations? Did William Morris, whose father commuted to work in the City by stage coach, and who amused himself by cursing bargees during his afternoon's rowing on the Thames, know about country life, or work on the barges, as it has been experienced by those who habitually laboured in these ways, Did he even know what the life of a craftsman was like when he was totally dependent – as Morris never was – on the products of his handwork to keep him alive? And would he have had the same feeling for the freedom and irregularity of a craftsman's life if he had not been able to say – without fear of hunger, 'When the mood of energy is upon me, I must be doing something, or I become mopish and unhappy; when the mood of idleness is on me, I find it hard indeed if I cannot rest. . . .'[5] How much could any of them know – how much do we now know about the real experience of people who laboured with their hands in remote ages? The silence of the past – for any but the words of the rich, the powerful or the clerical – is vast : those whose lives we would need to know about to understand this, spoke; they did not write; and their words have gone. How far then were the nineteenth-century critics justified in believing that there was any past age in which the ordinary experience of most men at work was dramatically more happy and satisfying than that of men at work in their own time.

And if an instrumental attitude to work is the product not of certain technological changes involving machines, but of much earlier conditions, or even of permanent elements of human experience, the question of its possible 'cure' – if it is in fact something that men should attempt to cure – is very much more complex. It may not be enough to get rid of assembly lines, for instance, in order to make men love their work and do it for its own sake, if before there were any assembly lines, or powered machines of any kind, most men other than the rich and the philosophers and artists already worked with more or less reluctance and – since the earliest times – more or less for the sake of consumption, money or exchange.

Part II

Experience of work in the past

8

Pastoral and machinery

The idea that industrialization was a kind of 'fall' is deep-rooted and can be found not only in subsequent theory, but also in the words of certain contemporaries. In 1835 a ballad writer sang

> Along the country roads alas
> But waggoners few are seen,
> The world is topsy turvy turned
> And all the past is passed away
> Like to a moving dream.[1]

In this century, when societies which resemble our own before the industrial revolution have been found, they have generally struck observers from big cities as beautiful, even where many of their inhabitants were eager to leave them for the cities. It was such an area for example – the remote Appalachian Mountains – which Cecil Sharp visited with Maud Karpeles, in 1917, to collect folksongs. His account of the visit in the preface to their book – *English Folksongs from the Southern Appalachians* – gives a clear idea of his reaction :

Their language, wisdom, manners, and the many graces of life that are theirs ar merely racial attributes which have been acquired and accumulated in past centuries and handed down generation by generation, each generation adding its quota to that which it received.

It must be remembered also that in their everyday lives they are immune from that continuous, grinding, mental pressure due to the attempt to make a living from which nearly all of us in this modern world suffer . . . In this respect, at any rate, they have the advantage over those who habitually spend the greater part of every eay in preparing to live, in acquiring the technique of life, rather than its enjoyment.[2]

Cecil Sharp may have brought pastoral expectations to the Appalachians, and there has been some doubt cast on the representative nature of the people he met : some critics have suggested that they were to a disproportionate degree people taught by the missions. But even if this is true, and if these singers knew a specially pure, unaccompanied way of singing which ultimately derived – like their manners – partly from the missions themselves, the same criticism can hardly apply to his general estimate of the people he met on his travels among whom he encountered not merely specially designated mission supporters, but strangers, as he vivdly describes, who could scarcely all have learnt their way of greeting from a single source :

> They have an easy, unaffected bearing and the unselfconscious manners of the well-bred. I have received salutations upon introduction or on bidding farewell, such as a courtier might make to his sovereign . . . Strangers that we met in the course of our long walks would usually bow, doff the hat, and extend the hand, saying 'My name is ——; what is yours?'[3]

There seems little reason to doubt that a particularly delicate way of life did exist – a way later distorted perhaps by prohibition as well as by the coming of mass communication – and that Sharp, who saw beauty where others saw only poverty, or some class 'inferiority', recognized it. He envisaged the question of industrialization, saw its effects on the fringes of the Kentucky mountains where mining or industry had brought money, and opted against it.

> Some of the women (missionaries) I have met are very nice and broadminded. But I don't think any of them realize that the people they are here to improve are in many respects far more cultivated than their would-be instructors, even if they cannot read or write. Take music, for example. Their own is

pure and lovely. The hymns that these missionaries teach them
are musical and literary garbage . . . The problem, I know, is a
very difficult one. For my part, I would leave them as they are
and not meddle. They are happy, contented, and live simply
and healthily, and I am not at all sure that any of us can
introduce them to anything better than this. Something might
be done in teaching them better methods of farming, so as to
lighten the burden of earning a living from their holdings; and
they should certainly be taught to read and write – at any rate,
those who want to, ought to be able to. Beyond that I should
not go.[4]

Whether this same judgement should be made now of similar less
advanced societies is a question that has to be solved by each,
individually. It is worth noting that Cecil Sharp did not in fact
settle in the Appalachian Mountains. We are reminded of
Montaigne's paradox about marriage : that 'those outside are trying to get in; those inside are trying to get out. We see the same
with bird-cages'.

To a generation of city dwellers used to going to the country for
holidays or weekends, the industrial revolution can hardly escape
seeming, consciously or unconsciously, like some gradually dis-
piriting train journey of the world from the fields and beaches of
Sunday afternoon through the thicker and thicker rows of back-
to-back houses to the hooting, Monday traffic of the city terminus.
Pastoral poetry seems to have been invented in the cities; and
the pastoral tradition has made it almost impossible for men to
see agricultural labour without some degree of idealization.

For centuries artists have had to react against it when they
have set out to depict rural life accurately : the brothers Le Nain
in the seventeenth century, for instance, with their peasants' faces
lined with misery and blank with lack of hope or understanding,
the only relief in the picture, a child, a musical instrument, and a
glass of wine; John Clare,[5] or Crabbe, in *The Village* (1783)
who, when he speaks of the misery of rural life, remind us that

the pastoral tradition in Europe is something a poet must fight
against if he wants to tell the truth about agricultural life:

> I grant indeed that fields and flocks have charms.
> For him that grazes or for him that farms
> But when amid such pleasing scenes I trace
> The poor laborious Natives of the place,
> And see the mid-day sun, with fervid ray,
> On their bare heads and dewy temples play;
> While some, with feebler heads and fainter hearts,
> Deplore their fortune, yet sustain their parts;
> Then shall I dare these real ills to hide
> In tinsel trappings of poetic pride?[2]

Writing of the everyday work of farm labourers at the time when
factories were beginning, Crabbe says:

> Go then! and see them rising with the sun,
> Through a long course of daily toil to run;
> See them beneath the dog-star's raging heat,
> When the knees tremble and the temples beat,
> Behold them, leaning on their scythes, look o'er
> The labour past, and toils to come explore;
> See them alternate suns and showers engage,
> And hoard up aches and anguish for their age;
> Thro' fens and marshy moors their steps pursue
> When their warm pores imbibe the evening dew;
> Then own that labour may as fatal be
> To these thy slaves, as thine excess to thee.[7]

Eighty years earlier a poet whose own work was agricultural
labour makes a smiliar protest against the pastoral convention

> The Shepherd well may tune his Voice to sing
> Inspired by all the Beauties of the Spring.
> No Fountains murmur here, no Lambkins play,
> No Linnets warble, and no Fields look gay.[8]

He writes of the dreariness of supposedly idyllic agricultural
labour; or returning home blackened with dust, horrifying his

wife and children; of the exhaustion; and also of the farmer's calculation and abuse.

> Week after week we this dull task pursue,
> Unless when winn'wing Days produce a new.
> A new indeed, but frequently a worse
> The Threshall yields but to the Master's Curse:
> He counts the Bushels, counts how much a Day,
> And swears we've idled half the time away.

E. P. Thompson, who quotes from the poem in a notable article on 'Time, Work Discipline and Industrial Capitalism'[9] finds in it a contrast: on the one hand there is the normal relationship in which the farmer drives the labourers on with relentless calculation, time-keeping and constant complaint; and on the other hand the harvest home, 'a moment at which the older collective rhythms break through the new' bringing with it 'psychic satisfaction and ritual functions – for example the momentary obliteration of class distinctions – 'and a shared sense of common achievement. Yet perhaps the poem is even bitterer than such a contrast suggests. It is true, there is 'huzzaing' for the end of the harvest, followed by a feast at which everyone gets drunk, as the 'too generous' farmer pushes round 'jugs of humming Ale':

> But the next Morning soon reveals the Cheat
> When the same Toils we must again repeat,
> To the same Barns must back again return
> To labour there for Room for next year's corn

Already in 1730 it seems that labour could be so monotonous and rest and celebration so short, and so far from expressing the reality of the working life, that harvest and harvest feast alike could be experienced as deceptive and unsatisfying. The 'older rhythms' of the harvest are in fact evoked by 'The Thresher Poet' only to show their fugitive, deceptive nature in the life of a working man. The reality is an absence of rests; a breaking-up of the natural work rhythm of effort and relaxation until instead there is a complete 'flow' of tasks – in early eighteenth-century agricultural labour just as in modern mass production.

> Thus as the Year's revolving Course goes round
> No Respite from our Labour can be found.
> Like Sisyphus, our Work is never done :
> Continually rolls back the restless Stone,
> New-growing Labours still succeed the past
> And growing always new, must always last.

If agricultural labourers had a hard burden in eighteenth-century England, there was probably a harder one still. Country women had to work both in the fields and also at home.[10] Thompson argues that the two parts of women's working life may have been experienced differently :

> such hours were endurable only because work with the children and in the home disclosed itself as necessary and inevitable, rather than as an external imposition. This remains true to this day . . . The mother of young children has an imperfect sense of time and attends to other tides. She has not yet moved out of the conventions of 'pre-industrial' society

Whether this was true, and whether it was a consolation, are neither of them certain. To know this one would have to know that inevitable tasks are generally felt to be less burdensome than those imposed 'externally' by the will of another person. And even if this were true, it would still not be impossible that a crying child could even then at times be felt to be 'another person imposing a task'. The suggestion again is that more easily endured or more deeply satisfying 'pre-industrial' tasks and rhythms were still present in eighteenth-century agricultural life, in areas not wholly organized in terms of wage labour; but in neither on the instances cited does the evidence appear unambiguously convincing. Whatever the truth of this, the life of labouring women in the English countryside shortly before the industrial revolution does not immediately present the aspect of an idyll.

Most of the manufacturing in England was still carried on in cottages and villages in the middle and late eighteenth century;

'the typical worker being some kind of village artisan or small-holder in his cottage, increasingly specializing, in the mid eighteenth century, in the manufacture of some product – mainly cloth, hosiery, and a variety of metal goods – and thus by degrees turning from small peasant or craftsman into wage labourer'.[11]

If the evidence of craftsmen today is anything to go by, crafts-men's work in the eighteenth century must have been more satisfying than that of most farm labourers or factory workers. People in most societies do seem quite simply to like making things in their own time, well, for a known community which values their products. They cease to enjoy this if they are called on to work excessively long hours, or if like the Spitalfields weavers of the nineteenth century for instance, they are starved through competition with machine products in mass markets.[12]

Craftsmen and artisans were able in some cases to keep a com-paratively free use of their time even into the mid nineteenth century. Those who worked at home could – and by all accounts did – spend much of the early part of the week in leisure and in drinking if they were paid on Friday. Only with Wednesday might the pressure of work begin. Similar behaviour is recorded in weaving, pottery and elsewhere, even where a rudimentary form of workshop or 'manufactury' existed.[13] Within this irregu-larity of daily work, rhythms of effort and recuperation could also sometimes follow a man's own pleasure if he worked on his own at an individual bench even in a large workshop. In eighteenth-century England many artisans and craftsmen were small holders or part-time labourers as well. But those who did not have con-sistent care of animals must have had a free-er use of their whole time than farm labourers. Festivals, wakes and feasts were not everywhere destroyed by the repeated assaults on them in the century after Cromwell.[14] Thus as late as 1755 a clergyman writes : 'common custom has established so many Holy-days that few of our manufacturing work-folks are closely and regularly employed above two-thirds part of the time.[15]

It is sometimes taken for granted that the coming of regular working hours must always have been experienced as a loss to working people. In the long run, this is not certain. However much cant there may have been in the homilies of clergymen and manufacturers in the eighteenth and nineteenth centuries on the virtues of early rising, regularity and thrift, the speed-up of last minute work from Wednesday to Friday under an irregular working pattern may also have been wearing and exhausting.

Furthermore, regular hours can be a defence against the incursions of overwork as well as a block to freedom and play. English working people, who have not generally heeded homilies and praise of work, have made use of regular timetables over the nineteenth and twentieth centuries to secure overtime pay on the one hand, and definite and regular spaces for leisure on the other. The cost may have been something that was noted as early as the nineteenth century: a certain inability in the modern English when contrasted with less-clock-bound peoples, to relax completely and spontaneously;[16] and again an 'industrial' structure to their leisure as well as to their work.[17] This may apply to the middle class much more. Perhaps the crocodile who swallows the clock in the pantomime, and is betrayed by its ticking wherever he goes, is a strangely appropriate fantasy to have originated in an industrialized Britain.

But over and above such freedoms of time as they enjoyed there must have been in most forms of artisan's and craftsman's work, a variety of demands made on a man's skills and energies, so that not only would he be required to think, plan and design, but also to use many muscles and many physical capacities in the course of a single day. George Sturt says, in *The Wheelwright's Shop*, that in his time – the late nineteenth century – 'a man's work, though more laborious to his muscles, was not nearly so exhausting yet tedious as machinery and "speeding up" have since made it for mind and temper'. Sturt has sometimes been thought of as an idealizing writer. But he is here on firm ground in terms of many findings of psychology since his day.[18]

However, a simple contrast between unhurried craftsmen working happily in their own time and sullen factory hands clocking-in each morning to a strictly regimented grind, would be too neat and untrue a picture of the changes that occurred in the industrial revolution. While many engineers and steel-mill workers retained or expanded their holidays and Saint Mondays well into the later nineteenth-century[19] craftsmen such as Sturt's grandfather – who was said to have had to make a wheel a day about 1810 – 'worked from five in the morning until eight at night', and apparently suffered from the same degree of exhaustion as certain modern assembly line workers.[20] So tired was he on returning from work that he could not eat in the evenings till he had laid down for an hour.[21]

Even longer hours could be characteristic of weaving and spinning in domestic industry. Workshop life, like family life, must have varied completely from instance to instance, depending on the nature of the parent or the master in charge. If he was kindly and not over avaricious the shop may have afforded a pleasant way of life; if not, the reverse. To some, the nuclear family with the handloom and spindle was a worse taskmaster than the factory itself. Cooke Taylor, in his *Tour of the Manufacturing Districts of Lancashire*, noted 'a village patriarch', born about 1760 who 'had been a weaver and remembered the conditions of the trade before the introduction of machinery. "The creatures were set to work", he said, "as soon as they could crawl, and their parents were the hardest taskmasters".'[22]

Nevertheless, pictures of the world of cottage industry survive, such as Wordsworth's in *Michael*, and the start of *The Excursion*;[23] and again later in the poem when destruction has come. E. P. Thompson, who quotes this last description, writes:[24]

> The existence of supplementary earnings from small farming or merely slips of garden, spinning, harvest work, etc is attested from most parts of the country. There is architectural evidence to this day testifying to the solidarity of many late eighteenth-century weaving hamlets.

He argues that the really important point was the 'difficult and painful nature of the change in status from artisan to depressed outworker.'[25] The change was not equally violent for all weavers. Not all had enjoyed the earlier prosperity to the same extent.[26] But from the end of the eighteenth century onwards, the decline was felt by all. Certain aspects of the artisans' world that were lost – the close relationships of family and neighbours tied together by mutual obligations of work and friendliness – have sometimes been described as constituting an 'organic community'. F. R. Leavis, who uses the phrase, argues that though the relations between work and the rest of life cannot in the future be modelled directly on the past, nevertheless 'the organic community' existed as late as the end of the nineteenth century in the way of life of small craft workshops, such as the one described by Sturt in *The Wheelwright's Shop*,[27] in which many excellent descriptions of craftsmanship and its relationship to the characters of the men engaged in it are given.

Sturt was the owner of his shop. In his own eyes this made him no more than one among equals – 'There were never any "hands" with us. Eight skilled workmen and apprentices, eight friends of the family. . . .'[28] But it may nevertheless have given him, just as it may have given Morris, a somewhat different view of craftsmanship from that of the men he worked with. Then again, he had been a disciple of Morris and of Ruskin, and by his own account it was under the influence of Ruskin's *Fors Clavigera* that he came to feel 'that man's only decent occupation was in handicraft'.[29] Thus while his life can certainly be seen as a test of these ideas in practice, and not entirely a vindication of them, the feelings he describes in the 1880s cannot be taken as independent evidence about Ruskin's or Morris' views about craftsmanship.

Furthermore, it has been suggested that the idea of 'the organic community' may have been arrived at partly by abstracting from such descriptions as Sturt's 'the penury, the petty tyranny, disease and mortality, the ignorance and frustrated intelligence which were also among its ingredients'.[30]

Another concept of 'lost' community has been based on the idea that most men in the country habitually lived in large groups centred on farmhouses and worked in relationships approximating to those of the family. Cobbett described the break-up of farmhouse communities in the early nineteenth century, and believed that it had already been going on for several centuries. This is also a matter of controversy, and it seems more likely that

the small nuclear family had for long been the normal household
in the English countryside.[31]

Raymond Williams writes simply : 'If there is one thing certain
about "the organic community" it is that it has always gone'.[32]

It has also been said that the nuclear family suffered from
industrialization. To some writers at the time, such as Fielden,[33]
the factories were an assault on family life itself, as well as on a
way of working surrounded by the family, set among gardens,
small-holdings and clean country air. There may be some
exaggeration in the pictures that men like Fielden and Gaskell
painted – pictures which did much to influence Engels' and
Marx's early ideas. It must be remembered that they were writing for the most part against a dominant view of the benefits of
mechanization, propounded by men like Knight in *The Working
Man's Companion* (1831) and Ure with his *Philosophy of
Manufactures* (1835); that they lived in a world where slogans
such as the Chartist cry – 'the lord of a thousand spindles against
the lord of a thousand acres' – could claim for the proponents of
the new machinery even the role of opposition to the established
order.

Thus Gaskell in *Prospects of Industry* (1835) wrote that 'the
great curse of the factory system' was to be found : 'not in its
hours of labour, nor in the slight unhealthy influences to which
those engaged in it are exposed. It is the breaking up of all home
and social affections ... the immense mass of social disorganiza-
tion, unfettered by domestic virtue'[34]

The accusations against the factories' effects on family life were
two-fold : it was said, first, that they separated families physically,
and secondly that they increased the relative earning power of the
wife and children – for instance when they were employed in a
factory and the father was, perhaps, a handloom weaver – and
thus inverted the natural order, depriving the father of his
paternal authority. This is a charge that Engels made against the
factories in *The Condition of the Working Class in England in
1844*. John Stuart Mill took a less jaundiced view of this second
development. In different ways both he and Marx saw in the

factory system possibilities for a change in the family and the beginning of an emancipation of women.

There is argument among historians about whether the former charge was true. 'The earliest inventions had the most disturbing effect upon the family life of the cotton workers' writes a local historian of Lancashire 'for much of the labour in the earliest mills consisted of apprentices who were separated from their families throughout the whole period of their apprenticeship. Generally speaking this phase of the factory system was of short duration and was succeeded by a demand for labour which could be supplied without breaking up family life'.[35] Other historians put more stress on the break-up of family and kinship relationships as a consequence of the industrial revolution; and it has been pointed out that the break-up of families was incidentally more clearly correlated with 'industrial unrest' than were changes in the standard of living.[36]

Whatever the truth of this, there is evidence from other countries besides Britain[37] that the move to factories could itself be traumatic. According to one historian, in the early nineteenth century 'factory discipline must have seemed as irrational, as irrelevant to one's own interests, as unfree, as army discipline today'[38] The employers' attempts to impose clock time from 1700 onwards often encountered intense opposition.[39] Savage penalties were exacted for unpunctuality and absence from work, in the early nineteenth century. Master-and-Servant laws entailed prison for breach of a workman's contract.[40] A wage of fourteen shillings a week in 1791 was to be 'abated in double Proportion for absence'; a child's pay of a penny a week and its keep to be 'abated not only ... proportionably, but also for the Damages sustained by such absence'.[41]

Play and singing, even talking, were to be stamped out:
'So there was profound silence enjoined?' – 'Yes'
'If any hand in the work is seen *talking* to another, *whistling* or *singing*, will be fined sixpence'

Deloney in the sixteenth century gave a picture of 'two hundred girls in a spinning room all singing one of the lovliest of the ballads, the Fair Flower of Northumberland as they worked.

Perhaps this was an idealized account. But perhaps there really had been better times in the distant past. It is not certain.

Weavers believed in a lost golden age; many of them had visibly enjoyed one. So it seems did many country people.

Crabbe talks of a ruined village, of better times in an earlier day. So, strangely, does John Aubrey a century earlier. Since the 'civil warres', all the old customs have died out and country life has been ruined. Even Shakespeare's time, which at first may seem a 'golden age' to which such memories might look back, was, we are told by historians, one of the worst ages ever known by the English country poor for low wages, unemployment and forced mobility.

There are three possibilities. English rural life perhaps declined from the Middle Ages onwards, especially from the period of comparative freedom and high wages that succeeded the Black Death. Or perhaps it never was as wonderful as men's memories told them it had been in some previous generation; and men simply have a rooted tendency, perhaps because of the childhood or womb that both past time and country life can represent, to believe the country past contained special happiness for those who lived in it.

There is a third alternative: that it was not some physical deterioration of country life – measurable in lower wages and smaller diets – but rather the break-up of a traditional culture which had given meaning to country life and made its labour bearable, that constituted the worst act of destruction.

The world that the factory towns displaced had been at some time in the past a world of ceremony and seasonal celebrations which neither Cromwellian theology nor commercial rationality had been able totally to destroy, though the destruction had been going on over two centuries.

Against Lord Snow's suggestion that 'with singular unanimity, in any country where they have had the chance, the poor have walked off the land into the factories as fast as the factories could take them',[43] F. R. Leavis quotes Hardy,

'This process which is described by the statisticians as the tendency of the rural population to the large towns, is really the

tendency of water to flow uphill when forced'.[44] Leavis argues
that : 'What Hardy describes is a positive civilization that made
the poverty and hardship he also describes (his point depends on
that) acceptable to the "rural population" who had, under
economic compulsion, to suffer, with the utmost reluctance, its
loss.' Which of these alternatives is nearer the truth is still an
important question, to other people than historians, since it is just
such a break-up of 'positive civilizations' and traditional meaning-
bearing myth, giving significance to an 'objectively' hard and
impoverished life, that many reformers across the world favour
today, in the name of development or of liberation. Yet it may be
that such a despoilation of imaginative culture can ruin what new
economic standards of living cannot alone restore : a dangerous
argument when used by a colonial governing people or an international organization to justify sluggishness in the offer of
development; but one that ought perhaps to be considered by
them and by 'developing' peoples themselves.

9
An early instrumentalist theory: Mandeville

And yet many of 'the poor' have in Lord Snow's phrase, undoubtedly 'walked off the land into the factories as fast as the factories could take them'. Does this provide 'convincing evidence', as R. M. Hartwell has suggested, 'about what the workers wanted'?[1] And does it also entail conclusions about how 'the workers' thought about their work and valued it, even before they reached the factories? Were they responding, already in the eighteenth century, while they world on the land or in hand-craft industry to the call of a higher wage elsewhere; and if there were advantages in their pre-industrial work, were they prepared to abandon these for the sake of more money – already taking what has been called an 'instrumental' attitude to their working lives before they reached the factories?

The latter question arises because such 'instrumental' attitudes to work – sometimes said to constitute 'self-estrangement' for an individual, and to contribute powerfully to his total 'alienation' – have been laid to the charge of factory technology and organization in the industrial revolution, which are said, if not to have created them, or to have greatly intensified them.[2] In the early stages of industrialization at least as far as the coming of the assembly line, 'instrumental attitudes to work' and 'alienation' are said to have increased as factory technology and organization advanced.

Other arguments put more stress on mobility, urbanization and the break-up of close-knit communities to account for a recent spread of 'instrumentalism'. As a single code of conduct learned from parents ceases to be adequate to the demands made on men by their changing environments – often environments sealed off from each other in which people play quite different roles – the sense of commitment in relationships is said to give place to a feeling for defined limits to obligation; relationships begin to be evaluated rather than simply accepted as inevitable, and come to be valued in terms of some 'return' to the individual that each offers.[3] If people's realtionships with their work can be seen as following a similar course to their relationships with each other, a significant increase in 'instrumental attitudes' should be expected to have occurred by this account as a result of the demographic changes of the past two centuries.

And yet neither theory accounts for the initial move from land to factory-town. Why, in the 'close-knit community', before they had experienced factory technology, should people have first wanted to make such a move? One answer, of course, is that they may have simply had no alternative at a particular moment of dearth and starvation, or because of the New Poor Law. In a bad harvest there was no way the poor in one part of the countryside could be assured of food from another part. Even in the age most often thought of as the golden period for English agriculture, records can be found of people dying of starvation in the villages.[4] Factory wages were not only, in general, higher than others; they were also more nearly stable.[5] Factory workers had their wages cut back in hard times, and suffered appalling fluctuations as a result of trade cycles and war. Yet factories must have extended a great promise in times of country famine.

And on the whole, as far as wages alone were concerned, they fulfilled the promise. The question of 'standards of living' in the industrial revolution has given rise to many controversies, the results of which depend largely on the base lines and definitions of 'standard of living' chosen. But historians generally agree that any general answer conceals enormous variations between the 'standard of living' of different groups within society in the industrial revolution. And among those groups, over the years from

1790 to 1850 at least, adult factory workers 'maintained their wages in the face of falling prices'.[6]

Many people from the country chose jobs with these higher wages. This does not show anything conclusive about what 'the workers' wanted. A great many 'workers' did not choose to move. And it does not show anything about the long-term wishes even of those who made the choice to go. People do not always 'welcome' what they have chosen. Even if they had an alternative at the time, the country people who moved may only have *thought* they were going to welcome the new way of life; when once they got to the towns, they may have had no way of going back. Such patterns of migration are certainly not unknown today.[7] They are particularly likely when past experience provides little guide to what can be expected in the new way of life, and when little is known about it but the rumour of its higher wages.

However, treating the evidence with all the caution it deserves, it still seems extremely probable that some people were already prepared to change their working life totally, before they had had any experience of factory life, for the sake of nothing more complicated than a higher money wage. Were they 'instrumentalists', then, before they ever came to industry?

Perhaps industrialization and the experience of mechanical mass-production have been made recently to bear too heavy a weight of responsibility for changes which may in fact have occurred earlier, or else may never have occurred at all, since they were more or less permanent elements in human nature – or some people's nature – and more or less constant features of at least some people's situation in most periods of the past. There was an earlier debate among historians about the 'effects' of capitalism quite similar to the more recent debate about the consequences of the industrial revolution. Marx, in his later thought, is dealing with 'two phases of capitalism (i.e. mercantile or commercial, and industrial) rather than with 'two technologically defined stages (pre-industrial and industrial)'. Thus 'it was not for Marx (in *Capital*) or Morris technology or the machine which debased work but mass production of standardized goods for a market : something which demonstrably preceded steam or "industry" '.[8]

Should earlier experience of the mass production of standardized goods for a market, then, explain the presence of instrumental attitudes to work in the eighteenth century? It has been said that England was wholly a market economy by 1750, in the sense that nearly all goods and services outside the family were exchangeable for money; and in fact virtually a single national market economy.[9] And 'mass production of standardized goods for a market' could apply to agriculture as well as to industry. *The Thresher's Labour* was published in 1730. It is not only hardship that it reveals in agricultural life, but a consciousness of time as money in the farmer's mind, and the attempt to impose a flow of almost clockwork conditions of the labour on his employees. Such attitudes both to time and to the employment of labourers – perhaps typical of mass production – are traceable earlier still.[10]

Instrumental attitudes to work on the part of the employees themselves cannot necessarily be inferred from a calculating attitude in their employers, or even from their awareness of this. The Thresher Poet, for example, seems to view his own labour almost as a duty, or at least as without alternative; in such a situation there is little to be calculated.

Nevertheless, when their feelings are revealed in more detail, and when they have fixed hours and wage rates to calculate with, employees can be seen taking characteristically instrumental attitudes to aspects of their labour well outside the factories. Even in 'the organic community' of Sturt's 'Wheelwright's Shop', overtime at six old pence an hour was the object of jealous seeking, while Sturt explains a familiar metaphor with exactly the sort of picture that Marx uses to describe the intolerability of alienated labour : Marx says that such work is 'shunned like the plague the moment it is no longer necessary'; Sturt says, 'To see the shop empty at the first stroke of the bell for dinner was to know the source of that metaphor for quickness "to go like one o'clock".'

Consider then a theory of completely instrumental labour which originated in the mind of an urban man, personally mobile, coming from one mercantile society to another in the late seventeenth century; but a man steeped also in late seventeenth-century philosophy with its drive to explain human nature by the smallest number of 'springs', like a mechanism; and also in late seventeenth-century urban drama and epigram, with their enjoyment of cynical motivation, yet also their roots in much earlier comedy, at least claiming to deal with permanent elements or 'humours' in a constant human nature. Bernard Mandeville published a short poem called 'The Grumbling Hive, or Knaves turn'd Honest' anonymously in 1705. It was later more widely known under the title of the second edition – 'The Fable of the Bees'.[12]

Mandeville was a Dutchman, and a doctor, who settled in England about 1696. Already in 1705, he treated the desire for money as almost the sole motive for work. He though that men in society were bound to follow private gain rather than public good in their work : though he did not believe that the effect on society as a whole was harmful. On the contrary, without 'private vices' there would be no luxury, art or science and also no employment. These – for him' constitute 'the public good' : for he says, 'I don't call things pleasures which men say are best, but such as they seem to be most pleased with'. Men 'seem to be most pleased with' their private gain. This, he argues, does not conflict with public wealth. His advice to them therefore is to cease lamenting about the vices of their neighbours, to accept these as fruitful as well as inevitable concomitants of civilization, and not to run the risk of impoverishment by putting into practice any radical notions of goodness, simplicity and virtue.

Thus :

> A spacious Hive well stock't with Bees
> That liv'd in Luxury and Ease

is shown at the start shocked at its own prosperous wickedness.

> No Bees had better Government
> More Fickleness, or less Content

The hive worked entirely by the harmonious interplay of actions in themselves vicious and done deceptively for private gain.

> Millions endeavoured to supply
> Each other's Lust and Vanity
> Whilst other Millions were employ'd
> To see their Handy works destroy'd

In this as in all other respects, it was the image of human society.

> These insects liv'd like Men, and all
> Our actions they performed in small.
> They did whatever's done in Town
> And what belongs to Sword or Gown;
> Tho' th'Artful works, by nimble Blight
> Of minute Limbs, 'scap'd Human Sight
> Yet we've no Engines, Labourers,
> Ships, Castles, Arms, Artificers,
> Craft, Science, Shop, or Instrument
> But they had an Equivalent :

He shows the bees in his hive dividing their labour into trades :

> Some with vast Stocks and little Pains
> Jumped into business of great Gains
> And some were damn'd to Scythes and Spades
> And all those hard laborious Trades
> Where willing wretches daily sweat
> And wear out Strength and Limbs to eat

This is the picture he gives, as a matter of course, of a labourer's life before the coming of industrialization. And the attitudes to work that he observes do not seem to have been fostered – as has been suggested – by labour; for they exist also among those who do not do any –

> As Sharpers, Parasites, Pimps, Players
> Pick Pockets, Coiners, Quacks, South-Sayers
> And all those that in Enmity
> With downright Working cunningly
> Convert to their own Use the Labour
> Of their good-natur'd heedless Neighbour.

The desire for gain and for fame are – for Mandeville the two main motives of men's actions in society, even for those whose apparent dedication to the public good is a familiar attribute of their profession. For instance

> Physicians valu'd Fame and Wealth
> Above the drooping Patient's Health
> Or their own Skill. The Greatest Part
> Study'd, instead of Rules of Art,
> Grave pensive Looks and dull Behaviour
> To gain th'Apothecary's Favour;
> The Praise of Mid-wives, Priests and all
> That serv'd at Birth or Funeral.
> To bear with th'ever-talking tribe
> And hear my Lady's Aunt prescribe . . .

The concluding parts of the Fable attracted the praise of Keynes, when he set out in *The General Theory* to persuade bankers and economists that thrift – long held to be a public as well as a private virtue – was not necessarily a virtue, and especially not in a time of chronic unemployment like the 1930's. In the first condition of the hive :

> When every part was full of Vice
> Yet the whole Mass a Paradise

luxury had :

> Employ'd a Million of the Poor
> And odious Pride a Million more;
> Envy itself and Vanity,
> Were Ministers of Industry;
> Their darling Folly, Fickleness
> In Diet, Furniture and Dress,
> That strong ridiculous Vice, was made
> The very Wheel that turned the Trade
> Their Laws and Cloaths were equally
> Objects of Mutability

But when virtue becomes the fashion suddenly everything is changed

> The Show is gone, it thins apace
> And looks with quite another Face . . .

The cessation of spending leaves men out of work

> In vain to other Trades they'd fly
> All were o'erstocked accordingly . . .
> The building Trade is quite destroyed,
> Artificers are not employ'd
> No Limner for his Art is fam'd
> Stone-cutters, Carvers are not named . . .
> The slight and fickle Age is passed
> And Cloaths, as well as Fashions, last.
> All Arts and Crafts neglected lie;
> Content, the Bane of Industry
> Makes 'em admire their homely Store
> And neither seek nor covet more.

The hive, shrunk in numbers and decimated by wars for which it can hire no mercenaries and must fight with all the strength of its native population, at last finds its new equilibrium in plainness, smallness and poverty.

Thus, Mandeville argues, the poor would not be benefitted by tying the rich to frugality; they would merely be put out of work since the spending of the rich creates their employment. He does not believe however that the poor should also be luxurious spenders and create more employment still.[13]

A critic publishing an anonymous rejoinder to the Fable accuses Mandeville of concealing, in the phrase 'the public good' which is supposed to be promoted by these private vices – the good of the rich; and he quotes Mandeville's remarks on his own poem:

> It is impossible that a Society can long subsist and suffer many of its Members to live in Idleness, and enjoy all the Ease and Pleasure they can invent, without having at the same time great Multitudes of People that to make good this Defect will

condescend to be quite the Reverse, and by Use and Patience, inure their Bodies to work for others, and themselves besides . . .'[14]

Marx praised Mandeville for giving what he thought was an unusually accurate picture of capitalist society. Mandeville argues – and he has been followed by many modern economists – that men's condition cannot be compared by any objective standards; that what matters is people's own 'expectations' and the interpretation they give themselves of their own situation. Everything should be judged in terms of people's wishes and feelings, nothing in terms of some supposed objective order of human needs. In his *Essay on Charity and Charity Schools*, Mandeville writes:

> There is not a more contented people among us, than those who work the hardest and are the least acquainted with the Pomp and Delicacies of the World.
>
> These are Truths that are undeniable; yet I know few People will be pleased to have them divulged; what makes them odious is an unreasonable vein of Petty Reverence for the poor, that runs through most Multitudes, and more particularly this nation . . .[15]

He raises the question that has troubled many writers since : what conclusions are to be drawn when men, in conditions that the writer would himself dislike, look cheerful at their work, or say they are on the whole satisfied.

> It being granted that abundance of work is to be done, the next thing which I think to be likewise desirable is, that the more cheerfully it is done, the better, as well for those that perform it as for the rest of the Society . . . I would not advance anything that is Barbarous or Inhuman. But when a Man enjoys himself, Laughs and Sings, and in his Gesture and Behaviour shows me all the tokens of content and satisfaction, I pronounce him happy, and having nothing to do with his Wit or Capacity. I never enter into the Reasonableness of his mirth; at least I ought not to judge of it by my own standard.

And with this he dismisses in advance the central critical tradition of thought about industrial society, in which writers, artists and philosophers have described the condition of those who work with their hands and argued that it should be radically improved – 'The greater the distance is between People as to their Condition, their Circumstances and manner of living, the less capable they are of judging of one another's troubles and pleasures.'

In arguing that with certain slight exceptions, men pursue their glory and their financial gain, Mandeville has constructed an early working model of economic man.[16] What is called Virtue is mostly pride; work, and the manners and customs that surround it, are given their shape by the pursuit of money, which determines matters in ever corner of life – even the choice of music in a brothel in Amsterdam, where the instrument must compete with the noise of boisterous sailors used to the noise of the waves. The phrase in which he describes this choice, in a phrase that did not need industrialization to inspire it, one which might well have come out of Denmark Street, W.C.1 today – is an example of pure

> The Musick in those Temples of *Venus* is performed by Organs, not out of Respect to the Deity that is worshipped in them, but the frugality of the Owners, whose Business is to procure as much Sound for as little Money as they can ...

Rousseau read Mandeville, remarking on his 'cold and subtle style', and much of what he describes is recognizably the same world, but seen from a radically different point of view. He does not accept the convenient arrangement whereby some are to live in Idleness while the poor 'inure their Bodies to work for others and themselves besides'. A philosophy that applies equally to all men entails a new attitude to work.

But the debate between him and Mandeville did not need machinery and factories to provoke it. Industrialization, on the contrary, may even have required as its precondition the existence in England, on the part of some men at least, of just such an 'instrumental' attitude to work as Mandeville writes of.

10

Habits and customs of working people

'The greater the distance is between People as to their Condition, their Circumstances and Manner of living', said Mandeville, 'the less capable they are of judging one another's troubles and pleasures'. How far can that charge be sustained against his successors in the nineteenth century, Marx, Ruskin or Morris? Did these men see the events of industrialization, and the changes in the nature of work that it entailed, in ways very different from those of the working people in their own time. And if so, has that been one reason for a certain failure in their ideas to find practical acceptance?

There can be no possibility of any final answers about the way working people in the nineteenth century and since have differed from Marx, Morris and their predecessors, on these questions of work, machinery, money, leisure and happiness.

But three main sources of evidence appear to exist : records left by working people themselves in writing; verbatim accounts of their words made by other people who could write; and oral tradition, especially traditional songs. There are also sources of indirect evidence – observations made by others, at the time, or inferences from behaviour to possible feelings. These sources are uncertain and liable to be speculative, while even the interpretation of the surviving words of working people involves some uncertainty. Thus the verbatim accounts of replies to parliamentary commissioners' and factory inspectors' questions, in the early nineteenth century, have frequently been attacked as evidence, on the grounds that they are answers to leading questions asked by the commissioners and inspectors, and selected in their reports to establish the existence of particular scandals.

Traditional songs have on advantage as evidence over the reports of parliamentary commissioners : they were sung by working people largely to each other and for each other; they were not answers to questions in the words of investigators from the outside.

But they have disadvantages too. They may give as much information about people's wishes as about the facts of their working lives; and it may be hard in retrospect to disentangle the two. The mood of songs may well depend on pre-existing conventions, and on the state of the art – whether there is enough dancing for a brilliantly happy rhythmic song to emerge, for example. Again, the kind of audience a song may have – of a single class or under surveillance, mixed or only men or groups to which people communicate their feelings, or rival groups to whom they display their front of pride or defiance – may determine how people sing and write, even when they are alone.

The songs of oral tradition vary greatly in what is called their 'authenticity'. Perhaps the most reliable songs, as evidence of experience and feeling, are those that have originated among the people whose life they describe; but even these have usually been sung and reshaped by succeeding generations continuously, as their way of life has changed. Such changes may have included decades of prosperity and of poverty, famine, enclosures, even industrialization without the song's disappearing; by the time it reaches us, or reaches print, it may not be evidence of the experience of any single generation. Transfer from place to place and even from country to country may have altered it in similar ways.

There are, nevertheless, in the songs of the last two centuries, some of the highest authenticity, recorded in many variants from oral tradition and found within a short distance, in space and time, from their origins, written by people doing the work they describe some anonymous, some known by name, like Tommy Armstrong, the nineteenth-century miner. There are others where the writers have been outside, yet still writing for a defined community: song writers, for instance, leading lives not radically different from the people they are writng for, like Robert Nunn, the blind Tyneside fiddler in the nineteenth century who wrote about the keelman he played for. Where such songs are taken into oral circulation, they may be nearly as reliable evidence as the first.

Other kinds of song are more uncertain from the point of view of evidence : broadsides and urban ballad sheets peddled in the country; or songs about carters, sung and perhaps written by miners rather than carters. These may well be preserved for the very opposite of their factual truth – for the wishful pictures they give miners of perpetual cheerful travel in a landscape full of girls and light, for instance; a king of working people's pastoral convention, or wishful singing.

Even songs written by people right outside working life, not living in any way like it, have occasionally been taken into oral tradition. Men have been known to sing lustily about the very opposite of their own experience – pressed men of the eighteenth-century ships, as John Bayley mentions having been heard chorusing 'Tis to honour we call you, Not press you like slaves'.[1]

Songs are not simple expressions of feeling, like cries of joy or pain. They do not give conclusive evidence about what people have felt. Often they reflect wishes as much as experience. But in many areas they may be the best available – or the only available – evidence of feelings left : feelings that were never set down in writing because those who shared them could not write, and those who wrote could not, for that very reason, share them.

There is one caution to be given here. This book's primary concern is with certain ideas about industrialization that are still alive and shaping the contemporary world today. If a single book of social history were to go through the entire range of evidence about work in the eighteenth and nineteenth centures, the variety and complexity of it, and its incompletemenss, would prevent any conclusive generalizations about working people's feelings in the past. And however important this question may be in itself, the importance of the nineteenth century critics' ideas for the understanding of modern industrial society does not depend wholly on the accuracy with which they portrayed working people's feelings in their own time. The critics of industrialization may have been prophetic; or they may have been subjective; but their ideas could still be of undiminished significance today. Thus, even if there were scope to do so in this book, it would be a mistake to look to eighteenth and nineteenth-century evidence alone for final answers to the questions that the earlier critics of industrial society raised.

But some part of that evidence treated with caution, should provide a limited ground for testing the critics' ideas in preliminary ways. Without offering answers, it can be a source of hypotheses to be tested against further evidence from the past and from modern society about the relationship of these ideas with working people's experience. If the nineteenth century critics were right, for example, about the overriding significance of the quality of work to all men, or if working people in their time felt towards machinery the same hostility as the most anti-mechanical of the philosophers, then in almost any part of the surviving evidence of working people's feelings about work that had not been selected consciously to include or exclude such evidence it ought to be reasonable to expect at least some traces of those feelings. Otherwise, there ought to be available some explanation of their suppression.

A dearth of such traces in any of the evidence consulted will not be taken as proof that these feelings did not exist to the degree that the critics of industrializing society believed; but it may be expected to raise such a doubt, and to pose such a question, for more detailed discussion elsewhere.

As far as can be gathered from the range of evidence consulted here, many working people do seem to have placed less emphasis than do the nineteenth-century critics on the significance of work itself, and on the virtues of production. They seem to have given greater value both to leisure and to play in all its forms, generally to play outside work, but sometimes to forms of play in their workplaces, usually independent of the work itself, and only very occasionally combined with work.

As we shall see, there is a possibility that Marx and Morris were closer to most working people than some of their predecessors had been on the matter of machinery itself; but not necessarily any closer on questions of work, leisure, play and what is called 'instrumentalism'. Whether they or the working people were right or wrong in the long term on either point is, of course, another question.

Marx's belief that voluntary productive activity was the essential nature of man may have been a great theoretical insight of universal application; or equally it may have been a private metaphysical prejudice, suggested by his early nineteenth-century German education and his reading of Carlyle and other contemporaries. In either case, it is not certain that it was shared by the majority of the working people he wrote about.

Modern sociological enquiries have suggested that about twice as many professional people as manual workers in western societies are likely, today, to say they give work a central place in their lives and expect it to be 'satisfying' or 'rewarding'.[2] The surviving song-words and their evidence imply that such an imbalance between classes might have been found in the nineteenth century also. The preoccupation of work and with the quality of work of Marx, or of Ruskin and Morris, is not simply a professional writer's prejudice. But from one point of view it may have been also that; at least the extreme importance they assumed work must have for everybody else also.

We have considered Marx's views on work in some detail. It is interesting to see how similar were the views of another product of the German system of education at that time who had also read Carlyle – Engels – already in the early 1840's, before their major period of collaboration had begun. Consider the following passage from *The Condition of the Working Class in England in 1844*:

Man knows no greater happiness than that which is derived
from productive work voluntarily undertaken. On the other
hand, man knows no more degrading or unbearable misery
than forced labour. No worse fate can befall a man than to
have to work every day from morning till night against his will
at a job that he abhors. The more the worker feels himself a
man, the more must he detest work of this kind – the more
acutely is he aware of the fact that such aimless labour gives
rise to no inner spiritual satisfaction. Does he work from any
natural impulse, or because he enjoys the tasks that he
performs? Of course not. He works for money. He works for
something which has nothing to do with the tasks that he has
performed. He works because he must. . . .

. . . How much human feeling or ability can a man of thirty
expect to retain if since childhood he has spent twelve hours or
more daily making pin heads or filing cog wheels, and in
addition has dragged out the normal existence of a member of
the English proletariat? . . .

. . . It is obvious that a man must be degraded to the level of
a beast if he is condemned to work of this kind.[3]

Now this passage contains many striking observations on the
effects of the division of labour and of work with machinery, not
only the parts quoted here. But consider the assumptions behind
the account, and the expressions : 'no worse fate'; 'no inner spiritual satisfaction'; 'it is obvious that a man must be degraded to
the level of a beast'. These are expressions and thoughts which
would scarcely have arisen either in the minds of working men
conversing mainly with each other, or from long and equal conversation with working men; they are essentially the thoughts of a
middle-class observer; a sympathetic one, perhaps generously
enough wishing to 'put himself in the place of' those he observes.
But it is still himself he puts in their place. Whom does he expect
to shock with the expressions 'he works for money' or 'he works
because he must? Only a rich man can afford to work, but not
work for money; and only a very rich man can afford to think it
natural not to have to work at all.

Engel's assumptions may be called in some sense 'higher' or 'more human' than those of the working people of the time. At this stage that is not the question at issue. The minimal point to be made here is that there is a gap of consciousness between the theorist and the people he is describing. When the assumption is, finally, that these people are liable to have been 'degraded to the level of beasts' and 'deprived of human feeling and ability' the gap is potentially a little dangerous.

Consider now a contrasting view. Thomas Wright the 'Journey man Engineer' who wrote *Some Habits and Customs of the Working Classes* in the mid-nineteenth century,[4] opens his chapter on 'The Real Life of Workshops' with a passage somewhat ominous for any belief in the overwhelming significance of work to all men !

In all phases of life, there is, I fancy, a sort of inner life – a life behind the scenes – that is known only to the initiated. At least, I know that such is the case in respect to the social life of the working classes. . . . To those particularly wise people who . . . arise in the House of Parliament and other public places, and in an 'I am Sir Oracle' strain assert their thorough and absolute knowledge of the wants, wishes, habits, virtues, and vices of the working-classes, life in a workshop will appear a very simple thing indeed. The people of this class would tell you that the be-all and end-all of workshop life was to labour for so many hours a day for a stipulated amount of money, and that all that was necessary to qualify a man for this life was that he should be possessed of a certain degree of technical skill, or physical power, or a combination of both. And it is by no means surprising that this should be an outsider's idea of what constitutes the life of a workshop. At the first glance, it seems the most natural, and is, *as far as it goes*, a really correct view of the case; and a view that is strengthened and confirmed from the circumstances that when visitors are taken through those 'show' workshops, which naturally form one of the sights of a manufacturing country, particular care is taken both by masters and workmen to arrange 'the show' in a manner that must impress sightseers with the notion that work, and work alone, is the beginning and end of workshop life. But any working man who entered a workshop with such an idea in his mind, and with no other qualification than being able to use his tools, would soon find himself in a very evil case. For him the shop would be 'made hot' – so hot, that, as a rule, he would have to leave it; and might thank his planets if he was fortunate enough to escape personal violence. This, however, is only a hypothetical case, for such a monster as a working man who considered work, even during his working hours, to be his being's end and aim is happily for himself rarely to be met with in the flesh.[5]

Wright was not a factory worker but a skilled engineer. What he says, despite his title, cannot be taken as evidence of the attitudes of the 'working classes' as a whole. However, any bias he has is perhaps more likely to be in the direction of valuing work; he is a skilled artisan.

For him, the alternatives to work are twofold. One is the 'real life of workshops' – a highly ritual life of games, many of them rough and cruel, guarded from supervision by an elaborate system of watch-keeping. The other is leisure : Sunday off, 'Saint Monday', or simply shorter hours.

Marx formed his early ideas in the 1840's, when for many who worked in factories 'leisure' did not exist. Consequently working in order to keep alive – instrumentalist – really was a vicious circle. But Thomas Wright speaks of a time only twenty years later, and he leaves no doubt about what change he values most in those years :

Artisans still young enough to enjoy a holiday are guilty of little exaggeration when they tell their younger brethren that when they (the old hands) were boys, they had to work – with the exception of a few hours for sleep – 'all the hours that God sent'; but all that sort of thing – the number of hours that constitutes a day's work being settled by the arbitrary will of a master, men having to hang about public-houses for hours before getting their wages, or having to take their wages in the shape of dear and unwholesome provisions – has been altered. But while improvements in such matters as these have been the most effective agents in producing that substantial improvement in the condition of working men which has taken place during the last thirty years, it is chiefly by the holidays that he has managed to secure that the Jack of the present day shows the earnestness of his conviction in the truth of the proverbial philosophy that awards him a time to play as a means of saving him from becoming dull.[6]

In these conditions, 'instrumentalism' can mean something totally different from its significance to the early Marx. It can mean working for the sake of leisure and family life, not merely to earn money to keep alive.

Even in the earlier industrial period, not all working people seem to have regarded the idea of working for the sake of money as itself so hollow as Marx thought. Some of the girls, for instance, were able to earn enough by their labour to dress up after work in the evenings. There is a record in one of the factory commissioner's reports of a young girl in Manchester – a silk winder at nine and now at eighteen a power-loom weaver – whose clothes, worn at the interview, would have cost her her entire wages for five or six weeks : 'she is a girl of high spirit for work'. Marx in the 1844 Manuscripts refers to such 'finery' as 'pathetic'; but it did not necessarily seem so to the people at the time, and only by a systematic under-estimation of play, leisure, and dressing up, by contrast with the quality of work, can such a judgement be made unreservedly.

Instrumentalism can be a matter of putting one beautiful thing in balance against many hours of drudgery – or perhaps not putting things in-balance at all, but simply uncalculatingly choosing something one wants. Readers of Huizinga's *Homo Ludens* will recognize in this girl's passion for dressing up; the familiar features of what he identifies, in primitive societies as 'play' the phenomenon to which he attributes the greatest significance in the building of civilizations. Only those who do not value any-

thing outside the sphere of work will automatically have condemned such an attitude in advance.

Marx and Morris were writers. In their own lives they gave a
very high place to work, and most of their own 'play', where it was
allowed at all, was integrated with their work, or ploughed back
into work, as Morris recommended. Marx, though a good father,
who apparently loved his family, seems to have been always working. This is still often true of writers today. People who have
worked with their hands have sometimes had other values in this
matter. Though in the early industrial revolution all kinds of play
were under attack together – the intrinsic variety of work itself,
the accompanying singing and social life at work, and the enjoyment of leisure activities outside – for any particular person even
then there may well have been a choice between defending one of
these at the expense of another. Thus there might be more money
to be earned in a more monotonous job, or more enjoyment to be
had in the social life of a low-paying job than in the most interesting or the most efficient work : the three objects may have been
alternatives to each other for any one person. They still often are.
It is the sense of this choice that we do not find in the reforming
writers. Thus the Manchester weaving girl could conceivably
have found less monotonous labour if she had been ready to
forego wages and silk gowns on Sunday. And this was the essential difference in the nineteenth century, between the situation of
the critics of industrial society and that of the working people
they were writing about. Perhaps in our own century it still is.

But if professional writers might be likely to rate play lower, in
contrast with work, than their hand-working contemporaries,
and may have been less aware than them of hard choices between
alternatives, there may have been other ways in which they
systematically saw things differently from the people they were
studying. For instance, professional people who observed working-
class life placed a very high value on sexual propriety. This was
something about which the working people were not unanimous.

Do the big boys see the big girls take off their stockings?
– Yes sir; some big pieces is married women; they have to
do the same.
Do the boys ever say anything naughty and pert?
– Yes, sir; some big boys is always doing it. . . .
Do the girls care about it? – Some doesn't like it; some
doesn't mind it.[8]

Working people in industry today are found to talk about sex
more freely at work than at home. Professional people are found
to follow the opposite pattern.[9]

Marx and Engels seem to have been as shocked as the commissioners they quote by working class divergence from professional norms of sexual behaviour and respectability at work;
and often to have given this very much the same priority as their
informants. Marx quotes a report on the girls in the tiling
industry in which he repeats, without comment, the Church
Commissioners' opinion of the 'greatest' evil :

the greatest evil of the system that employs young girle on this
sort of work consists in this, that as a rule, it chains them fast
from childhood for the whole of their after life to the most
abandoned rabble. . . . During mealtimes they lie full length in
the fields, or watch the boys bathing in a neighbouring canal.
Their heavy day's work at length completed, they put on better
clothes and accompany them to the public houses.[10]

In repeating conversations between commissioners and working
people, Engels' responses also seem often to be less close to the
working people's than to their interlocuters'. He seems unaware of
the way children's minds might distinguish between subjects that
do and do not interest them : for instance, he quotes the following
report on working-class education.

Some (of the children) have never heard the name of Her
Majesty, nor such names as Wellington, Nelson, Buonaparte
etc. But it is to be especially remarked, that among all those
who had never even heard such names as St Paul, Moses,
Solomon etc there was a general knowledge of the character

and course of life of Dick Turpin, the highwayman, and more
particularly of Jack Shepherd, the robber and prison-
breaker.[11]

And having written of some appalling facts about child mortality
when women worked in factories, he continued

> But we have not yet discussed the worst results of women's
> work in factories. The moral evils are worse than those aspects
> of the problem we have already discussed. In the factories,
> members of both sexes of all ages work together in a single
> room. It is inevitable that they should come into close contact
> with each other.[12]

Engels is not exceptional here, among reformers. For instance,
one commissioner's only reaction to a group of miners' voices
mingling together in noisy merriment in a pause in their work is
that their jokes were course. Another found such a party round a
fire in a mine and reported only its state of nakedness.[13] Most
observers seem not to have understood such people as the pit bank
women in the Welsh coalfields. The commissioners are amazed to
find them so happy, but because they do not fit the standards of
femininity of the time, a chemist, in evidence, calls them 'the
lowest and most degraded class' and says that

> When the men come up at night half stripped, they change
> their clothes in this hovel, and these girls are there mixing with
> them; these girls are generally in their teens, seldom above
> twenty, and become very immoral and obscene.

While a commissioner says:

> One of these girls, in her coarse great-coat, with her hands in
> her side-pockets, presents a picture of rude jovial independence
> of life. . . . They drive coal carts, ride astride upon horses –
> sometimes two or three together upon a large long-backed
> horse – drink, swear, fight, smoke, whistle, and sing, and care
> for nobody. Being very happy, they are certainly no objects for
> pity, but surely their circumstances are of a kind in which girls
> should never be placed.[14]

Some of the working people had forms of social gathering and of play both in work and out of it, which had nothing to do with the intrinsic nature of the work itself. Where these amusements or ways of life seemed 'coarse' to middle-class observers, including Marx and Engels, they were missed or undervalued. But they may have been very important to the people who took part in them: to whom the idea that they were 'coarse' might in some cases have come as a surprise. This may account for a further devaluation of the surviving elements of working people's play, in work and leisure; and Engels, Marx and even Morris may – without realizing it – have allowed such a misunderstanding to widen the gap between them and the people they wrote about.

Ruskin and even Morris seem to have excluded the possibility that some people may actually like machinery, and prefer mechanical and man-made environments to all others. Such a sensibility is quite rare among writers yet it may be largely the traditions of romanticism that makes it seem such a monstrous impossibility for other people. Ruskin seems not be be conscious even of the kind of wonder and interest people showed at the Great Exhibition in his own time:

> Round every object more wonderful than the rest the people press, two and three deep, with their heads stretched out, watching intently the operations of the moving mechanism. You see the farmers, their dusty hats telling of the distance they have come, with their mouths wide agape, leaning over the bars to see the self-acting mules at work, and smiling as they behold the frame spontaneously draw itself out, and then spontaneously run back again. Some, with great smockfrocks, were gazing at the girls in their long pinafores engaged at the doubling-machines.
>
> But the chief centres of curiosity are the power-looms, and in front of these are gathered small groups of artisans and labourers, and young men whose red coarse hands tell you they do something for their living . . . indeed, whether it be the noisy

flax-crushing machine, or the splashing centrifugal pump, or the clatter of the Jacquard lace machine, or the bewildering whirling of the cylindrical steam-press – round each and all these are anxious, intelligent, and simple-minded artisans, and farmers, and servants, and youths, and children clustered, endeavouring to solve the mystery of its complex operations.[15]

Anyone may be interested in an exhibition. But in everyday life can the same hostility to machinery be ascribed to people who have actually worked with their hands, at machines in factories, as exists in Schiller, Ruskin and their anti-mechanical contemporaries? The maiming and deformity, the dust and cotton fly, the speed of the machinery and the cruelty of employers and overseers are all mentioned repeatedly by the working people as well as by the commissioners, in the parliamentary reports of the early nineteenth century. Yet it is asserted by some people at least in the nineteenth century – both observers and working people – that the factories were not the worst places to work at the time. For instance, many held that at least for women and children the mines were worse than the factories.[16] Perhaps Scotland is a special case because of the late survival of serfdom; but in Scotland the mining women's demands in the industrial revolution seem to have been not so much for reform of the mines as to be released from the mines altogether. Now the mines were at the time of the industrial revolution unmechanized : this was the trouble. And the evils of the Scottish mines were by no means new in the industrial revolution. Women had for centuries worked underground. If such work was among the worst experienced by anyone at the time, mechanization cannot be blamed for it directly. It can be blamed only indirectly for its effects on the unmechanized areas of the half-industrial economy : women and children were doing work which subsequently would be taken on by machinery, yet were forced to perform it in an economy making expanding, and increasingly mechanical, demands on their labour.

References to other trades can also be found in the industrial revolution – closer to skilled hand-work than to the heavy labour of mining – suggesting that in some people's eyes they were also worse than the factories: lace-running, needlework, milliner's work, embroidery, staw-plaiting. Despite such obvious manifestations as Luddism and machine-breaking in the nineteenth century, despite the campaigns waged by skilled workmen, sometimes to the point of murder, against the introduction of machinery that would ruin their crafts and trades, there have been contrasts in working people's lives by which, for their own employment, machinery has been the lesser evil. A violent hatred of machinery as such has not always been as easy to find on the surface of working people's life as in the texts of social critics and aesthetic pamphleteers. This may be merely a matter of surfaces. But it is at least possible that the ways of feeling of working people on the one hand, and of writers and artists who have criticized society on the other, have generally diverged on this point.

Marx, faced with machine-breaking, attributed it to the workers themselves, whom he perhaps imagined rising up against the 'congealed labour power' confronting them in their machines' as an alien world! In fact it appears that most machine breaking in the early nineteenth century was done on the one hand by skilled workmen of all kinds, by craftsmen, who were being undercut by the new inventions and whose products were being undersold by cheap but inferior substitutes; and by small farmers or spinning entrepreneurs frightened that larger men with more machinery would drive them under; and on the other other hand by country labourers whose livelihood in the comparatively idle season – threshing – agricultural machines threatened.[17]

Those who broke the machines were not in general the men who used them, but the men they displaced. People have always hated and feared those machines that make their work redundant and particularly so when there is no other prospect of earning a living. On the other hand there is a quite different tradition of hostility to machinery among professional people, especially writers, and those who live in the country without working on the land. Machines can be ugly and noisy, for instance, and can disturb a view. But a machine, ugly as it may be to the spectator, and in fact harmful as it may be to men who use it, is not usually the first thing that a labourer is likely to attack if his alternative might be either no work, or doing the same job in the same circumstances for the same pay, or less by hand and arm, and back.[18]

Operators of some machines often in fact speak of them in anthropomorphic terms, even with affection; a large turbine is 'man enough' for a certain job; a railway engine is sometimes treated as almost human by its driver, and was so particularly in the days of steam.

Nevertheless, even if such broad generalizations are valid as a whole, the question of working people's hostility to machinery in the nineteenth century is far more complex than this.

On many points there was a convergence with the ideas of the literary and philosophical critics of industrial work. Concern with the quality of manufactured goods – the anxiety about 'shoddy' goods that Ruskin and Morris so frequently express – was not restricted to literary men. When 'A journeyman cotton spinner' in an Address to the public of Manchester during the strikes of 1818 describes 'those terrible machines . . . called steam engines', he attacks not merely the heat in the factories, the food, the hours, and the tender age of the children employed and the supersession of human labour; he also adds that the 'more marketable' article they make is not in fact a better one.[19] Working men in other parts of the country also objected not merely to the conditions created by machinery, but also to the quality of the goods they were required to produce in factories.[20] Again, even historians who argue that Luddism was in most parts of England 'a means of coercing employers into making concession on wages, working conditions and other specific grievances'[21] – that in fact it was a new instance of a traditional phenomenon which Eric Hobsbawm describes as 'collective bargaining by riot'[22] – nevertheless point to exceptions : to places such as the Spen Valley of Yorkshire, which includes the woollen manufacturing areas of Leeds and Huddersfield, where 'hostility to machines' as such (though particularly to new labour-saving machinery such as shear-frames and steam-looms) was 'a striking feature of the disturbances'.[23]

No separation between literary attitudes to machines and those of men who worked with their hands could have been complete in nineteenth-century England. The two worlds were not sealed off from each other and the fact that critics in both worlds were in reaction against a similar dominant philosophy of entrepreneural expansion was bound to create a convergence. Thus an idea that has been found frequently, with different variants, in the literary and philosophical tradition – the idea that mechanization makes men mechanical also – can be found equally early (1794) in the writings of a Jacobin and artisan, Thomas Cooper, 'who had experienced the early stages of the Lancashire industrial revolution';[24]

Finally, at least one of the poets of the time was an agricultural labourer – John Clare; another was a craftsman who experienced the mechanization of his trade and the destruction of his way of work in his own lifetime. William Blake's *Songs of Innocence and Experience,* and the prophetic books are not simply 'responses to industrialization' although they are that too.[25] Blake and Clare, like the songwriters we shall consider next, show how far from rigid any distinction can be between 'writers' and 'working men'. If the evidence of a gap between the traditions is in general significant, the exeptions to it are not for that reason any the less remarkable.

11
Songs in oral tradition

Although the greater part of most people's waking time in the past, at least in temperate climates, has probably been taken up by work, the evidence to be found about the experience of work in surviving songs is perhaps less than might be expected.

Songs sung to accompany work are found among all peoples. They may even be the earliest form of all singing. But when they acquire words, their words are by no means always about work. Nor do songs sung after work always centre on what must have been, in terms of time, often the main experience of the day.

There are a few fragments of a milling song from ancient Greece. Shepherds' songs, shanties, work songs for men labouring rhythmically in gangs, milking songs and so on, are common to all countries. In more modern times there are numbers of printed songs praising the various trades and showing how indispensible each one is to the survival of the world as a whole. Some of these have gone into oral tradition.

But in general, songs from oral tradition in Britain specifically about work and about the feelings associated with it, are not in a majority among traditional songs If they did once occur they do not seem to have been preserved as frequently as those dealing with what one nineteenth-century collector summarized shortly as 'Love, war and murder'.

Of course this may be only because work changes more rapidly than love changes, and the songs that went with old ways of working are abandoned with them. Again, men sing about, and remember, the remarkable, even when they live the unremarkable. But on the evidence of the songs alone, work might appear to have been experienced through most of the history recorded in our own oral tradition, as a form of inevitable background to life, so continuously present that men are not conscious of it except in times of crisis.

If work – and creativity in work – has been even latently as important in all human life as Marx, Ruskin and Morris supposed, it is surprising that there is so little hint of it in the orally preserved songs, in contrast with the lovemaking, fighting and dying that are the subjects of most songs of the pre-industrial era and since.

In the assumptions of orally preserved traditional songs the subordination of work to lovemaking is almost complete. Even factories first appear in the traditional songs, surprisingly enough, as places to look for love in. Here is the final verse of an early nineteenth-century broadside from Oldham, quoted by A. L. Lloyd :

> Where are the girls? I'll tell you plain
> The girls have gone to weave by steam
> And if you'd find them you must rise at dawn
> And trudge to the factory in the early morn.[1]

Most references to machinery in early British songs seem to occur in erotic metaphor[2]

> . . . As I walked between Bolton and Bury, 'twas on a
> moonshiny night,
> I met with a buxom young weaver whose company gave me
> delight,
> She says : Young fellow, come tell me if your level and rule
> are in tune,
> Come, give me an answer correct, can you get up and square
> my new loom.
>
> I said : My dear lassie, believe me, I am a good joiner by
> trade,
> And many a good loom and shuttle before in my time I have
> made.

Your short lams and jacks and long lams I quickly can put
them in tune.
My rule is now in good order to get up and square a new
loom. . . .[3]

As A. L. Lloyd points out, there is nothing new even in songs like
this except the details of the machinery. The handcrafts had long
had their own erotic metaphors,[4] not only that of blacksmiths
and millers but of cobblers, tinkers, chimney-sweeps, ploughmen
– all the gear of all the trades seems to have been adapted to
symbolism.

When work does occur in the earlier songs, plain and without
metaphor, it very often again supplies only the background to
love. Work is never so good, the songs seem to assume, as when it
is interrupted by love. Here is a typical opening – a song that was
once about a knight, but became adapted to a working life :

> There was a bonny shepherd lad
> Kept sheep on yonder hill-o
> He's laid aside his pipe and club
> And gone to sleep his fill-o
>
> And when he's woken up again
> His heart is gi'en a turn-o
> For there he's spied a well fav'red lass
> A-swimming inth e burn-o.[5]

There are plenty of songs in oral tradition, and many more in
print, that show men as proud of their trade – ploughmen's songs,
miners' songs, and weavers' songs like The Work of the Weavers'.
But very often among those that have been preserved exclusively
in oral tradition the pride they show is in the success in love of
ploughmen, miners or weavers, or else that is the metaphor
through which the pride is shown. Some of them are highly
lyrical :

> I've travelled east and I've travelled west,
> And travelled ower Kirkaldy,
> But the bonniest lass that e'er I spied,
> She was followin' a collier laddie, . . .

'O whaur live ye, my bonnie lass?
Come tell me what they ca' ye.'
'Bonnie Jean Gordon is my name,
And I'm followin' a collier laddie.' . . .

'Ye see yon hills the sun shines on
That the sun shines on sae gaudy
They all are mine and they'll a' be thine
If ye'll leave your collier laddie.' . . .

Her faither then he vowed and swore :
'Though he be black he's bonny;
She's mair delight in him, I fear,
Than in you wi' a' your money.'

'Oh I can win my five pennies a day,
And spend't at nicht fu' brawly,
And I'll mak' my bed in the collier's neuk
And lie doon wi' my collier laddie.'[6]

Apart from love itself, play of all kinds – music, dancing or just
fooling about with the equipment – seems to make more appearance in the songs than intrinsically 'good' or 'interesting' work.
This may of course have been precisely because such 'good' work
was quite out of people's reach and they had to make do with
play for consolation. But it may also be because play has been far
more significant to people in the past than early nineteenth-
century schoolboys in Germany, like Marx, were told :

Call the horse, marrow
For I can call nane.
The heart of my belly
Is hard as a stane :
As hard as a stane
And as round as a cup,
Call the horse, marrow,
Till my hewer comes up.

Me and my marrow
And Christy Crawhall
Will play with any three in the pit
At the football;
At the football
And at the coal-tram,
We'll play with any three in the pit
For twelve-pence a gam. . . .[7]

It is not often, in the whole body of traditional songs, that we find
a reference to work as an activity valued in itself, independent of
love, of the chances of interruption by girls, of play, or of the
rewards; in fact of all the songs that have survived in oral tradition in this country possibly only one – 'The Recruited Collier' –
shows something like Morris' or Marx's vision of work itself as a
binding element in human love and life :

'Oh what's the matter with you, my lass,
And where's your dashing Jimmy?'
'The soldier boys have picked him up
And sent him far, far from me.
Last pay day he set off to town
And them red-coated fellows
Enticed him in and made him drunk,
And he'd better gone to the gallows. . . .
As I walked o'er the stubble field,
Below it runs the seam,
I thought of Jimmy hewing there,
But it was all a dream.
He hewed the very coals we burn,
And when the fire I's lighting
To think the lumps was in his hands
It sets my heart to beating.
So break my heart, and then it's o'er,
So break my heart, my deary,
And I'll lie in the cold green ground,
For of single life I'm weary.'[8]

And this reminds us again that the weight of evidence of songs cannot be taken simply as an indication of what has been significant to people in the past : that people do not always sing about what is most important to them; that they do not in fact always notice what is most important to them until it is about to be taken away. This is as true of literary poetry as of traditional songs. There are few lyrics of married love; and few poems of any kind that celebrate it except those that deal at the same time with its loss – like the lines in the Iliad when Hector takes leave of his wife and child before his final battle. And so with this song, a feeling about relationships expressed through work is shown exposed at the moment of destruction. Despite everything that has gone before, such feelings may well have existed, and have been divined by Morris and Marx- below the surface of other lives also.

The gap between consciousnesses may be superficial; perhaps there is greater community of feeling below. We shall meet this possibility again, in comparing what Marx and Morris believed with the words of people working in docks and motor factories today. A feeling for the importance of creative work appears to be strong in many people doing such work; though often lying beneath more immediate concerns. But even when it does appear, it is usually only side by side with a care for family life, love, a home leisure and plays not necessarily – as in Marx – having primacy over them.

However in one respect Marx in *Capital* was close to the feelings of working people. Perhaps the most bitter of all the work songs in Britain is not about factories but about handcraft work in an age of industrialization. It comes from early nineteenth-century Lancashire, and is known under many names, such as 'The Oldham Weaver', 'The Four-Loom Weaver' or – 'Junior', from the title of the half humourous tune with its strange unrhymed last line on which it is based 'Jone O'Grinfilt Junior'.

... in th' mind that I'm in I'll ne'er pick o'er again
For I've woven myself to th' far end.

I'm a poor cotton weaver as many a one knows,
I've nowt to eat in the house, and I've worn out my clothes.
Tha'd scarce gi' me tuppence for a' I've gotten on,
My clogs are both baws'n and stockings I've none.
You'd think it were hard to be sent into th' world
To clem and do best that you can . . .[9]

The realities of factory life itself – the enclosedness, the monotony, the dirt, the danger, even the length of the hours and the harshness of heat and cold – do not seem to emerge from any surviving song quite so bitterly as the experience of unemployment and starvation for those craftsmen whom factories and war displaced.

This may of course be because factory life destroyed in many places the capacity to make songs, with all the prohibitions on talking, whistling or singing at work, with the sheer noisiness of the machinery – in machine weaving for instance – and with the severance of traditions involved in factory people's exodus to big cities. Noise in particular could have had a devastating effect on the possibility of singing and song-writing. In many mills people had to lip-read. Occupational deafness was and still is, far from rare. But perhaps it is also, as Marx saw in his time, because, for many people over the last century and a half, going into a factory has been the alternative not to agreeable Ruskinian stone-carving with the support of a private income, but to unemployment and starvation.

Songs about the quality of work – for instance complaints about monotony – do exist: songs written about weaving and spinning in the nineteenth century that could almost equally well apply to the mass-production of contemporary motor factories.

Poverty, poverty knock!
Me loom is a sayin' all day.
Poverty, poverty knock!
Gaffer's too skinny to pay.
Poverty, poverty knock!

Keepin' one eye on the clock.
I know I can guttle

When I hear me shuttle
Go : Poverty, poverty knock !

Up every mornin' at five.
I wonder that we keep alive
Tired and yawnin' on the cold mornin',
It's back to the dreary old drive.[10]

Yet it is not monotony and futility alone that the song complains of. 'Poverty, poverty knock' is so sad and accurate an onomatopeia for the sound of the loom that it is pssible at first to forget that it has a surface meaning also : 'Gaffer's too skinny to pay'. It is not merely the work that the Batley weaver complains about. And the refrain does not necessarily apply to factory work. Handloom weavers were also called in nineteenth-century Yorkshire, 'poverty knockers'.[11]

Even when we seem closest in the songs to the assumptions of the nineteenth-century critics, there are differences of starting point. Where for Morris the focus of criticism has been on the monotony and the notorious lack of creativity of the work itself, in the workmen's songs there are things that are experienced with monotony, equally or even more the objects of complaint – the machinery going wrong, cruelty, injustice – and, inside or outside a factory, low pay or no pay.

The same association of dreary work with harsh management and low pay is the theme of a song written recently by Mrs Mamy Brooksbank of Dundee. This kind of song is no more extinct than the conditions that have produced it :

O, dear me, the mills' ga'in fast,
The puir wee shifters canna get their rest;
Shifting bobbins coorse and fine,
They fairly ma' you work for your ten-and-nine.

O, dear me, I wish the day was done,
Running up and down the pass isna fun,
Shiftin', piecin', spinnin' warp weft and twine
To feed and cleed my bairnie aff'n ten-and-nine

O, dear me, the world's ill divided,
Them that work the hardest are the least provided,
But I maun bide contented, dark days or fine;
There's no' much pleasure living aff'n ten-and-nine.[12]

Songs sung by working people outside the world of powered
machinery tend to show a similar set of concerns. Whereas the
pastoral literature and drawing-room ballads of those who have
done little labour have been full of praises of farm-work and sea-
faring as intrinsically satisfying ways of life – particularly when
'uncorrupted' by modern technology – the songs of people
actually engaged in these activities day after day suggest an at
least equal concern with factors that are not intrinsic to the work
at all – such as payment, conditions, justice and cruelty at work,
and love after it. It has sometimes been argued[13] that instrumentalism in working people is the product of industry itself : the
outcome of working with machinery, or of some increase in
'alienation' dating more or less from the industrial revolution. If
this were so, we might expect to find quite different concerns in
non-industrial songs : praises of the soil or of the sea, rather than
complaints about pay, conditions and injustice in ploughing or
sea-faring. But consider – from the same world that produced the
'Shepherd Lad' – this bothy ballad from Aberdeenshire.

DRUMDELGIE

At six o'clock the mill's pit on
To gi'e us a' straicht wark,
An' twal' o' us to wark at her,
Till ye could wring oor sark.
At acht o'clock the mill's taen off,
We hurry doon the mair,
To get some quarter through the fan
Till daylight doth appear.

The cloods begin to gently lift
The sky begins to clear,

The grieve he cries : Oho, me lads
You'll be no longer here.
An sax o' ye'll gang to the ploo'
Sax to ca' the neeps
And the owsen they'll be after thee
When they get on their feet.

At puttin' on the harness
An' dra'in' oot the took,
The drift dang on sae very thick
That we were like to choke;
The drift dang on sae very thick
The ploo', she wid na go.
Twas then the cairtin' did commence
Among the frost an' snow.[14]

This is a song from the later nineteenth century when many itinerant labourers housed temporarily in 'bothies' worked on the farms of Scotland. Yet similar forms of work, seem earlier to be accepted without complaint when there is no overt sense of personal injustice, and when money is not a source of intense complaint in itself.

This is true of other songs besides the agricultural ones. Consider the sailors' songs of the early nineteenth century, particularly the forebitters sung by the crew of a ship in their own quarters to each other, rather than at work under the supervision of officers and boatswains. It is possible to find whaling songs that describe the same conditions, sung by the same men, who experience the conditions in opposite ways. In the songs that complain about injustice, personal cruelty, or cheating over pay, there is also suffering from wind and ice and exhaustion; when the pay is good, and there is hope of return to a home port, and to a chance of love rather than to robbery in a brothel, these same conditions and the work itself appear in a totally different guise. The cheerful songs seem to take in their stride, as it were – in the conscious expectation of reward in terms of pay, rest, drink, warmth, and lovemaking – just the intrinsic conditions of work which the bitter songs complain of. It is generally true that the more bitter sea-songs are the later ones.

Here is a song of the first kind from the 1860s or 70s portraying an experience of work wholly without 'meaning' or 'interest'; just the kind of nakedly instrumental labour that Marx writes of in 1844. When injustice, cruelty and low pay are the rule, the ship is as grim as the factory, or worse :

> When first I landed in Liverpool, I went upon the spree,
> My money at last I spent it fast, got drunk as drunk could be;
> And when my money was all gone, it was then I wanted more,
> But a man must be blind to make up his mind to go to sea
>   once more.
>
> I spent that night with Angeline, too drunk to roll in bed
> My watch was new and my money too, in the mornin' with
>   'em she'd fled;
> And as I roamed the street about, the whores they all did roar
> 'Here comes Jack Spratt the poor sailor lad, he must go to
>   sea once more.'
>
> As I was a-walking down the street, I met with Rapper Brown
> I asked him for to take me in and he looked at me with a
>   frown;
> He said : 'Last time you was paid off, with me you chalked no
>   score,
> But I'll give youse a chance and I'll take your advance and
>   send you to sea once more'
>
> He shipped me aboard of a whaling ship bound for the Arctic
>   seas,
> Where the cold winds blow through the frost and snow and
>   Jamaica rum would freeze;
> And worse to bear, I'd no hard-weather gear, for I'd spent
>   all my money ashore,
> It was then I wished that I was dead so I'd go to sea no more.

Sometimes we're catching whales, my lads, and sometimes
  we're catching none,
With a twenty-foot oar stuck in our hands from four o'clock
  in the morn,
And when the shades of night come on, we rest our weary
  oar,
It was then I wished that I was dead or safe with the girls
  ashore. . . .[15]

On the other side, a song like 'The Bonnie Ship the Diamond'
which dates from the earlier nineteenth century seems to describe
the same general conditions, but in a totally different light.

The Diamond is a ship, my lads, for the Davis Strait she's
  bound,
And the quay it is all garnished with bonnie lassies round;
Captain Thompson gives the order to sail the ocean wide,
Where the sun it never sets, my lads, nor darkness dims
  the sky.

So it's cheer up, my lads, let your hearts never fail,
While the bonnie ship, The Diamond, goes a-fishing for the
  whale.

Along the quay at Peterhead, the lasses stand around,
Wi' their shawls all pulled about them and the saut tears
  rinnin' doon :
Don't you weep, my bonnie lass, though you be left behind,
For the rose will grow on Greenland's ice before we change
  our mind. . . .

It'll be bricht both day and nicht when the Greenland lads
  come hame,
Wi' a ship that's fu' o' oil, my lads, and money to our name
We'll make the cradles for to rock and the blankets for to
  tear,
And every lass in Peterhead sing 'hushabye, my dear' . . .[16]

The songs come from different points in a folksong tradition –
and that undoubtedly is responsible for part of their difference.
No doubt also, under the intensely competitive pressures of nineteenth century sailing, conditions between the two songs degener-
ated. But the main form of work itself, the absence of women, the
discipline, the sea and the cold are all the same. The difference
that the songs display is not so much between two forms of work
as between different backgrounds to work – in one of which there
is injustice which leaves work unrewarded, and in the other a
context that makes it meaningful, however simply – in terms of
pay and love.

If some kind of instrumentalism – of this sort at least – is an
habitual assumption in working-men's songs like these, it may
have long been an habitual element in working-people's feelings
and expectations, even if it has existed side by side with the more
elusive concern for creativity. If so, Marx, Ruskin and Morris,
who wish to focus attention on the quality of work itself, on its
creativity and its intrinsic nature irrespective of its rewards, may
have an extraordinary difficulty in appealing to many working
people for whom such an abstraction is traditionally strange; few
of whom in the past have been craftsmen, and for whom work has
perhaps for generations been felt to be satisfying or unsatisfying in
proportion as it is well or badly rewarded and humanely or
cruelly conducted, not in the degree to which it is interesting,
creative, or akin to art.

There are, however, a few songs that do show men enjoying their
work positively. It is striking that they are nearly all about either
carters, millers, tramps, tinkers or haymakers; they are not, in
general, about men who produce things, or about craftsmen.
Even songs about blacksmiths are generally erotic. And in the
enjoyable work a strong element of either play or the possibility of
sudden interruptions by love-making seems again to be present.
At the same time, in those rare cases where work is shown as a
direct source of enjoyment, the diction suggests either literary or
music-hall composition. The nearer the work itself is to being

enjoyed, the less convincing are the songs in their immediate popular origin.

Nevertheless, even if written by outsiders, songs like 'Jim the Carter Lad' and 'The Merry Haymakers' have both been taken into wide circulation among working people. If they do not necessarily reflect the labourers' experience in work as it was they are unlikely to be wholly unrealistic, and by their popularity and survival among certain working people they may still say something about what they have wished for.

> ... It's my father was a carrier
> Many years ere I was born;
> He used to rise at daybreak
> And go his round each morn,
> He'd often take me with him
> Especially in the spring,
> When I loved to sit upon the cart
> And hear me father sing.
>
> So it's crack, crack, goes me whip
> I whistle and I sing;
> I sit upon me wagon,
> I'm as happy as a king;
> Me horse is always willing
> As for me, I'm never sad;
> There's none could lead a jollier life
> Nor Jim the Carter Lad.
>
> It's now the girls all smile on me,
> As I go driving past;
> The horse is such a beauty,
> As we jog along so fast;
> We've travelled many weary miles
> But happy days we've had,
> And there's none can use a horse more kind
> Nor Jim the Carter Lad ...[17]

This song has been sung, mainly, by men who were not carters, but who watched carts go by; it may show something of people's feelings about the kind of work they liked to think of. The following song originator as a ballad-writer's broadside in 1695, but it has survived and been recovered from oral tradition, in some cases sung by men who actually do make hay:

'Twas in the pleasant month of May
In the springtime of the year,
And down by yonder meadow
There runs a river clear.
See how the little fishes,
How they do sport and play,
Causing many a lad and many a lass
To go there a-making hay.

Then in comes that scytheman
That meadow to mow down,
With his old leathered bottle
And the ale that runs so brown.
There's many a stout and a labouring man
Goes there his skill to try,
He works, he mows, he sweats, he blows
And the grass cuts very dry.

Then in comes both Tom and Dick
With their pitchforks and their rakes,
And likewise Black-eyed Susan,
The hay all for to make.
There's a sweet, sweet, sweet and a jug, jug, jug,
How the harmless birds do sing
From the morning till the evening
As we were haymaking.

It was just at one evening
As the sun was a-going down,
We saw the jolly piper come
A-strolling through the town;
There he pulled out his tapering pipes

And he made the valleys ring.
So we all put down our rakes and forks
And we left the haymaking.

We called for a dance
And we tripped it along,
We danced all round the hay-cocks
Till the rising of the sun,
When the sun did shine such a glorious light
And the harmless birds did sing,
Each lad he took his lass in hand
And went back to his haymaking.[18]

As evidence of actual experience, this song is open to the objection of fantasy and compensation. It survived in Rottingdean through a period when Sussex was the centre of rickburning and machine breaking : it can scarcely therefore represent the real conditions of agricultural labout in that county over the whole period of its survival.[19]

However, certain things shown in this song as an integral part of work have apparently appealed to singers all over the country, many of whom have worked in quite different conditions. Several of them are present in the carting song as well. If we have to spell these things out, the first is an enjoyment of fresh landscape – of the clear water of the river and of the 'springtime of the year'. Then there is a delight in the presence of other lives than the singer's own, especially lives smaller and more playful than an adult man's – 'the little fishes how they do sport and play' – and the birdsong – 'There's a sweet sweet sweet and a jug, jug, jug, how the harmless birds do sing'.

Thirdly, this more playful life includes a powerful suggestion of erotic happiness, present already as an element of work and capable of interrupting work or of growing naturally out of it. The couples lay down their rakes and forks to dance when the piper comes, then return to their haymaking, or 'haymaking' – for in this song, as in many other songs about work, erotic suggestion fuses in metaphor with the work itself.

Fourth, there is a rhythm related to the rhythmic work, and this again is related to the whistling, singing and dancing that occur in the action of the song, as in the carting song – and even in certain lines in the song, with their dancing half-syllables, 'such a glorious light' or 'tapering pipes' – this last phrase a fine example of Tolstoyan detail incidentally, which probably originated accidentally as labour and pipe gradually grew obsolete.

Finally, there is a great feeling of freedom, of ease of movement, choice of speed, space and air around, an absence of close supervision and of clock time.[20] There is even a suggestion that the haymaking, like the carting, is some voluntary work, to which the haymakers have been somehow drawn, by the springtime, the landscape and the playing of the fishes in the clear river nearby, as the carter is by his love of the trade.

Certain wishes or fantasies of an uninstrumental kind of work have survived, then, in traditional songs. They appear to have been partly suggested from outside working life, then taken up by working people; and they may represent wishes more than everyday experience. They are not particularly concerned, even then, with the decoration or craftsmanship that preoccupied William Morris, or with Marx's kind of work – in the most deadly earnest, really hard effort, for example, composing. They are not even concerned with 'production' in the sense of making new physical objects.

But in the idea they suggest of a fusion of 'play' with work – play not unlike the leisure and freedom for the sake of which man with an 'instrumental' attitude at least hopes to labour – they contain a possible alternative ideal, in working people's own inherited consciousness, both to the routine hand-labour of farms and factories, and even to the ideals of craftsmanship, serious productive labour, and instrinsic satisfaction in work itself with which the nineteenth-century critics planned to 'humanize' their conditons.

The idea that working people might have ideas of their own on these subjects is sometimes disturbing to those who would improve their condition. However, it may be true.

12

Levin in the fields

One of the finest descriptions of satisfying physical work in any novel echoes the impressions left by these happy working songs, but makes them perhaps more explicit. It is about a similar form of labour – haymaking. But it sheds light also on an enjoyment discernible even in some of the less obviously happy working songs. It apparently came from first-hand experience, yet was written by a man who did not do this work regularly – Tolstoy. In Anna Karenina,[1] Levin the landowner tries his hand at mowing : here he is seen losing himself gradually in the rhythm of the work.

He heard nothing save the swish of the knives, saw the receding upright figure of Titus in front of him, the crescent curve of the cut grass, the grass and flower-heads slowly and rhythmically falling about the blade of his scythe, and ahead of him the end of the row, where would come rest. . . .

Levin lost all count of time and had no idea whether it was late or early. A change began to come over his work which gave him intense satisfaction. There were moments when he forgot what he was doing, he mowed without effort and his line was almost as smooth and good as Titus's. But as soon as he began thinking what he was doing and trying to do better, he was at once conscious how hard the task was, and would mow badly. . . .

The longer Levin mowed, the oftener he experienced these moments of oblivion when it was not his arms which swung the scythe but the scythe seemed to mow of itself, a body full of life and consciousness of its own, and as though by magic, without a thought being given to it, the work did itself regularly and carefully. These were the most blessed moments. It was only hard work when he had to interrupt this unconscious motion and think.

This is a wonderful description of the effects of a working rhythm; effects which may be present in quite different work, even as we shall see – in an alternative form – in unlikely places like factories today. The old mower in front of Levin seems to have attained this state of self-loss in his work consistently, and is so relaxed in the rhythm of it that he is intently aware of everything around him.

> The old man, holding himself erect, went in front, moving with long, regular strides, his feet turned out and swinging his scythe as precisely and evenly, and apparently as effortlessly, as a man swings his arms in walking. . . . And while he did this he noted everything he came to : sometimes he would pick a wild berry and eat it, or offer it to Levin; sometimes he threw a twig out of the way with the point of the steel, or examined a quail's nest, from which the hen-bird flew up from right under the scythe; or caught a snake that crossed his path, lifting it on the scythe as though on a fork, showed it to Levin, and flung it away. . . . In the wood their scythes were continually cutting birch-mushrooms, grown plump in the succulent grass. But the old man bent down every time he came across a mushroom, picked it up, and put it inside his smock. 'Another little treat for my old woman' he said as he did so. It was easy enough to mow the wet, soft grass but going up and down the steep slopes of the ravine was hard work. But this did not trouble the old man. Swinging his scythe just as usual, taking short, firm steps with feet shod in large plaited shoes, he climbed slowly up the slope, and though his whole frame and the breeches below his smock shook with effort, he did not miss one blade of grass or let a single mushroom escape him, and never ceased joking with the other peasants and Levin.

Seeing something of the same image of life lived fully in a young couple stacking hay in a nearby farm a short time later, and believing in the peasants' uncalculating willingness to work and to enjoy, Levin envisages, for a time, a better life for himself too :

> Some of the very peasants who had most disputed with him over the hay – whom he had been hard on or who had tried to cheat him – those very peasants had nodded happily to him, evidently not feeling and unable to feel any rancour against him, any regret, any recollection even of having intended to cheat him. All that had been swallowed up in the sea of cheerful common toil. God gave the day, God gave the strength for it. And the day and the strength were consecrated to labour, and that labour was its own reward. For whom the labour? What would be its fruits? These were idle considerations beside the point.
>
> Levin had often admired this life, had often envied the men who lived it; but today for the first time, especially under the influence of what he had seen of the relations between Vanka Parmenich and his young wife, the idea came into his mind that it was in his power to exchange the onerous, idle, artificial, and selfish existence he was leading for that busy, honourable, delightful life of common toil.

But only a few days later Levin is listening with approval to an old landowner who wants to restore serfdom. Now he can see only the struggle and opposition between himself and the peasants, because he has been trying to improve the system of agriculture in his own interests. This is not what the labourer wanted.

> What the labourer wanted was to take it as easy as possible, with rests, and, especially, not have the trouble of worrying and thinking . . . all they wanted was to work light-heartedly and irresponsibly, and his interests were not only remote and incomprehensible to them but fatally opposed to their own most just claims. Levin had long felt dissatisfaction with his own position in regard to the land. He saw that his ship leaked, but did not look for the hole, perhaps purposely deceiving

himself. But now he could deceive himself no longer. The farming of the land, as he was managing it, had not only ceased to interest him, but had become distasteful, and he could no longer give his mind to it.

Thus ultimately the picture of physical labour that emerges from Tolstoy's description is as ambiguous as any other account. There is a state in which work is done without conscious resistance – where 'it does itself' – and this is characterized by a loss of self-consciousness, by a keen perception of everything around and above all by rhythm. Work is then still full of effort yet light-hearted and can be interrupted momentarily at will – for eating berries or picking mushrooms – without disturbance to the underlying rhythm. At its best it is done in the open and in summer, and there is joking and company : it is surrounded by the life of other creatures. Yet even this 'good' work involves toil, and people want 'to take it easy with rests', and 'especially not to have' the one thing Marx believed essential to redeem manual labour – the trouble of worrying and thinking. Tolstoy does not attempt to focus these two distinct visions. He leaves them as they came to Levin, simultaneous and strangely contrary.

13
The search for golden ages
of labour

How far are any beliefs in 'golden ages' of labour without an instrumental attitude to work to be credited? There could be both a strong and a weak definition of an 'instrumental' attitude to work. A weak definition might apply when clear consciousness of a later reward, outside the work itself – in terms of money, consumption, affection or respect – is a significant element in the experience of work, though not the only one of which men are conscious; a strong definition where work is experienced consciously as nothing else than a means to such a later reward, or a means of avoiding punishment or starvation.

If there was in fact a spread or a strengthening of instrumental attitudes in the industrial revolution, we have seen that the factors involved in this may have been not merely technological but cultural – the loss of traditions, or ritual, of songs, religions and closeknit relationships; but that even these may have been exaggerated, both at the time, and subsequently; so that a 'golden age' of labour may continually have been projected into the past, irrespective of the facts of previous working experience. When this is said, it is still not evidence that better conditions and more spontaneous enjoyment of work never did exist; fantasy of a golden age, and the reality of genuinely happier work, may both be located at different times in the past. There is at least a possibility, for instance, that the centuries after the Black Death really were much better for many people on the land than those that preceded or followed them.

Let us see what evidence there is for the existence of less instrumental attitudes in pre-industrial societies, and, if there is any, how far this may have been due to differences of technology and the division of labour, and how far to the existence of songs, customs, beliefs and rituals giving meaning to forms of work perhaps no more rewarding in themselves, or perhaps also in other ways intrinsically more enjoyable.

Perhaps a disproportionate amount of evidence about work from the distant past comes from the recording of disputes, and it sometimes seems as if working people's disputes are similar in any civilization where they are recorded. Men who have to live by very small sums of money, or with little to barter, anger those who live or compose the morals of the society, by arguing about these small sums. The rich and the learned complain that the poor are so obsessed with money, and so mean-spirited, that they dispute about the most minute amounts. To show their high-mindedness, the rich frequently refuse to pay their bills.

Meanwhile reformers and moralists, whom someone somehow supports without their having to labour, often take an even sterner line than the rich : they say that everyone should labour, and no one should care about money; both the idle rich and the disputing poor are at fault. Meanwhile to write reforming books, to tell parables, to preach sermons or simply to pray is to be regarded as morally equivalent to the very hardest labour; and those who do these things, unlike the rich, are rightly to be excused from labouring. 'Soldiers, be content with your wages' says St Paul; and his Master : 'It is easier for a camel to go through the eye of a needle than for a rich man to enter the kingdom of heaven'. The labourers in the parable of the talents argue against the fairness of a flat rate of a penny for a day's work or for any part of a day; the master, in defending his flat rate payment, manages to imply that tired workmen ought to be as far above such disputes, as he is, surveying his vineyard in the cool of the evening.

Certainly in the Middle Ages, where William Morris would look for wholly different attitudes to work, this three-sided pattern can be seen – though perhaps it was not so often to be found before the Black Death and the extension of wages; nor is it true of those monks who built the monasteries some of whom continued to labour with their hands. Among those who did not actually do any labour themselves, the prestige of work seems to have stood extraordinarily high in the fourteenth century. The sermons are full of praises of work. Both prayer and labour are useful and blessed; but the inactivity of the rich is one reason they will not – as Scripture warns us have much chance of getting into heaven.

Such praises of work from the outside, by those who do not themselves do any labour, might almost be said to count as evidence against feelings of enjoyment among labourers and even craftsmen; for it these all loved their work as much as Morris believed men did in the Middle Ages, it would hardly have been necessary to exhort them; not could the rich or even the priests have been easy to deter from joining in.

Yet apparently they were. Even in those medieval texts where work is recommended as an activity to be integrated with study, and in the Renaissance books that follow them, there is little suggestion that work will itself be pleasant. The monks who are said to have been among the first to use regular time did so initially for contemplation and services rather than to organize their lives round work;[1] and there is no evidence that they went to labour itself more willingly than their contemporaries. When St Benedict says his monks ought to work, he adds that they should not complain when they are obliged to get in the harvest, 'for then they are truly monks when they live by the labour of their hands, as did our Fathers and the Apostles'. He assumes that they will complain.[2] And equally Sir Thomas More, when saying that everyone will share the work in his *Utopia*, makes no suggestion that labour will be intrinsically pleasant. Those who would voluntarily choose a life of labour rather than ease would be laughed at, unless they made the choice from motives of religion.[3] In *Utopia*, it will need care to make sure that 'no man may live idle but that every one may follow his trade diligently'.[3]

One modern historian sums up the available evidence about agricultural work in the Middle Ages:

It seems clear at least that labour services were deeply un-
popular with those who had to discharge them, and the un-
satisfactory nature of their performance was one of the factors
leading to commutation. The famous passage in Aelfric's
Colloquy tells us how hard the Anglo-Saxon ploughman considered his lot to be, while Walter of Henley says that labourers
must be watched all the time because 'customary servants
neglect their work'. The manorial overseer accordingly carried
a stick. We know that the medieval peasant swore when his
cart got stuck in the mud. . . .

However, he adds 'But under less trying circumstances, what
the free peasant working his own plot as opposed to working
for others thought about it all I have no idea.'[4]

As far as the peasants are concerned the prospect of gain, including money wages, appears to have been a factor affecting actions
from at least the fourteenth century. In the mobility that followed
the Black Death, people moved off the land to which they had
been tied, beginning to work other and sometimes better land,
often apparently moving for marginally higher wages. Peasants'
revolts at the time do not appear to have involved calls on the
part of the peasants for more interesting or varied or intrinsically
satisfying labour but for less labour and fewer taxes – in rather
similar claims to those that organizations of working people make
today. Meanwhile Langland's complaint in Piers Plowman
against the peasants of his time – that they like idleness and do
not work hard enough – sounds strangely like the one made by
many modern non-labouring commentators – clergy, politicians,
newspaper leader-writers and the like.

Of course, it is possible that certain forms of work were enjoyed
in ways we do not know about. Very little is known of medieval
working people and it is as wrong to build sceptical generalizations on the basis of a lack of evidence as to accept Morris' or
Ruskin's beliefs without question. What evidence there is suggests
that here again elements of life quite outside work may have
contributed to people's enjoyment more than any supposed benefit of agricultural or craftsmanlike work themselves. The very

large number of holidays was almost certainly an important factor; one hundred and eleven saints' days and festivals have been noted in the French year under the ancient régime,[5] and, in medieval English records, a working year of forty-four weeks, with Sundays off. Though some records cast doubt on the ubiquity of the 'third of the year's leisure'[6] and though perhaps only those who did not have to tend animals ever gained the full benefit of it in any case. It is not until very recently that anything like so many days away from work have been recovered by working people in the West.

Such holidays were generally passed in communal activities in the same village, activities quite different from work – and sometimes in customs that inverted the normal order of hierarchy, such as the Saturnalia, the dominion of the Lords of Misrule. The possibility cannot be excluded that in this period everyday life was at times unmeasurably better because of such rituals and ceremonies, or even because of social relationships now lost, inspired by belief in an order higher than the earthly one to which all men were equally subject. Perhaps Simone Weil, for instance, is right in arguing that in the civilization of Languedoc up to the twelfth century, equality, hierarchy and loyalty had been uniquely harmonized. Absence of evidence is no guarantee of the truth of a more sceptical view.

Craftsmanship, though it was probably never the occupation of more than a small minority, could apparently bring freedom of movement and a comparatively high standing in society.[7] Unfortunately, however, little more is known about the feelings of craftsmen than about those of peasants. A notebook of Walter de Honnecourt survives; it shows among other things that the originality and spontaneity of medieval craftsmen was perhaps exaggerated by the nineteenth-century philosophers. A lot of de Honnecourt's time seems to have been spent in copying models or noting down ideas from other people's work. But of personal feelings and 'experience of work' the notebook contains no trace. The historian quoted previously writes:

The model craft guild, maintaining standards and a sense of professional pride, permitting all to work their way up from apprentice to master allowing masters and journeymen to work side by side, involving the comforting patronage of a saint, helping the poor and sick among its members, and combining economic functions with religious and carnival ones, must have produced a very different attitude to work from that to be found today in a large factory or steel works. But how common was this arrangement? (How can we test the statement ... that 'There was satisfying work for more people in sixteenth-century England than today')[8]

It is only as they begin to be thought of as 'artists' rather than 'artisans' that detailed records of craftsmen's lives exist. And then evidence for the theory that they were all interested only in the intrinsic nature of their work is not to be found. The first medieval artist known about in any detail as an individual is Giotto, and it appears from the facts recorded in Giotto's time that to live in the early fourteenth century, and to paint pictures, gave no guarantee of freedom from a passionate interest in payment. The earliest records suggest that Giotto

> combined the highest artistic skills with an acute business sense. In 1314 four, perhaps even six, notaries were looking after his business interests. ... We cannot be certain that he wrote the poem sneering at 'those many who praise poverty' to which his name is attached ... but there is nothing in his life which makes it improbable.[9]

Interest in money has not been called here a 'strong' criterion of an instrumental attitude to work. A medieval artist could quite possibly be interested in both money and the intrinsic nature. But this could be equally true in our own day; and not merely painters, but some factory workers also speak of their work as both a source of intrinsic satisfaction and a source of money. The point is that here, in what might have been expected to be a paradigm case of Ruskin's and Morris' Middle Ages, and in the very painter Simone Weil singles out as having necessarily had a purity inseparable from his paintings, a complete disinterest in the financial rewards of work is not to be found.

Perhaps, it will be argued, this is because capitalism had already developed sufficiently by 1300 to give Giotto 'modern' feelings about money, as well as a known name. If so, then the idea that the industrial revolution marked the main incursion of instrumental attitudes into people's feelings about work needs to be revised. And if this is so, the critics of industrial society must look further back than the eighteenth or nineteenth centuries for those quite different attitudes to work and money that they believed in and hoped to recreate.

Ancient Greek society is among the earliest and most consistent objects of idealization in the tradition we have been considering. Schiller says that only after the time of the Greeks was enjoyment separated from work. He did not make clear whether he meant that everyone in the time of the Greeks enjoyed work; or whether he meant that work was enjoyable only for those who were not slaves. Of course, if slaves do the most unpleasant and monotonous labour, it is not so hard for the others to enjoy the work that is left over. A modern scholar writes that although

> a count of heads would probably show that even in Athens the citizens who did work of some kind, including agriculture, outnumbered the others ...

Yet

> as far as the managerial level slaves were the sole labour force in all manufacturing establishments exceeding the family circle, while trade, on which far more than on manufacture, the growth of ancient cities depended, was in Athens dependent on a vital minority of alien traders either transient or 'metic', needed for the import both of luxuries and of necessities.'[10]

Thus 'what we call the economy was properly the exclusive business of outsiders'.[11]

In that case, if the Athenians did in fact avoid unenjoyable work, it may have been through no miraculously harmonious or 'unalienated' approach to living such as Schiller supposed; rather through the use of slaves to do the bitterest labour and by 'ways and means' to earn more profits and buy more slaves, to the end that every Athenian may be maintained at public expense'.

And this is surely true. Apart from some sayings of Hesiod, and a few remarks of Socrates, there is little praise of work itself, or even respect for it, recorded in any ancient Greek texts, at least in the Classical period.

According to Klingender, although

> art was intimately associated with productive labour in primitive society and in the mural decorations in Egyptian tombs ... and ... craftsmen at work are depicted in the early black-figure pottery of Attica; and tablets of the same period from Boeotia contain the earliest surviving drawings of miners. Yet work scenes are scarcely ever found on the red-figured vases of the Classical era, except as illustrations of myths, such as the Labours of Hercules. ...

He holds that the contempt for manual work first appeared when industrial production, based on slave labour, began to supersede craft production in Classical Antiquity.[12]

Plato, in the *Republic* and the *Laws*, praises the division of labour on the grounds that a man who specializes makes better products more easily :[13] Xenophon also praises specialization, not only because the final product is better, but because a man can live by one trade, or by less than a whole trade, in a large city with labour highly divided.[14] Neither of these justifications suggests any attitudes to work that would disturb a modern production manager, nor any direct evidence that would support Schiller's idealization of the experience of work itself in Ancient Greece.

Where the originality of the Greeks is striking however – and this is a point picked out by Rousseau – is in the sense of sufficiency. Aristotle contrasts 'money-making' with provision for a household by pointing out that the householder's needs are limited. He is therefore capable of freedom. The money-maker by contrast is under constraint, precisely because there are no limits to his needs or desires.[15]

Men in modern society, in this sense, are under constraint. Much work is now done for rewards which are not themselves limited, and it is the business of the modern economy to keep demand constantly buoyant at whatever cost to the sense of sufficientcy of those who must strive in it in production and consumption. The products of work and its technical equipment are required to be in a state of perpetual development and expansion, and so is demand itself. The Greeks by contrast had no notion of 'an economy' outside the individual household. The word cannot be translated, according to the scholar quoted above, and though he notes that this view is disputed, the Greeks probably did not believe material 'progress' to be either likely or desirable.

Although wages for labour in Ancient Athens were never high, it is possible, though not certain, that individual working people also chose rest rest rather than more money where they could. Thus according to one story, some of the stone-masons who worked on the Erectheion – despite the beauty of the view and what would seem the extraordinarily absorbing nature of the work – knocked off for at least a fifth of the time, for more days than there were holidays in the Athenian calendar. The poorer labourers seem to have complained of this, since they got no work when the masons were not there, but could not live on the wages they earned when there was work going.[16] If this is accurate, it is remarkably similar to the complaints that can be heard today in factories where men work on assembly lines at piece-work wages much higher than the day wage of the labourers who supply them : when the assemblers have earned enough – so the day labourers complain – they down tools on some unimportant pretext, and stay away till they need more money. Ruskin might explain the similarity by the repetitive nature of marble-cutting according to the Greek method; each of the six groups working on a different pillar being required to flute it identically.[17] But if one had hoped to find, in Greeks working on a classical temple, attitudes to manual work dramatically different from those of our own day, the parallel, if it is in fact correct, is disquieting.

The idea of sufficiency went also with a sense of limits in scale. The Greeks were aware of the large numbers of men employed in the enterprises, for instance, of the Persians. But Classical Greece had very few large factories. One mine in the late fifth century had a thousand slaves. The largest workshop in Attica may have employed a hundred and twenty slaves. A workshop left to Demosthenes by his father was not thought small : 'it employed between fifty and sixty slaves'.[18]

The Germans of Schiller'e day praised the Greeks for their 'naturalness'. It was even believed that, being closer to the origins of mankind, they preserved some essential simplicity that had been there at the beginning of time. And it is true that simple peoples and perhaps most civilizations before the European Renaissance have had some sense of limits to the scale of human needs, if only because they have had few means of exceeding them. But the Greeks' sense of sufficiency was not 'natural' in the sense of merely inherited from a primitive civilization – something inevitably to be superseded by more 'developed' peoples later. Their neighbours, they knew, behaved differently. For them it was also a philosophical attitude, derived from a religion and a cosmology. If there was an unusual relationship between work and leisure in ancient Greece, it was perhaps that men saw the object of work as the production, simply, of 'enough'.

Can anything be learned about work in the most remote societies of all from our own – the societies which early in his life Rousseau praised, and which some of his followers, to his distress, seem to have believed were the main objects of his devotion?

In the songs of 'primitive' peoples engaged in hunting and gathering, herding and simple agriculture today, some evidence may be found of what men feel in forms of life when their activities are hardly divided into work, consumption and rest. Of course modern 'primitive' peoples have mostly had some contact with civilization; perhaps we can now see only partly civilized people wherever we look. But certain songs survive, recorded as early as the mid-nineteenth century from unlettered peoples; and they may give suggestions, if not conclusive evidence, of how hunting and gathering, herding and agriculture have been experienced in the simplest forms of life.

The first striking fact about them is that there is so much good poetry to be found among them, not only of that aspect of poetry that can be best appreciated in translation – what Pound called *phanapoeia*, or the casting of images on the eye of the mind – but also signs of craftsmanship, apparently valued everywhere. Song-making for instance, is found in nearly all those 'primitive' societies that we have evidence of:

'Every Dobman is a song-maker'; 'The Meo (are) a people of poets'; 'The Nuer are poetic'.

Most men and women compose songs which are sung at dances and concerts and composed for the creator's own pleasure and chanted by him in lonely pastures. . . . Youths break into song, praising their kinsmen, sweethearts, and cattle, when they feel happy, wherever they may be. A man composes his song as he cuts a canoe or a bow or as he paddles a canoe, singing it over softly to himself until he is satisfied with it. He then awaits an opportunity to sing it in public.'[19]

The second thing that stands out is that – though it may be hard to translate our concept of work into any primitive language – nevertheless activities at least resembling work and done apparently with a conscious eye on subsequent consumption already seem to be present however simple the stage of the society we examine – though in the very simplest, least clearly.

The distinction is usually drawn among so-called primitive men, between on the one hand hunters and gatherers and on the other those who pursue simple agriculture and pastoral life.[20] Marx, in his early philosophical writings thought of 'instru-mentalism' as beginning with the first exchange.

Perhaps the concept of work also occurs first with the exchange of present pain for future satisfaction in agriculture. For agriculture, even of the simplest kind, must always involve some loss of immediacy of enjoyment. In all work there is exchange, between the present and the future; but agricultural man sows for the sake of a later harvest, while hunting and gathering man, by contrast, hardly defers his gratification. Hunger, hunting and eating are separated not by seasons for him, but by the running of a particular animal and the burning of a single fire. In this sense, it seems that the hunters and gatherers – and only they – fit the nineteenth-century critics' demands, that men should engage in activity that absorbs them wholly, done for its own sake rather than for the sake of a future reward of which they are conscious at the time.

The idea that all 'primitive' men have so much pleasure or absorption in the immediacy of their activities that they carry them out without any thought, at the time, of reward or result seems doubtful. From Polynesia comes this song – in translation – of a man paddling a canoe : it seems to show the most brilliant pleasure in his action :

> It is laid by the canoe-side,
> Held close to the canoe-side,
> Now, it is raised on high – the paddle !
> Poised for the plunge – the paddle !
> Now, we spring forward !
> Now, it leaps and flashes – the paddle !
> It quivers like a bird's wing,
> This paddle of mine ! . . .
> . . . Ha ! the quick thrust in,
> The backward sweep !
> The swishing, the swirling eddies,
> The boiling white wake
> And the spray that flies from my paddle ![31]

But this is a war canoe; not a hunting boat or a ferry.

> There before us lies our ocean-path,
> The path of strife and tumult,
> The pathway of this chief,
> The danger roadway of this crew;
> It is the road of the Great-Sky-above-us.[21]

When the King of a West African tribe commanded a song to be sung after burials, he identified the pleasures which the dead do not enjoy in much the same way as might be expected from a modern man who works instrumentally. They do not include the pleasures of anything like work :

> I see it : There is no pleasure for the dead.
> I say : What you eat in this world, the pleasure of it goes with
>   you.
> I say : The drinks you drank, the pleasure of them goes with
>   you.
> I say : The meat you ate, the pleasure of it goes with you.
> I say : The drinks you drank, the pleasure of them goes
>   with you.
> I say : This pipe you smoked, the pleasure of it goes with
>   you.[22]

And when an Australian aboriginal woman complains of her husband's straying, it is not of his wandering in search of more interesting craftsmanlike tasks :

> Ah, our daughter was taken ill –
> You didn't sing for her as a father should !
> You are foolish and silly, you sing only to please the ears
>   of a woman !
> You like to lie close to a young girl, a virgin, and give her
>   a child !
> You will not stay in one place !
> Here and there, all over the place, you go among the camps,
> You go walking hither and thither, looking for sweethearts.
> Ah, before, it was here that you used to stay.[23]

We find an Eskimo singing of the seal he hunts, and singing of it quite simply in terms of what hou it will be to eat it.

> Over there I could think of nothing else,
> Beneath me when it breathed loudly through the water.
> When the broth-provider was going to rush up to me,
> Beneath me, I could think of nothing else.[24]

There are some moving modern accounts of hunting and gathering among the forest pygmies of the South West Sudan

> They drift through the forest in sizeable groups, men, women and children, looking for edible plants, berries and, most eagerly, for honey. As they ramble they sing, or yodel rather, in sweet harmony, and the ingenuity of their performance reminds us that the term 'primitive' certainly doesn't mean 'unskilled'.... Each person seems to make an independent contribution to the collective blend. Pygmy performance has been compared to a treeful of singing birds. . . . In their music they hardly use words at all, just a melodious web of vowels.[25]

But even here, in the opinion of one folk song scholar at least

> Each song has a purpose, and . . . the power of their song is to awaken the god and ensure good luck, because God awake will surely put the bees in their path to lead them to . . . honey.[26]

Here is part of an elephant-hunting song of the Gabon pygmies, who do use words. Their activity is seen vividly in the song; but so is its purpose :

> Meat is in front of you, the huge piece of meat
> The meat which walks like a hill
> The meat which makes glad the heart
> The meat which will roast on the hearth
> The meat into which the teeth sink
> The fine red meat and the blood that is drunk smoking.[27]

On the other hand, there are profound differences between this world and that of a modern urban man who works 'instrumentally'. The songs of most 'primitive' peoples share with the folksongs of agricultural peoples a strong sense of relationship to other living creatures besides men. This last element occurs often in the songs as part of the experience of hunting.

> I could not sleep
> for the sea lay so smooth
> near at hand.
> So I rowed out,

and a walrus came up
close beside my kayak.
It was too near to throw,
and I thrust the harpoon into its side,
and the hunting float bounded over the water.
But it kept coming up again
and set its flippers angrily
like elbows on the surface of the water,
trying to tear the hunting float to pieces[28]

That was part of an eskimo hunting song from Canada. Identification with the hunted animal gives a vivid anthropomorphic
image for it. Such identification can be seen equally in the rest of
the Gabon pygmy elephant-hunting song mentioned above:

On the weeping forest, under the wing of the evening,
The night, all black, has gone to rest happy;
In the sky the stars have fled trembling,
Fireflies which shine vaguely and put out their lights,
On high the moon is dark, its white light is put out.

The spirits are wandering.
Elephant-hunter, take your bow!
Elephant-hunter, take your bow!

In the frightened forest the tree sleeps, the leaves are dead,
The monkeys have closed their eyes, hanging from branches
    on high.
The antelopes slip past with silent steps,
Eat the fresh grass, prick their ears attentively,
Lift their heads and listen frightened.
The cicada is silent and stops his grinding song.
Elephant-hunter, take your bow!

Elephant-hunter, take your bow!
In the forest lashed by the great rain,
Father elephant walks heavily, baou, baou,
Careless, without fear, sure of his strength,

Father elephant, whom no one can vanquish;
Among the trees which he breaks he stops and starts again.
He eats, roars, overturns trees and seeks his mate.
Father elephant, you have been heard from afar.
Elephant-hunter, take your bow!
Elephant-hunter, take your bow!

In the forest where no one passes but you,
Hunter, lift up your heart, leap, and walk.
Meat is in front of you, the huge piece of meat,
The meat which walks like a hill, . . .[29]

An Australian aboriginal song-maker seems able to respond
similarly, at least at its early appearances, to a machine as well as
to other living things.

You see the smoke at Kapunda
The steam puffs regularly,
Showing quickly, it looks like frost,
It runs like running water.
It blows like a spouting whale.[30]

Perhaps it is not the activity but the poetry of songs like this,
together with ritual that mainly distinguishes hunting and gathering and simple pastoral and agricultural life from work in our
time.

According to Levi-Strauss in a recent lecture, a North American Indian tribe, given a cine camera to make a film of their own
activities, devoted the majority of the shots when filming a hunt
to the ritual details of preparation; and incidentally, in putting
the film together, separated actions which few film editors would
have considered separate, so that the shots were of far fewer
frames than in most films conventionally made, because of the
importance of every ritual detail. When the hunt began, they
filmed little and cut less. It was ritual which bound together these
activities with the hunt and its conclusion in eating. To them, a
film of their hunt was mostly a film of what modern Europeans
would call its preparation.

It may therefore be only indirectly – because it brings about the decay of poetry and ritual – that the growth of exchange and rationality allows a distinct concept of 'work' to form, and allows the intrinsic meaning of activities other than the final gratification to vanish. If this is so, hunting could follow agriculture and become an activity done almost entirely for the sake of its outcome; and with competitive sport and the industrialized whaling and bison-herding of the nineteenth century, perhaps it has. Perhaps in general it was only the vivid poetry present – in ritual and song – in much of 'primitive' life that gave immediacy to a world that for modern man has become one of abstraction, delayed enjoyment and work.

Rousseau, who noted the fineness of mind of the 'primitive' men of his day, was not perhaps as fanciful as he has been said to be, in the centuries of mechanized optimism that have succeeded him. Certainly this vividness is something men search for now in poetry, though in life they usually want it allied with comfort and security – perhaps its two inevitable enemies.

In either case the making of songs like the ones quoted, and the distribution of beautifully composed songs in all corners of the world confirm one point that the nineteenth century critics stressed. They praised craftsmanship and said that it had once been important to most men. If this has been less easy to substantiate in the Middle Ages – though it may have been true then also – it certainly accords with the high value which most so-called 'simple' peoples seem to place on craftsmanship, in poetry and song-making as much as in any other aspect of life. 'We have no art' said some Balinese, according to Marshall McLuhan. 'We do everything as well as possible'.

Craftsmanship thus seems to have a universal significance, uniting men over many generations and in many societies, and the making of household objects in a man's own time, skilfully and with oranment, accompanied by song-making and singing, may not be an idealized picture of the way men have worked in many simple societies even if not in all.[31]

But the young Marx's ideal of some primitive simplicity before the first exchange, where all action was wholly its own reward and nothing was done for the sake of anything else, is nevertheless not easily to be traced. Men cannot live by craftsmanship alone. Though 'work' as a distinct concept may not arise in the simplest forms of life, some activities resembling work, and done with a keen consciousness of their outcome, seem present even among hunters and gatherers.

However, an awareness of the outcome need not prevent ritual or poetry from surrounding an action and enhancing it – or perhaps it is truer to speak of our ideas of distinct actions as having been mined out of an ore of earlier ritual and poetry in which they were once wholly embedded. A girl who sings as she milks, hunters who prepare for pursuit with ceremony and dancing, may be 'aware' of what they want; but the awareness may be very unlike that of modern men. Whether the changes happened suddenly or unexpectedly is less certain. Certainly once agriculture and something like a concept of work arise, there is little evidence of many men doing it consistently in any age except under the pressure either of necessity or of reward in terms of consumption for themselves or those they were responsible for; the main exceptions being the rich or the clerical, who have either done lighter labour than the poor, or who have laboured intermittently in sport or warfare or writing. There is one case of a civilization in which agricultural work has been held to be satisfying in itself : Persia in the time of the Zoroastrian religion.[32] In that religion the earth is sacred; and the word for 'work' is related to the word for 'holy'. The exception suggests again the sigificance of culture rather than bare technology in determining what is held to be satisfying.

We have seen everywhere the difference that a religion, ritual and poetry can make in giving meaning to actions which, severed from their culture, can become onerous. Perhaps those writers today who argue that industrialization and urbanization, if they harmed men, did their main damage by depriving them of their inherited culture, are at least partly right.

Part III

Work and leisure today

14
The London River

Between the world of the nineteenth-century songs and that of the mid-twentieth-century numerical control machines and computers lie the forms of work of a lighterman and of a docker working on the River Thames.

The majority of those who work on the river in London are dockers. Dockers, whether they are working on shipboard or on the quayside, belong to the life of the shore. They work shifts by the clock. Lightermen and watermen, by contrast, come home and leave home by the way the tide changes. Lightering – with the driving of the tugs and pleasure boats – is a skilled trade, with a five- or seven-year apprenticeship. It has a certain amount of ritual. Watermen and lightermen are 'freemen of the river' and they start their apprenticeship at a ceremony in Watermen's Hall, replete with versicles and responses which no one has yet abandoned.

WATERMAN ... Oh I went up there. You go into a hall, and there is the – I forget what you call them now – the clerk of the Court, dressed up in his waterman's outfit – the Queen's Waterman's outfit; he is a Queen's Waterman of course. And there were the Board – the Watermen's Board, you see – you go in there, and they ask you – your Master not you, they ask your Master who he brings with him, as if they didn't know of course; but these are just old laws. They ask him who he brings, and he says he brings an apprentice to be bound for so many years, as a bound apprentice, and then they ask you a few questions, you know, and they read out the apprenticeship paper to you which is still the same today, of course, as it was, and the first apprenticeship papers have never been altered at all. Something about you mustn't frequent taverns, playhouses, gambling houses, or anything else, and your master is not compelled to give you any money at all, but must keep you in meat and clothing apparel, which is all rubbish of course. I mean it is the old law and is still read out. And that is it, you sign your indentures, and then you come out.

To become freemen of the river lightermen must know its course so well that they can find their way about it by oars, using the tide, in daylight or by night, alone.

Docking, by contrast, has historically been almost without skill, and without formal ritual. Only in this century has any system of registration preserved it for a definite body of men; in the nineteenth century anyone could come for a shift in the docks when there was no other labour going in London. Even with registration there was a pool of surplus labour, and men trying to get a living by dockwork had either to know a foreman who would pick them at a 'call' or bribe the foreman to pick them, or else fight their way to the front when men were being picked for a job.

DOCKER   You didn't have any sort of friends. You made out you had friends, but when it come to getting a job, if you hadn't no work, you was pushing and shoving like the next man, because we used to line up like cattle, you know, over an iron bar, and the man used to come along and take our book and you used to struggle and push to get your book in front so that you'd get work.

MR RILEY   The hardest time was when I first went there; the first few years at the docks, that was the hardest time. The old chaps they were pushed over on one side, you see, and the young fellows they'd pick the hats off the old chaps at the front and throw them at the back, you see, that's what they used to do. At the West India Dock. say, they used to do that. They used to walk in there at six o'clock in the morning and wait there for nearly two hours so they would be first on the barrier, along the barrier, so they would be in the front to get their tickets and some of them, I've seen them, get the hats, take the hats off them men's heads and fling them at the back so that they could get into the front. Every man for himself, doesn't matter who you were, and as I say, it was a struggle.

The theme of the documentary study that follows is the contrast between three attitudes to work : the attitudes of an old lighterman, a docker of the same age, and his sons. Work is here treated in isolation from home life and leisure – perhaps the programme was to some extent a product of the thinking that has been criticized in the nineteenth-century philosophers – but the next chapter hopes to restore the balance by dealing with the same people's lives outside work.

The two central characters – both approaching retirement at the time – are 'Mr Coles' a lighterman who had worked on the river since he was a boy; a man well known along the Thames for his paintings and also for the eloquence with which he described life on the river; some one who clearly loved his work and the river he worked on, and found in his job scope to exercise his skill and to stimulate his imagination.

By contrast 'Mr Riley', foreman in one of the docks, had worked through the slump and the war, had survived, kept a home together and brought up his children. These – with his fishing – were his main interests, and his work was to him largely 'instrumental' to those outside concerns. But he did not seem to be discontented on the whole with the arrangement.

His two sons who worked with him, however, were discontented. They represent the third attitude to work – 'instrumental but grudgingly so – unhappy to have no greater satisfaction in the work itself.

The contrasts are not, of course, clear-cut and simple, and the documentary was not made simply to show them. Not all lightermen like the work; the script opens in fact with two who resent it.

The study has been left, except for a few details, as it was originally made for radio :[1] only the songs that were written for it have been omitted. When it was broadcast some of the dockers played it over the tannoy loudspeaker system of the ships moored in the docks and some of the lightermen came to tie up by the dock gates to listen. They said that it was a realistic presentation of their work. Perhaps as evidence then it can be regarded as roughly on a par with the words of some of the songs composed outside working life; not a first-hand source because the selection of the spoken words is the work of some one from outside; but equally and not remote from first-hand experience, composed only of the words of the people who do the work themselves.

FIRST LIGHTERMAN We are not human beings, we are just working animals; animals are taken in when its raining, but we are told to stop out on our craft.

SECOND LIGHTERMAN We are in a barge's cabin which is patrolled by lightermen, day in and day out, and this is what you have got to come down to. You've got no coal, you've got nothing to light a fire with have you? This is what you have day in and day out, and they want you to do nights out in these barges and all.

FIRST DOCKER One of the hardest days work in my life was going to a wharf called Laurence's Mill which was only dealt in rice, and rice is in 2 cwt bags and we used to have to load a hundred ton of that, on our own, one man.

I did 75 tons on that first day – that was to save me being out at night to shift the barge – and when I went home – I was in diggings then – I was a young man about twenty-four then – the landlady cried when she saw me shoulders.

That's the truth, they was all raw red. Anyway, the next morning I got on with the other 25 and finished the barge, covered it up and that was done.

FIRST LIGHTERMAN The only shelter we do get sometimes when

we are on a jetty – we borrow other people's accomoda-
tion – and when you're in the barge you use the cabin –
then we stand in the shed – we have got no shelters like
the dock workers have. We are out in all weathers – if it
rains, snows or hails we're still out there. If the sun is
shining it's a good life. When it's raining and wet you say
'Who'd ever be a lighterman,' . . . but you still plod on.

MR COLES   You are not one man in winter, you are not a man,
you are only about a quarter of a man. I've known it, I've
known a time when the spray has absolutely frozen in
mid-air – it has been that cold – frozen almost before the
water has touched the deck, and there have been little
pellets of water. The cold is so intense there that if you're
climbing aboard or something and you put your naked
hand on the iron, it'll freeze to the iron, and it feels like a
burning feeling. You'd feel like you were rowing from the
knuckles.

SECOND LIGHTERMAN   It's clear as a bell one minute, then fog.
That is what they call a blanket, all stay on deck and look
out for different lights or buoys that you can get a turn
on, and you can't sleep that night.

MR COLES   Yes, fogs are funny things; come down all of a
sudden at times; and the most funny part about being in
the fog is that you imagine that there are ships coming at
you all the time. You see, fog floats about in the air, and
you get a thick layer of fog, and you get a thin layer of
fog.

FIRST LIGHTERMAN   A tug running into a ship would be just as
disastrous as a ship running into an iceberg. A tug don't
take long to sink once she's got a hole in her.

SECOND LIGHTERMAN   What was that tug – the Servia? She went
down in 25 seconds, and she turned over – so heavy aren't
they – there's not much out of the water. If you hit them
– whoop – down they go.

FIRST LIGHTERMAN   Would you like to be out on a barge on a
night like this? This is your living, you are supposed to live
down here while you are waiting. Now you see the state of

the living quarters, where we are supposed to be. They're
your home for the night when you've got a night out with
them. We are not human beings we are just working like
animals.

SECOND DOCKER Johnny, what was that thing we had? Tigers,
yeah. We had a circus here once didn't we? Proper cages
for them you know, and dockers used to – you know,
being curious you know – you'd go and look. You know
'Lion . . . Grrr . . .'

FIRST DOCKER Then at Tilbury Jetty I've seen ships come in
with crates and wild animals aboard, going out to South
America. I've seen lions, tigers, elephants on that ship.

MR RILEY They brought one over about, let me see, a year ago,
and they straddled this elephant up, it's true, they
straddled this elephant up, they had special nets for him,
to go under his belly part you see.

FIRST DOCKER And he was strapped to the deck of this ship in
the West India dock, all he was doing was trumpeting all
the day long, till they got rid of him, then they put a big
canvas strap under his stomach and lifted him up on a
crane and put him out on the quay and then he was taken
away in a van, but, oh, the noise he was making, all the
morning until the van came for him. Big elephant too.

MR RILEY They couldn't put slings round him, see, so they had
special nets sent down to go underneath his belly part,
and when they took the weight off the deck . . . it tilted a
bit. You should've seen them run. They run. Up to the
cabins, hop in the captains, on the bridge. They thought it
was going to break loose. Yeah! But he just give a couple
of bellows you know like.

FIRST DOCKER So we had some queer cargo in our time. One
of the filthiest cargo we ever loaded was camel bones from
Egypt, raw, with the flesh running off them and loaded
with maggots. That is true.

MR COLES We carry wheat, flour, timber, cork. We load marble.
You got to be an expert in loading marble. Another day
you will be loading puncheons of rum or brandy; another

day you would be loading butter. There's different smells, especially when you are unloading the spices. What about when you are loading spices? You get pepper – don't want to smell that too much though. You got to be a Philadelphian lawyer to know about these things, especially when you are signing for the goods that you load in your barge.

MR RILEY Cement, cement, it's terrible. Years ago it used to come over in jute bags. If you had three or four days work at that, after that, you've a job really to touch your boot-laces, I know, I have experienced it. The tips of your fingers were red raw. They didn't bleed, they didn't bleed, but there was something in it, just the tips of the fingers, that's all, it was painful even to do your bootlaces up. That was cement.

FIRST LIGHTERMAN As a docker you're just an out and out labourer – your using your body muscles – and really some of these gangs, with these heavy cargoes to shift, I think they shorten their lives with the strenuous effort they have to put into it. As a docker you're just a unit in a gang. But as a lighterman you're the unit – you are individual – you work solely on your own. You use your own brain and use your own brawn. But in a gang, one man uses the brain, the rest of the gang use the brawn, one man has an easy time, the rest of them just pull, pull their cods out, if you want to put it that way.

MR JOHN RILEY (YOUNGER SON) I used to work for radio and television people, and I was interested in the job, because to me, if I went to a house to repair their wireless or television and it wasn't working when I went there, especially if there were children there, after I repaired it, and I left, there was a family there, happy, happy with the work that I'd done. And that made me happy – I could come home at night and knowing that I'd made several families happy. Where I can do a day's work in the dock and what have I achieved? All I've achieved is money. I've not made anybody happy in the work I've done. I can see nothing from my work in other words.

MR GEORGE RILEY (ELDER SON)   We goes to work and gets called
from here to there, he gets down to the dock and he's got
a load of stuff to unload. Well, now, well it's just a sort of
manual work isn't it. Well, it's just sort of shifting it from
there to there. He hasn't done anything sort of mechanically, he hasn't – I don't know – he hasn't done anything
to say 'Well, I've made this' or 'I've done that'. It's all
graft, it's all brute, it's all do it. You load up a lorry with
this and the lorry goes out. Now you can't see the finish of
that. It's gone. You've just loaded the lorry; it's out it's
gone.

But when you've been at it a while you get used to it,
and it's the atmosphere it creates I mean, it's free and easy
you got no sort of foreman hard on you, you know; there
is no clocking-in business; you're at liberty to do within
reason what you want. I mean you're your own guv'nor
within reason – you go out to tea when you like, you come
home when you like, it's sort of freedom; it's the atmosphere it creates, it's the characters you meet.

FIRST DOCKER   We have one of our mates, he is a painter. We
call him Picasso.

MR GEORGE RILEY   The flute Dooly, well he is a character on his
own, really I mean, I've seen him march the whole gang
right round the dock out to tea in the afternoon, playing
the flute, and he marched them all out for tea.

MR RILEY   Just like the old pied piper, with the rats. That's how
it was Jim Dooly going out the front. 'It's a long way to
Tipperary' and its about twelve men behind him.

MR COLES   Another bloke, Old Spittem and Blinkems . . . he
always, when was speaking, keep blinking his eyes and
spitting. Yes, he used to keep pigeons, that bloke, and he
threatened to throw the pigeons out of the window one
day and break their necks.

MR JOHN RILEY   I have actually seen this man chase a rat, which
was eight or ten inches, length, caught hold of him by the
body, and I didn't want to watch this, but I had to, to

believe it of this man – and I seen him put his mouth over the head of this rat, bite it, twist the body of the rat and pull. I actually see the men down here walk away feeling bad to watch it. I felt bad myself.

MR COLES   A rat is a good connoisseur of food. You get them on the rubbish barges. They'd even come down the chute when a ship is like discharging grain. All different rats. Of course I don't know their nationality because they don't carry a passport, but we do get all kinds of rats; long haired ones, like the Beatles, short hairs, like the boys under government control.

MR GEORGE RILEY   It's the atmosphere, it's the characters you meet. I mean that's the main thing, it's the different characters. I mean you talk about writing a book about the docks, the characters.

MR COLES   We've fallen in love with the Thames. Oh yes. I think it is a good life, and if I had my time over again I think I'd do exactly the same thing. Could you imagine, coming to work on a lovely summer's morning with plenty of food – you know, you've got your food with you and all your meals for the day – going off in the boat, and you are going to do your day's job in the glorious sunshine; and especially if there is a nice breeze, if there is a lovely breeze blowing up or down the river – there are other people stuck in an office, slogging and sweating away there like billy-o and all you've got on is a pair of short trousers and a singlet. Would you sooner have a job like that? Summer time it is lovely on the river. As a matter of fact it is, it is worth – I should say it was worth paying to go to work; to go to work in the summer time, that is; but only in the summer time. Chaps on the tugs – off shirts, and they are just in their birthday suits almost and, come to the end of the summer, their skins are just like brown paper. If you hit London Bridge, it's strange but it's true, you're bound to hit the next one : Southwark Bridge – Cannon Street, you usually hit the lot. It's the set of the tide. I couldn't work in a factory, sat doing the same thing every day, day in and day out. See, on the river, during my life on the river, it's been a variety. Variety is the spice of life. You drive a barge one day, you lead her the next and you take her to one place one day and you take the barge to another place the next day.

MR GEORGE RILEY You're your own master, actually. You're given a job to do and you do it, and get on the 'phone and you're given other orders. You haven't got no one pushing you. It's up to your own ability.

MR COLES We used to take it in turns having a little swim while we were driving down or driving up. That was about twenty-five or thirty years ago, perhaps longer than that. The water used to be lovely and clear – you could swim. But if you go overboard today the police they pump you out in case you've got any of the river water inside you. When I as an apprentice, we'd take it in turns undressing : just a pair of shorts on, over the side you'd go, come back again, take our turn with the oars, and the other chap would go over. But these days if you go overboard there's so much oil and filth that if you get a mouthful of water you might get typhoid fever, so they put the stomach pump on you, pump you out. It's oil pumped from the ships bilges – all kinds of muck from the wharves shovel it over the side, which they're not allowed to do. We love our river you see.

A WATERMAN I remember the time when there were a thousand punts here, and er – you used to go out in these punts at night, and they all had covers on, should it rain, and you would go out for picnic suppers and that. People used to go out with coloured lanterns and an old candle – lanterns they were, made of glass – and you would put a night light in them and hang them up for light. There was nothing else to give you light. And then they would go out and have supper parties and enjoy themselves, you know, and come in. Now it is dead at night in the summer. Nobody goes out and enjoys themselves, at all; they don't want the quiet.

MR RILEY   When I first went in the docks, it was in 1922, and
things then, they were very hard, you're really lucky to
get one or two days work a week.

Sometimes you'd get two weeks with nothing you see.
Take myself, me and my wife and two children, thirty-
four shillings a week to pay your rent and everything.
They gave you one shilling to keep a child up till he was
fourteen years of age, one shilling a week to keep that
child.

Within five minutes walk of us in them days we could
count six pawn shops. Now you got to walk a mile now
before you see one. On Monday mornings, you could see
people lined up before eight o'clock with their parcels,
ready to go in that pawnshop to pop in and get a few
shillings. There is no doubt about it, it was hard days.

You don't know, you'll never know. But I know, I
know the difference, I know the difference when you
went in the docks and you may be lucky to get one day a
week. Today. . . .

GEORGE RILEY   . . . Yeah, yeah . . .

MR RILEY   That's it, you don't want to know!

GEORGE RILEY   All that's like donkey's years ago.

MR RILEY   Yeah, yeah . . .

GEORGE RILEY   You forget them times now!

MR RILEY   All right!

GEORGE RILEY   It's like you was to say 'Let's light the gas' when
we've got electric.

MR RILEY   All right! That's what I was trying to tell you. You
are my family. I am trying to tell you that you don't know
what the old people went through years ago. You don't
know how lucky you are, you're living in modern times
today. . . .

GEORGE RILEY   But you don't keep thinking about it then, do
you?

MR RILEY   But I'm just telling you the difference. . . .

GEORGE RILEY   You don't keep thinkin' of those days dad, do
you? You must think you are living today, not years ago.

MR RILEY ... Yes, but I'm just trying to tell you how lucky you are today. You're lucky, because you just can't realize what your old people went through. The old cry is this ... they don't want to know. Because why? Because they will never know the poverty in the East End of London especially when I was a young man. They'll never know and nobody knows unless they've been through it, and this is the truth. I've been through it, I know what it is. When the workhouses were open – there was a workhouse within fifty yards of me where I've seen men and women chopping wood to make bundles of firewood and chipping stone, within fifty yards of the little old house where I used to live in – well it wasn't a house, it was one room that I had – four shillings a week, four shillings a week.

You see, with the docks – for years and years – it's been like a family affair. It's handed down from the grand-father to his son, and down to his son ... in the family.

MR COLES You get a spring tide, you get a neap tide, you get a harvest moon tide, you get a birds' nesting tide. You see they're all different tides. You see it's the time of the year – say the birds' nesting tide – it all works with nature, the tide is worked by the moon as you know and it's all nature. You see, it's what makes the river so lovely, because you're working with nature all the time. You see, going back, birds' nesting tides, they are very low – it gives a chance to the birds to nest and bring up their young. Harvest moon tides; they're very high. See it's according to the moon.

WATERMAN I think we've seen the best of it. It will never come back to the river I used to know. I've seen the changes from sail to rowing. The whole life of the river has changed. I remember the end of what, to me, were the glorious days of the river. The sailing barge has gone. It was the largest spread of canvas ever handled by two men. 1,000 square feet of canvas; well, that's gone. River trade is dying in our capacity. The barges are so big. The tonnage is not done on the river as it should be, therefore there is not so many men wanted.

And they don't get the same – love of the game, if you like. It is also a sense of pride. That has gone these days, completely gone. Well, not in every case, but compared to years ago, pride in watermanship today doesn't exist.

MR COLES   They are beautiful things, a swan, they look so grace-ful. They are good lightermen, they know the tides and they never harm you. They're good watermen : they'll always get out of your way; they seem to know what you're going or where you want to go, when you're in the boat. They are good watermen really.

WATERMAN   Once the towing of these craft came in – that's when you began to get your hustle and your bustle, and it all ties in together you see with quick profits, fast tugs, nothing done properly. Now your tug is in charge of everything. Whereas a man before under oars – every-body gave way to him. They had to by law. You had a sort of sense of purpose about what you were doing. But, of course, in other ways, thank God it has gone. It wasn't all honey, you know.

MR COLES   It is a lovely river, easy-going, easy to navigate.

Yes, yes, it is, it's God's gift to London, I think, the River Thames and the work it creates and the living it's given to millions. It is alive, it is alive all the time. There's a continuous ebbing and flooding. It's always alive, it's always on the move, even when you're alseep, it never stops. That'll be the day when they try to stop it. There's been an attempt to dam the Thames at Gravesend, but it has never happened yet, to stop the ebb and flow. It's never happened yet.

15
Family life and an
'instrumental attitude'

The contrast, then, between the way lightermen and dockers are inducted into their work is reflected in many other aspects of their lives. Lightermen work mainly on their own or in pairs. They are their own masters, with a skilled job to do. They also have a great variety in their work, moving up and down the river, taking responsibility for constantly changing cargoes and working irregular hours by the tide. They have a different view of London from most people; it is a total city to them, with slower rhythms than those of the clock. And they are out in all weathers – which means hardship in winter, but in summer almost the ideal conditions of work that the folks songs from the past described.

For Mr Coles many aspects of the job, even the changing cargoes, contributed to this variety. He did not sentimentalize the effects of winter and the cold. Many lightermen die early through pneumonia and bronchial diseases, and the fog, when it comes, means constant fear and can mean sudden death.

Like most of those who work on the river, Mr Coles has seen great changes in his lifetime : sail giving way to steam, then diesel, the clear water getting fouled up with mud in the blitz and with oil from the tankers and the ships' engines. However, the changes in the conditions of work have not altered his love for the river, nor his vivid perceptions of it, which he derives in part from his painting and in part from the slow and loving observation that his job, with its easy rhythms, makes possible.

Not all the lightermen are eloquent painters. There are others who resent their jobs and feel exploited and left behind by progress; who see little of the beauty in the river and have little care for the variety of the work – a reminder that the sense of injustice can easily affect all other feelings about work. It would be wrong to suggest that lightering is an 'ideal' job for all who do it; the individual expectations that people bring to work determine every detail of the way they feel about it and can make two men experience identical conditions in diametrically different ways.

Nevertheless, lightering does offer scope for those who want and expect satisfaction from it. By contrast, dock work is a frustrating task for people with this temperament and these expectations; however much they are looking for variety and intrinsic satisfaction in their job, they find it hard to discover. Those who appreciate dock work most are frequently men who have experienced much worse conditions in the past and are grateful for the comparative security of the job : a man like Mr Riley. He was looking forward to his retirement. It meant long days of fishing for him : he had found a cottage near his favourite stretch of river in Kent, and already went there every weekend that he could. Many of the cargoes he had had to load had been physically damaging. He tended to accept this stoically, even with a certain pride at what he had been through. The work did not seem to interest him particularly in itself. Yet he did not complain of this. For him, as he constantly reiterated, looking round his home, 'Life's good.'

His sons, by contrast, were looking for something more in work, and yet could not find it in the docks. They do not have any sense of achievement from having come through the hard times of the past. On the contrary, they dislike talking about these times, and clearly regard them – however humourously – as a theme the old tend to harp on excessively.

Nevertheless, there is much that Mr Riley's sons appreciate in the docks besides the pay : not the work itself exactly, but the social life that is bound up with it; the friendly atmosphere of dock work, and the freedom that dockers enjoy, for all the insecurity of the old casual system.

There seems to be at least some continuity between what these different men say in the study and some of the themes that have emerged from the traditional songs. The mixture of play with work seems to be at the root of the appeal of the two trades, and what is enjoyed about both sounds much more like Fourier's idea of work, which Marx dismissed as mere fun, than his own notion of free and conscious productive activity in deadly earnest. Thus, though there was much to complain of in both trades, the things Mr Coles the lighterman liked about his work were very much the same as the carter in the traditional song was said to have enjoyed. The job was mixed with a good deal of fun, with lying out on the barges getting his skin 'like brown paper', slipping over the side to swim, watching people hurrying past in the city and contentedly laughing at them – in the summer at least. He also seemed to enjoy some of the same things as the hay-makers in the other 'ideal' song : the open air, the life of the water birds around him, and even the movements of the river, which he spoke of as 'alive'. Beyond that, he liked above all the variety, and the exercise of a skill.

Again, what the dockers picked out as enjoyable about their own work was a quality of fun or play that does not quite seem to emerge from Marx's ideal of intense effort. They were free from supervision, free to come and go and do jobs in their own time; but they also liked the company, and the 'characters'. They had in fact created their own world of informal ritual. But this was a partial consolation only. The dockers who spoke on the whole did not like their work. Quite apart from the misery of the casual system, they disliked the fragmentation and the aimlessness, the heaviness of the work, and the need to be out in all weathers and conditions. Yet they did the job, and one of Mr Riley's sons mentioned that he had given up a more intrinsically satisfying job to do it. He 'quite liked' the characters, and the ease and freedom of docking.

If both he and his father were in their different ways, as they said, happy men, the explanation is not likely to be found in their work alone. If the father and one of the sons are followed to their homes it may be possible to see, in a modern context, the reality of the notorious 'instrumental attitude to work'. First, Mr Riley, the father whom we have already seen in dispute with his sons over the relevance or irrelevance of the past. He settled back in his armchair one evening, with one of his sons and a daughter-in-law beside him and waited until his wife had gone out to fix more cups of tea before he began to speak about the past. His wife entered with a tray of tea things just as he began to talk about one spring in the past.

MR RILEY I come out of the army, and I can always remember the wife when she was a little girl. We lived in the old Court then you see. I didn't see much of her while I was in the army, but when I came home she'd grown into a young woman see, and one or two nights I used to have a walk up under the arch, and she'd be standing there all on her own, so one night I said : 'Here Rose, would you like to come up the pictures with me.

A couple of weeks after that I took her down the market and I rigged her out with, you know, a few clothes, pair of shoes and all that, and then I went in to see her mother, and told her mother what we were doing. Oh yes, all above board. And we were together like that for two years, and then we got married.

The greatest enjoyment the wife's got was to see her children growing up. . . . It's a marvellous thing, you know . . . you look after them and they grow up. First they're in arms crying. . . . Then they're crawling, then they start toddling along. Then all of a sudden before you know where you are, they're reaching on the table and you've got to shift the cups of tea away from them in case they pour the tea over them. And before you know where you are they're walking round and they come round and see you, and you say to yourself 'Cor, luverduck, look how big they're getting.' That's right, ain't it. And you say to youself, 'My God, ain't it marvellous to see the way they grow up . . .', and a little while goes by and their children's walking round themselves to come and see their grandfather and grandmother on a Sunday morning.

There's one good thing about the wife. She's been all right you know. That's why I look after her now. Yes, we've had a happy life right through, if you think about it. We've never been apart. . . . That's the best way to go about it. They say happy in love, happy in life.

The best day – I love Sunday . . . because it's a day of rest and when you get away from London, and you meet these different people and you go to these old . . . houses, the atmosphere is entirely different. . . . Sitting at a little old table : you meet different people that come in. You sit there, you've had a nice drink. . . . You walk along the river, find a nice little spot. . . . I do a few hours fishing. . . . About seven o'clock you say, right. You've had the lovely air, the old birds are singing. . . . We find a nice little house . . . a drink. People come in. About nine o'clock they start having a little sing-song. . . . Everybody's friendly. 'Goodnight, goodnight, see you next weekend', and home we come. What's better than that?

I love autumn. And the spring. When the little buds start breaking forth on the trees, and your garden, you see your few plants that stop in year after year. You see them come through the earth. Isn't it wonderful to see that. And you say, 'Spring is here, now we can go out together.'

MRS RILEY   But I have to get him up first.

MR RILEY   What I like is a little bit of gardening, But I love fishing most of all. They're my two hobbies. . . . Fishing, it's like what they call, you've read it in the books sometimes, the mystery of the deep. . . . You're all anticipation. It's pleasure, it's restful, but at the same time it's excitement, because you're watching that little float. . . . All of a sudden you get a bite; you don't know what you're going to fetch out. It could be a little gudgeon . . . or it could be a bloody fine roach – a couple of pounds. . . . It's the excitement.

I've been fishing on and off fifteen to twenty years – only weekends and Sundays.

But this is a true saying. . . . There is something in fishing that makes you so good tempered, and when you walk along the river bank and see these fishermen sitting down. You'll never see an angry fisherman, they always have a kindly word.

With fishing, you can sit there all the morning, or perhaps all day and not catch nothing, but it's a funny thing, it's a really funny thing, that you're still happy, you feel just the same as though you've caught a big catch of fish. . . . To me it seems as though when you're sitting on the bank and you've got that rod out, and it's a nice day, you're sitting on top of the world somehow.

MRS RILEY   Hop-picking? I ain't been since I been here; because of the machines. From a babe of six weeks old till about ten year back, we always used to take him and his brother hop-picking. Oh it's a lovely life – out in the fields singing, picking, you're earning money all the time. Then you come home, have a good old feed. . . . Six weeks hop-picking. . . .

Up at five, hop-picking, seven in the morning till five at night. Then you come home and have your cooking and do your hop house all out, sit round the fire, have a good old sing-song.

MR RILEY   A lot of people in the East End of London miss hop-picking, because it was the working man's little family holiday. Because it was a good life, rough and ready, but you enjoyed yourself. Don't matter what the weather was like, it seemed as though it was rough and ready and everybody was the same. You always come home with a pound or two, and you'd had a good holiday in the old sunshine, and what's better than going in the old Garden of England, Kent? Out in them lovely hop gardens. Yes, it used to be very nice. But now it's finished, nearly finished. The machines have taken the place.

When I retire, I shall get myself a little place outside of London, and then I shall enjoy myself. Six o'clock on that river, no one about, what wonderful sport it must be.

Forty-four years in the docks. You get used to the winters. . . . The dampness – your clothes damp, the next morning they feel so cold and wet.

But once you've had a good wash and a cup of tea, you're all right for the day. . . . You feel fit to go out and you laugh it off. . . .

Isn't it wonderful to say, 'Well, come on, let's have a run out.' And you jump on a train or a bus for a couple of bob's ride, and you come out into the lovely fields and you can see the flowers and you hear the birds singing and perhaps a nice little river running through the fields. . . .

When you look at that, life is worth living, isn't it? To know you can get away for a few days and see the beautiful things, the beautiful countryside. I love the country life . . . there's none of this madness of London. . . . You've got the nature there . . . when you see the river flowing along and the wild ducks, it's lovely, isn't it, to see it.

I think of it all the week. So you put up with all the hardships and squabbles.

It's like me, when I'm at work. Roll on five o'clock. I know that when I get in here, there's a nice big fire, there's a cup of tea poured out for me. I sit in the old armchair and what more could you wish for? A millionaire couldn't live better, could he? Because, one thing, you're happy in life, and that's everything.[1]

His younger son John was the docker who had worked previously for a radio and television firm, and who said :

JOHN RILEY If I went to a house, to repair their wireless or television, and it wasn't working when I went there – especially if there were children there – and after I repaired it and I left, there was a family there happy – happy with the work that I'd done – that made me happy. I can come home at night, knowing that I've made several families happy.

Whereas I go to do a day's work in the dock, and what have I achieved? All I've achieved is money. I've not made anybody happy in the work that I've done. I can see nothing from my work in other words.

This statement was not prompted, as far as I am aware, by any suggestion of the ideas of the nineteenth-century critics. The suggestion that was brought up by that strange song *The Recruited Collier* is recalled by these words; that though the nineteenth-century critics may have put their ideas in forms that make little immediate appeal to working people today, they may nevertheless have divined feelings that were below the surface in their day, and are in ours – feelings which some sensitive minds may bring to the surface unexpectedly.

Yet there is a difference. It is not the intrinsic nature of the job, repairing television sets, that appealed to the younger Mr Riley; but the immediate effects of his work on the people he came in contact with – especially the children. And these are precisely what he finds in his life after work when he labours in the docks. Even if at first it may seem a slight difference, in reality it may be a profound one. The idea of craftsmanship – of which solitary writing or composing, in deadly earnest, may have furnished Marx with his paradigm examples – made no appearance in John Riley's account of his previous, satisfying job – though it was a craftsman-like job. Instead it was the direct contact with children and the immediate effect of his work on people's happiness – effects which might be more readily available in many people's leisure than in their work – that above all satisfied him most. And it was this in turn that he spoke about when he talked about his life after work in the evening :

JONH RILEY   Well, when I left school and went to work for a radio firm, I was called out to do a repair to a radiogram, which when I got there, a valve went wrong in the gram, which I repaired, and there was this girl there which I got talking to, and – er – we made arrangements to go to the pictures, this particular night. I took her to the pictures, and saw her occasionally afterwards, went out, and then I believe about six months afterwards we got engaged to be married. We were engaged for three years, and in that time we saved up, and tried to get the deposit for a home, or a house. Then we got our house, we got married, and now we are quite happy, we've two children.

I've always been quite happy, and no regrets sort of thing. Clothing is dear for the children; some of their clothing is dearer than mine I mean I'm about to buy them a pair of shoes, and their shoes is probably dearer than what I would pay for my own. But – er – otherwise I'm happy. It's more like – well, I like to see them looking nice and smart.

Oh I like to be with them. I mean they are, to me they are everything, they are my life, I live for them. I love children. I wouldn't be without them. The girl is Susan, and the youngest one, the boy, is John.

The wife was in a maternity home at the time, and it was near time, and I was on the 'phone like, 'The wife is all right, and you have got a baby girl.' So I asked when I could go up and they said that morning – to see the wife and the baby. I went up and then I first saw the baby. To me, being – everything was perfect like, you know, to me it worried me to see the hands – and everything was perfect with the baby like you know, and er – her hair, the mass of hair she had, that was – when she was first born. Oh it was a surprise, it is one of them things, it is a miracle, it's a marvellous thing to my mind.

Coming home from work, coming home from work, and coming through the street door, my street door, the moment I put the key in the door, I can hear the kitchen door open, and the youngest one, crawling and scrambling up the passage, and the eldest one, she has either got a book or a toy, or something which she has been bought that day, and she wants to eagerly show me. As I open the door, I ordinarily have got to pick the youngest one up in my arms, and also talk to my eldest one, they are both at me all the time, I've still got my overcoat on, and I can't even sit down when I get in, but as I say, I look forward to it, and I wouldn't want it no different, knowing that they want me like, you know.

On Sunday is a regular day for the park in the summer. I take them when they are both ready, and out to the park we go, outside. The oldest one, Susan, she wants to go on the swings, that's all right if John's asleep in his pram, and he don't realize what's happening. The moment the pram is stopped I push Susan on the swings. Then it happens that John wakes up, then I've got to get Susan out of the swings, and then we automatically carry on round the park, see the flowers and one thing and another, and always as long as the pram keeps going round, then John is happy like, in the pram.

I've never felt that I was married until I had children, because it is children to my idea that binds one another. Then you realize you are married, married in respect of responsibility. But without children you can't feel as though you are – you're – er – married enough – in a way like. It holds you both together, children.

By contrast, when Mr Coles the lighterman talks about his work and leisure, there is much less separation between them. Lighterage is if anything even more of a family affair than docking : the trade is inherited, and many people marry within it. In his early years on the river, hours were so irregular that leisure had no day-to-day pattern. Even now hours go by the tide rather than the clock.

The river is there in leisure as well as at work, and a conversation ostensibly about leisure continually goes off at tangents towards the river, the canals and the waterways of England. Many lightermen row for sport. Mr Coles, unlike some of his family, never gave much of his time to rowing. He is a painter. But many of his paintings turn out to be of the effects of light on the river.

MR COLES   Oh, father, grandfather, great grandfather, they were
all lightermen. My great grandfather on my father's
mother's side, he won Doggett's Coat and Badge in 1832.
And you see the lighterage business, the watermen and
lightermen, it used to run right the way through into
marriage you know, like they'd marry, so come to the
finish you're related to about, well, a dozen different
families on the river you see by marriage.

I was an apprentice just after the 1914 war. Time off
was very very uncertain in them days. We might get done,
for instance say like about five o'clock in the afternoon.
And then perhaps be home till the next tide, you see. That
night we'd turn out at ten. And then probably we'd be
out all night again, you see, and not get home until the
next evening tide. It was . . . it was a very busy job, you
know. Plenty of work

Surprising how this river . . . I never thought it would
go like it's gone today. All the freight taken off the old
river and put on the road. No wonder we've got road
congestion. But I see in the papers that they're going to
open up all the canals that branch off like Brentford and
the Grand Union Canal and going to restore them,
because they was bought over by the railways. When the
railways come into being all the canals and the locks, they
was neglected and left to go derelict, you see. And we can
get anywhere in this, in this Britain, this . . . this England,
anywhere by water. Right up to Gloucester, Birmingham.

In the early days we'd most probably be out, you know,
from Monday till the next Monday, and only just a
couple of evenings at home. And of course years ago we
used to entertain ourselves. With the piano, you see, and
the gramophone. And there was always a party, you
know, you could go to of a weekend. Somebody was
having a party, you know. You made your own entertainment, which really and truly is better entertainment than
what you get on the television today. Some programmes
are very good. And it's a waste of time looking at others

... other programmes. And so I cut out and perhaps I paint. You know I paint, don't you? I've been painting ever since I was about five year old. As far as I can remember – and that was the age of about three and a half years – all my presents and all my gifts were in some form of a drawing material or painting. They knew what I was, they knew. It started off with slates and the old slate pencil, you know. When I was very young. Then I used to paint in water-colours, and then a young fellow – he was related – a relation, he used to paint in oils, but he passed on, and they gave me all his gear, his painting material. We visited his place, it was somewhere up above Battersea. And that's what started me in oils.

Time goes very fast, when you're painting. Sometimes I've been up at the easel, which I think has been about a couple of hours, and I've been there four hours.

As regards for sport or anything like that, I've done a bit of rowing pf course in regattas, in fours. And I did start to train for Doggett's Coat and Badge, but we didn't get the time, you know, like through being at work so many hours, to do justice for a training period to row for this honourable and very lovely race. It's the oldest race in the world, you know, Doggett's Coat and Badge. It's the oldest annual organized race. Way back, it dates back to 1714. . . .

16
Theories of leisure

The contrasts between these three men working on the river can be considered now in terms of some general theory about work and leisure. It has for some time been questioned whether people on the whole try to compensate in their leisure for the frustrations they experience at work, or by contrast tend to have similar experiences to those they find in work. The question was put by Harold Wilensky in terms of two hypotheses, one of 'compensation' versus one of 'spillover'.[1]

Rather than attempt to answer this question in a general way some sociologists, notably Stanley Parker, in *The Future of Work and Leisure* have more recently suggested a three-fold typology.[2] First, some people can be seen pursuing a pattern of 'opposition' between work and leisure: deep water fishermen[3] or oil-rig drillers, may be cited as examples. After work, they may well tend to seek some compensation for its deprivations and exhaustions; and this pattern will be more likely among those who do very physical labour, or who are away from home for long periods. In the songs of the nineteenth century we have seen evidence of such a pattern in the seamen's forebitters, with their contrasts to the womanless monotony of sailing ship life: 'When first I landed in Liverpool I went out on the spree' or 'We'll make the cradles for to rock and the blankets for to tear'. And in the London Docks the elder Mr Riley, with his choice of fishing as his favourite leisure activity, perhaps shows a smiliar pattern in a modern context. What he values about it – the peace and quiet, the tranquility of relationships to other people, the absence of effort, and the unspoilt countryside to which it takes him – are in direct contrast to what he finds in his work, and in still stronger contrast to the work he experienced in the most formative years of his life, with the competitive jostling at the call, the dashing from dock to dock to get work, the heavy labour on the job and the dirt, smoke and what he calls 'madness', of London.

A second pattern in such a scheme has been called 'neutrality'. As work becomes physically lighter and economically less of a struggle, without necessarily becoming any more rewarding or interesting in itself, people may develop increasingly 'neutral' feelings towards it; they experience neither strong attachment nor a violent need to restore themselves after it, while work gives them neither a set of interests that can readily be extended into leisure hours, nor a level of attention that requires absorbing activity to sustain it afterwards. Thus they may tend to choose leisure activities that are similarly neither very strenuous nor very tranquil, but rather undemanding, and mildly entertaining without necessarily providing any extreme contrast to their work. Some of the demand for broadcast entertainment is arguably of this kind. Such a pattern may be typical of many people in industrial and office jobs; and may be becoming more prevalent as more work becomes lighter without necessarily becoming more interesting.

In our own three-fold contrast, Mr Riley's younger son, whose experience of docking has been so much less rigorous than his father's, does perhaps have some such 'neutrality' in his attitude towards his work; and by contrast with his father, seems to have less need to vary in his chosen activities in leisure also, not perhaps having had the same degree of damage and deprivation at work to restore, in the considerably easier conditions of docking in the fifties and sixties.

The third pattern in such a scheme is known as 'extension'. People whose work is highly demanding and absorbs many aspects of their life – many artists for example, craftsmen, teachers, managers, some nurses, doctors and others frequently find their work leaves them in their leisure looking for the same kind of absorption, either in some other activity or in a continuation of their work itself. In general, those who have the most interesting work may tend to be those who seek the most interesting leisure, or seek to continue their work in leisure.

Mr Coles is a man who finds his work absorbing. It is a trade requiring skill and training. It takes him out in the open air, and brings him into contact with the varied aspects of river life – the tides, the changing weather and light, the different wharves and reaches from above London to the Kent marshes, the life of the sea-birds and water-birds and the different cargoes of the ships from many parts of the world. In his conversation, leisure and work intermingle. His trade is connected with his family relationships; and (in his eyes) it includes elements of 'play' in summer at least, by contrast with the orderly schedule-keeping and monotonous labour he imagines in the factories and offices he passes by.

In his leisure Mr Coles pursues something equally absorbing and equally based on craft and skill – his painting. Painting and his river work are again related to each other : he paints what he sees at work, while conversely the scenes he paints create much of the interest he finds in his work, supplying the imagery and the observations of light, of birds and of water that enrich his conversation and his experience of work. The relationships between work and leisure for him then could be said to be largely one of 'extension'.

The three-fold typology leaves many questions open. It is a classification of people's activities only. But people do not necessarily find either the work or the leisure they want; so their needs and wishes cannot necessarily be assessed from their actions. There may be more people seeking 'extension' or 'compensation' in leisure than actually find it.

Again, from the existence of patterns of 'opposition', 'neutrality' and 'extension' between people's work and leisure there is no guarantee that there is any causal relationship between experiences in the two areas of life. According to one theory it may be simply that the same man will choose both interesting work and absorbing leisure; and undoubtedly in certain cases this 'integrated man' explanation, as it has been called, is the reason for any correlation found.[4] A man's education or his curiosity may equip him and motivate him similarly for both.

But in other cases, as we shall see with a day worker in a motor factory who had once been a builder, and with another who had spent most of his working life making levers by mass production, exposure to a particular kind of work may shape a man's capacity in his leisure. In the terms used by some earlier sociologists, the 'spillover' hypothesis of the relationship between work and leisure, rather than the 'compensation' hypothesis, or what is called the 'integrated man' theory, does seem to apply to some people at least, and these effects may be particularly likely where work entails both long hours and the kind of 'neutral' form of personal involvement that the threefold typology described.

We cannot yet tell how many people are affected in their leisure by the experience of work, or to what extent. But any instance of such an effect is inconsistent with the economic assumptions by which wage bargains are normally struck in our society, and perhaps with our normal conception of economic progress as something measurable exclusively in terms of productivity and real income per head. If work experiences limit or determine the way leisure can be imagined and spent, even for some people and to some extent, then it is not enough to see the relationship between work and leisure as mediated by pay alone. To increase one's pay, or even marginally to shorten one's hours, may in fact be no compensation for the replacement of a satisfying or absorbing job by a less interesting one; for the leisure in which the new pay is spent, or to which the further minutes are added, may be made difficult to spend enjoyably by the persistence into it of habits, routines and levels of interest set at work by the less absorbing or satisfying job. Yet compensaion by more pay or shorter hours is what 'hard-headed realists' may be liable to suggest as the only adequate one. As so often, 'hard-headed realists' may turn out to be the least realistic of human beings in practice.

17
A factory

In their opinion of factories as an alternative, dockers, lighterman and other people working along the river were fairly unanimous.

MR COLES Well, I couldn't work in a factory. I don't think I could work in a factory, sat doing the same thing every day, day in and day out. See, on the river it's, during my life on the river, it's been a variety.

A DOCKER You see in a factory you could have a foreman behind you all the time, pushing you and pushing you, I worked for the Delta Melta when I first come out the army, and I worked for the Gas Company and I used to clock on and clock off, and I tell you there's no comparison.

A BARGE REPAIRER If you were in a factory, well, it gets so stuffy in there, fumes from everything, and it just clogs your lungs up and you can hardly breathe.

FOREMAN BARGE REPAIRER One man to have one job is all wrong, that's what I think. That's what my opinion is. One man to do just one job or one bit towards that job is wrong. To work in those conditions, same as on the production lines in a factory, it would get any of us, I think, welll, right on the floor.

They come here and ask for a job because they want to work on the river, and you ask them why and try to tell them, try and warn them that it's hard work, heavy work. They say : 'Well, as long as I get a job on the river.' It's the fresh air that's calling them, that's what it is; the fresh air calls them – I suppose it might be that. It's the tugs and barges moving; something moving, you know – as a child; because you've just left childhood, and now you start work and you want to move on something which moves through the water. . . .

Let us see how far dockers' premonitions about factory life were born out by experience at the same period in a large motor works with two factories, one for pressing bodies and one for assembling cars.

Again, it is considered briefly here in a similar documentary form.[1] We will then look in more detail at both the experience of this kind of work and of the changes such work is undergoing at the moment as a result of technological development.

MR ANDREWS   Could you imagine getting up tomorrow morning at six o'clock to have your breakfast, and clean yourself up; get to work at 7.15? And when you get to work at 7.15 you put a little card in a slot and you hit it dong! You've clocked on. And there you must stay until the hooter goes. . . .

MR BANNISTER   When I first came into the factory, I was scared to a certain extent, because they've got huge presses there. On going there first of all you go past these presses and they go down with a tremendous thump, and you feel as though everything is going to erupt any time.

I wouldn't say it's noisy like as far as that is concerned, but it's the thump, you see. Working on the floor itself, tremendously noisy, with pneumatic hammers, and machines going, and very often if you wanted somebody you made signs.

MR COLLINS   All you saw was rows of bodies coming down the line, chaps in and out of them and running all round them, drilling and discing and things like that, and then a chap whistling, one singing. They seemed a happy crowd.

MR DERWENT   It's terrific really, the amount that comes off that line. Terrific. To see it start: within a minute as it's gone through there's a car coming off. It's nothing when it starts, and yet it's a car at the finish. You see certain models, a car comes off every minute. It's astounding, to what it used to be. It was all done by hand once upon a time.

MR ANDERSON Well, you see, it's like a beehive; everyone's got a job to do and you've got to move to do it. You can't just stand still and do the job, the lines are moving by.

MR O'FAOLAIN They're a good set of people that work in there. They're not a crowd of morbid people. They've got to do a day's work and they go in there and enjoy themselves. They have a good crack and a laugh. It's pretty good like that. They're not just robots that walk in and do a job.

MR GARNER They're quite a happy crowd at work actually. There's a lot of fun. Much more fun than people realize. It's not all sweat and work.

MR HARRIS I mean, we have all nationalities in the factory, and yet the coloured boys are the easiest to work with. They laugh at you, they love a laugh, you see, and I'm just the same, I'll laugh, I'll laugh with anything. I even look in a mirror and laugh when I'm shaving, it's a wonder I don't cut myself.

MR BANNISTER It's pretty heavy, but then when you acquire the skill you get a thythm – especially if you're working under piece work conditions – you get into the rhythm and it doesn't take it out of you like it would in the first instance.

MR IMESON Well, I say I can make a thing by hand out of the flat ... there's nothing more satisfying. Being able to do a job that nobody else could – you know, being able to shape these forms. Very satisfying.

MR JENKINS It's our bread and butter. We have to like it; because it's our bread and butter. We could choose another occupation, I suppose, that's not in the factory; say 'Get your cards and get out!' To have to work and

MR COLLINS I mean you cannot get the money anywhere else. Or the conditions as far as that goes. Anyone that's interested in anything mechanical like that, it's a marvellous job. Of course, when the majority go there they're not tradesmen, but after they've been there a few years you could almost rank them as tradesmen, first-class at that too.

MR GARNER   The spirit of the work was better in those days than it is now. Although It was a hard job and a dirty job, everyone was very matey in those days. There was a different spirit altogether. They used to help each other much more. Today they're on piecework which kills all the helping each other feeling.

MR O'FAOLAIN   You hear these people talking about the good old days but I think that's a lot of hooey. There was no such thing as the good old days. In the good old days you had to graft like hell, didn't you? They'd just come along and say Get your cards and get out!' To have to work and wander round the country looking for jobs. You had to take what was going on the job, and if you didn't like it you had to move around, there was no barbed wire round the hut like – you just had to get out and that's it.

MR KENNEDY   The way food and material are wasted by the young blood in the factories. When I was a child at school I've had to stand at six o'clock in the morning outside the pawn shop, and take things to be pledged to get the money for the week's food; and today the poor pensioner suffers because the men in the factory are getting that much money that they can go into a butcher's shop and say well 'That's a pound, I'll have that.'

MR LAWRENCE   Prewar, men were like rats, scavenging for food. That's what they used to remind me of – fighting for food. I mean if you see a rat and you throw it some food it'll fight for it. Well, that's just what it was like before the war. You'd grab anything that was coming your way.

MR BANNISTER   You were paid by result. If you didn't earn your money you didn't get it. Well, of course, today it's a different matter. You have a guarantee, you have a guaranteed waiting time and so on, which is a good thing what the unions have done. And at that time the union wasn't in being.

MR CARR   You can show a man a job that's going to take him three minutes. Well, he becomes proficient at the job and he's probably interested in it for a day, perhaps three days, but at the end of three months he hates the sight of it. He's got no interest whatsoever, and at the end of three years I don't think you can imagine what it is like. . . .

MR EDWARDS   If a man starts, he is told that he has got to put eight nuts in a certain part of the car; he'll do that day in, day out for perhaps years and years, and it's all he damn well knows at the finish. He'll go to bed some nights and think about nothing else, will he?

Well, after coming out of the building line which is an open air job, well, I felt shut in; I felt like a bird in a cage, what's been used to wild life. It wants some sticking, the machinery.

MR LAWRENCE   There's one department there which they call Trip-Hammers, and you can't even hear yourself think, let alone speak – it's terrible. One trip-hammer is about twice as bad as one pneumatic drill and you've got at least six of those, or eight, all going at once.

MR ORAM   Yes, hold it up by hand, put it between these things – we call them a trip-hammer – put your foot down on the pedal and it starts, and it makes a hell of a din. Just up and down. It's terrible. What can I liken it to? Have you ever heard an Oerlichen gun? You know, where there's boom, boom, boom, boom, boom, boom.

MR CARR   You get the dirt in the factories that's making the bodies. Oh yes, yes, when you come out your overalls will stand up on their own very nearly with the oil and dirt in the body department, working on steel.

MR LAWRENCE   In the cleansing department, they're the lowest paid men in the works and yet they've got the dirtiest and filthiest jobs. Because everything's got to be cleaned you see. It must be clean and tidy, And sometimes, well, to clean out a pit, a sludge pit, that's where all the dross is going, well the smell's enough to drive a man insane.

MR EDWARDS   We used to get a special price for that job because it was very dangerous. You were only allowed down there so long, ten minutes, quarter of an hour. Because the fumes coming from the bottom when you start digging now, it's like a lot of putty at the bottom, the sediment from the paint. We used to have safety belts to go down, then dig it out in buckets and you used to be pulled up out of these tanks – a dangerous job. You were only allowed down there so long and you hollered when you'd had enough. We used to wear a mask. But no more of that; it's a terrible job and it could only be done at night.

MRS NORRIS   I have done night work in the past myself and I know that you don't get the same amount of sleep. There's so much background and different noises; and it doesn't matter if you sut up your windows or black out your windows with thick curtains, there are still noises, and your body knows that it's daytime. You don't eat properly and you don't feel refreshed after your sleep. And after a time it does begin to get you down.

MR PARKER   You get a half-hour from twelve 'til half twelve and you get another half hour from half three to four. That's the worst time of all the night actually. You're feeling depressed and upset. You're more inclined to drink a lot of water or milk or something than you are to eat, like.

MR O'FAOLAIN   You take a Friday evening for instance, you finish on a Friday morning and then you've got to go and do four hours in the Friday evening and then you've got to go to sleep again, and then you wake up about two or three in the morning and you're finished – you know what I mean? It knocks you around. Because you're used to working at that time and you're sleeping. I wouldn't say it does your system a whole lot of good you see.

MR CARR   In the upholstery department you get the smell of leathers and the smell in the dips of the enamels and the paints, all these fumes – terrible things. And two hundred men spread out at perhaps four feet apart and all of them perhaps going just as hard as they can go. This was the thing that impressed me. This is what I said to myself. You've got twenty more years left in you of work. Are you going to carry on like this for the rest of your days? And I stood at the end of the line and watched them and they all looked at me as though they'd gone stark raving mad, you know, everybody was moving fast.

MR JAMESON   We've got boys up at the company now. They've come from outside – from the building sites – and they hate it you know. They simply hate it, because they're enclosed. I worked with one last week and he said 'I detest it in here', he said – just like that. 'I detest it', he said. 'Well', I said, 'the money's good. . . .'

MR CARR   The most of them become victims of this – they can't give it up, because first of all they were in there to get this money to get married. Then they get married and they carry on – things are going nicely on thirty pound a week. Well, can that man give up and go and do a more interesting job for half the wages or just above half the wages?

There's no interest whatsoever in anything that you do. The only interest is queuing up at the end of the week to collect your money.

MR GARNER   At the Friday end of the week you feel a different person. You're free for a couple of days and you've got something to take home.

You stick the card in the slot and push a handle and that registeres the time at which you clock in. It's nothing much. But it's a much happier sound at night; the whole thing sounds much happier when you're clocking out than when you're clocking in. I don't know whether it's psychology but it always feels that way.

I think that the average workman gets some fun out of his job. He has a joke. I think if they're out for a couple of days they miss it, the companionship of their pals and the cross-talk. There's a lot of fun in working even though it's hard work.

MR COLLINS There's one thing that sticks in my memory. We had a chap called Tiny. It was when they first started fitting the tyres, putting the tyres on the wheels. Well, he could pick up a tyre and put it on with his hands without using a lever of anything like that. He was a tremendous man, about six foot four; but he had shoulders about as broad as he was high.

MR GARNER He actually died young, but he used to put the tyres on with his hands; and now they have to get an implement made for the job, with lots of people all fiddling about. But Tiny used to sit there all day long screwing the tyres on with the strength of his hands. He had huge hands.

MR DERWENT Oh, yes. Old Tiny Newman. He had hands like legs of mutton. And he could put tyres on blooming near as quick as they could put them on with machinery today. And people came from all over the world to see him put them on.

MR COLLINS I remember one instance, he lived at Headington and on a bus going up Headington Hill he picked a chap up and held him over the side of the bus – it was the open-top buses in those days you know. He annoyed him, and he picked him up and hung him over the side. He was that sort of chap. Very inoffensive.

MR DERWENT We can't all be white collar merchants. Somebody's got to do the hard work. It's as good as any other job, provided your interested and do your job; but with any job you've got to be interested.

MR ORAN Some day all this is going to change. I feel absolutely sure about this. I mean animals have to hunt and scavenge around for things to eat and they have to make their own shelter, but we want something different.

MR O'FAOLAIN I've had a good run. We've had our ups and downs, strikes, and everything like that, but I don't regret it. I only hope it'll keep on for another twenty years. I can stick it. As long as the money's there – I'll stick it.

18
Some effects of repetitive
work on leisure

This documentary study, short as it is, may illustrate some of the findings about repetitive mass-production that have emerged from many studies done over the past generation.

The motor-assembler is perhaps the paradigm figure of contemporary industrial production, just as the cotton-spinner was in early nineteenth-century England.[1] Such popular images depend partly on myth, and it is easy to find elements of people's experience that do not fit into stereotypes at all; aspects of the work of a motor factory – the very symbol of 'alienation' in contemporary literature – that are felt by some people to be satisfying and productive.

There is in fact a minority of people who like such work for its own sake. A majority dislike the work, but like the money that it pays, but even for these, sources of satisfaction can be found in the work itself. Many enjoy the fun and companionship which they find in the social life at work. There are also sources of intrinsic satisfaction in the flow of rhythmic work itself, of which people are frequently less aware until they are interrupted; the sense of being carried along with what some psychologists have called the 'traction' of a job.[2] Some people derive satisfaction from being involved simply in making things.

MR DERWENT   The amount that comes off the line : terrific. To see it start, and within a minute as it's gone through, that's a car come off. It's nothing when it starts, and yet it's a car at the finish.

MR COLLINS   Where I'm working at the moment, there is bits
and pieces of iron floating all over the place, and gradually it begins to take shape, and you stand there and
watch it take shape. Just like growing up with your
children; you don't notice the growth of the child, but
somebody else walking straight in and looking at him after
about twelve months would know the difference.

    We stand in a good position : we're way up above the
line you see, and you look down at it, and, you wonder
where all the cars are going to. They keep rolling off and
rolling off and rolling off.

    There's no machinery there, really. All the machinery is
hidden. You see, with mechanization or automization it's
all hidden, you see. You know exactly what's going on in
your mind's eye, you see, and all you can see is just a line
of cars going along. But you know just exactly what is
going on underground.

MR ROGERS   There's something satisfying about seeing the various operations other people are doing, and all this non-
sense you know. And to see a piece of metal or several
pieces of metal and about two hours afterwards you see a
car body all joined together in 'Car Bodies'. Then in
about four hours' time they're turned out trimmed and
everything. The same metals as you've seen in the raw.

    Statements like those of the early Mark about machinery wage-
labour and 'man' – as if these were indivisible entities – may lead
his reader to expect a uniformity in human responses in working
life. Sociology, when its results are put in statistics, can make such
pictures clearer, but with a danger of its own : the idea of 'the
average'. A minority, or an individual, may be forgotten if these
satatistics are used as evidence for broad generalizations such as
'the average assembly line worker is discontented with his job'. In
reality within 'averages' the most dramatic differences can exist.
But in general the evidence, even from those with very different points of view about the nature of factory work, supports
rather than challenges the assumptions of the critical tradition :
that the feeling of doing good work is important to people, and

that variety, freedom, a self-imposed rhythm and skill are necessary elements in most intrinsically satisfying work. People who
said they positively liked factory life, far from treating their work
as a mere source of pay, or enjoying repetition for its own sake,
seemed to find in factory labour some of the same variety, skill
and rhythm that others sought outside it. But for most people,
assembly-line mass-production is in strong contrast to the most
satisfying forms of work, and it is done largely for the sake of
money.[3]

We have already seen that such 'instrumentalist' patterns of
work and leisure – 'alienated' and 'self-estranged' to those who
judge them with the concepts and assumptions of Marx's 1844
Manuscripts – are often said to be comparatively satisfying by
those engaged in them. Meanings and roles can be found in
leisure and family life perhaps more significant than those which
work fails to provide. This is just as true of many people in
factories as of some who work on the river.

AN ASSEMBLY LINE WORKER   To me sex is a way of life. This
tranquility after the act where you just lay there satisfied
in each other's company. You have this rest which is more
potent than sleep. It's just a relaxation of every muscle in
your body; and nothing could be finer. But unfortunately
the old alarm clock wakes you in the morning, and that
must call you back to the life of reality.

I'm happy in my work. The point is, you've got to keep
the home together, and you've got to keep going, so
naturally you've got to work. And as long as I've got
enough to keep my family going, I'm happy. I'd rather be
working than, say, be on the dole. I'm happy to be working. Whether I'm happy in my work is . . . well, sometimes you'll get browned off, but there you are, you're
happy to have a job and the money to go on, and there's a
lot of people that are not in that position. They haven't
got a job at all, have they?

Personally speaking I've got four children of my own.
I've got a nice wife, I've got a nice home. I've got to work

to keep it and at times, like everything else, work gets people down. Sometimes you mean to say 'I don't feel like going today'. But it's an obligation, and obligation plays a big part in people's lives – when you have a family and children, responsibilities.

As long as they've got a roof over their head, a nice warm bed, clean clothes and bellyful of grub, good shoes on their feet, that, to me, is what counts.[4]

But although in reply to questions about 'satisfaction' people will very often say, like this, that they are 'satisfied with their lives as a whole; and although very large majorities, usually between 60 and 90 per cent do say they are satisfied with their jobs in most surveys, there are frequently large differences between occupations in this respect; while when people are asked whether they would choose the same life again if they could go back to the age of fifteen, as few as 16 per cent of unskilled workers may say 'yes' while by contrast, 91 per cent of mathematicians may say they would choose the same life again.[5] In a survey covering a wide range of trades, only between 20 and 40 per cent of those in various professional occupations said they would do different work if given a second choice, while by contrast 69 per cent of the car-workers interviewed said if they could go back and start life again they would start in another trade.[6]

There are, then, deprivations in the lives of people in work like car production for which the wages do not entirely compensate. This study will be concerned, in concluding, with only one : the effect of repetitive work on the area in which its financial reward is mainly available to be enjoyed : home life and leisure.

Two illustrations may show what the 'spill-over' from monotonous and unsatisfying work to leisure can mean in everyday life. The first speaker here is the wife of a day-worker in a motor factory, who had previously worked in the building trade, and had gone into the factory quite simply to make money.

He has always been used to being out in the open, and now he's got this sort of feeling, I think, that there is someone always coming up behind you, if you sort of stop for a few minutes. My husband's always been a pretty healthy man. I don't remember him ever being off work when he was outside. But since he's been in there he's always got a bad stomach – pains in his stomach, pains in his back.

My husband always says that the work – what they call hard work in the factory – well, there is no such thing. He says they don't know what hard work is. He'd much rather be out on the railway lifting half a dozen fifty-foot rails or something, and he would feel that he had gone and done a good job. But in there . . . it's tiring. It's not harder, but it's tiring. Much more frustrating too, so he finds.

My husbnd kind of gets bogged down, and even when he's at home he can't seem to get up enough energy or enthusiasm to do other things. He used to go out for a drink with his friends, but he doesn't go now. He just doesn't bother. He just meanders about home and potters out in the garden.

He's altered in every way. I mean, before he went up there, well, he was rather, shall we say, happy-go-lucky. He used to work quite hard. I mean, it was more harder physical work that he did, but he used to come home and eat an enormous meal, and then he'd sort of say, 'Well, get washed and changed now, and let's go to the pictures', or 'Let's. . . Do you want to go out somewhere, let's go out', you know. I mean, though he'd been out all day, he still wanted to go out again; and at the weekend we always went out somewhere, or did something or other. But since he's been there, in the week he's got no appetite, when he comes home he doesn't want to eat, he's tired and just sits down in the chair after tea and falls asleep over the paper.

Given these conditions, despite all the extra hours of leisure gained since the 1840s, if the work is sufficiently monotonous the leisure can be monotonous also. A man who worked in a factory which Goldthorpe, Lockwood, Bechofer and Platt investigated

recently in a well-known study – a man who, like many of these
they interviewed had once been a skilled craftsman – told me of
the regret he felt at his choice of mass-production instead of the
furniture-making he had started in.

> In the back of your mind, you was often thinking about
> 'Shall I go back again to the other firm to create some-
> thing?'[8]

But he went on, with a shake of his head, to say that he never did,
and that instead of making the decision he 'would go and have a
pint', as his only way of escaping the 'number' that had worked
its way, year after year, into his brain.

> You come in each day : you're timed on this job, When
> you first start on it, you come in. All right; today's
> output : 240. And that's your number; and you think of
> the 240 until you've done it; and you're number-minded;
> and when you go home the boredom is there with you.
>
> Now people are talking to me, and I've got one thought
> on my mind, to get to work and finish a number. And that
> number is hanging in my mind all day long until it's
> finished. Then I've got nothing else to think about.
>
> And when you get home, you are just the same. To my
> opinion, they only break you get, you go to have a pint
> and then you forget it. But when you come back to work
> the next day, that number still comes back into your
> mind, and that's how that number works into your mind,
> and after years and years that's still there.

The Cambridge study argued that the lives of 'instrumentally-
oriented' men were 'sharply dichotomized' between work and
non-work. But if two aspects of human life can be distinguished
conceptually, it does not follow that they are distinct in reality.
And this is true even if the people concerned believe they are
distinct. Even if some assemblers do believe that their work and
leisure are tightly compartmentalized, and have no influence on
each other, in reality there may still be influence. Thus there is an
ambiguity in the definition Goldthorpe, Lockwood and their col-
leagues give of an 'instrumental' attitude to work :

Since work is defined essentially as a mandatory and instrumental activity, rather than as an activity valued for itself, the ego-involvement of workers in their jobs – in either the narrower or wider sense of the term – is weak. Their jobs do not form part of their central life interests; work is not for them a source of emotionally significant experiences of social relationships, it is not a source of self-realization.

Consequently, workers' lives are sharply dichotomized between work and non-work.[8]

This may well be an accurate account of how work appears to a man who treats it instrumentally. But there is an ambiguity in it; for we do not know that such an attitude to work does not really 'involve the ego'. Perhaps, instead of 'not involving one's ego' in work, it is possible that in some cases one 'involves one's ego' in an apathetic, routine-bound way. There may be as great a difference between the two possibilities as some have observed between chastity and prostitution.

> After years and years that number has worked its way into your head. And when you go home that boredom is there with you.

Demanding work, on the other hand, far from exhausting people or preventing the enjoyment of leisure, can, at least in some cases, have the opposite effect. The man who spoke previously about the 'number' working into his brain changed at the age of sixty to a job on a numerical control machine which ran taped programmes, and which required him, instead of repeating a single action, to watch its whole complex programme constantly. It is not an exaggeration to say that the change of work transformed his entire life.

> All of a sudden we get up to the present-day. Here's a challenge. Here's a new machine, everything is nice – well – to me it looked like an octopus, for being honest; there's lights, lights all along it, there's arms going in, there's probes going in, there's up and down movements – to me it looked like a jigsaw puzzle when I first looked at it, but

it was a challenge. Something you could get your teeth into. You were interested. It's absolutely changed your life, from numbers to something interesting. Now I want to get on to something perhaps a little bit more complicated, because I've really got my teeth into something. The old grey matter had got dull and now it's livened up and I'm away with it.

It's alert. The machine to me, it seems as if it's a brain. It's just as if this brain, the machine, is working, and it's telling what to do and what not to do. If it makes a mistake, you're the father, you've got to put that right.

To me it's revolutionized my thinking of mass production. You are creating something, you are doing something really good. I'm sixty-one now. You see, there's such an old saying goes 'You can't teach old dogs new tricks'. This is one that's been wrong.[9]

This man had been on his new job for only about six months when he spoke about it, and it is possible that some of his interest might have been an interest in the novelty of the work rather than in the work itself. If so, one would expect to find people who had had several years' experience of such new machines less happy with them now. But this does not seem to be the case with Californian numerical control operators for instance, who sound at least contented after five or ten years of the new machinery, and generally compare it favourably with hand-production.

Even within the present system, people working in the most monotonous jobs may find an improvement in their work through the development of the technology itself, out of hand-production to tape-programmed numerical control machinery. At the moment, in England, they are only a small minority – less than half a percent of the people who worked in his factory at the time that man spoke. But it would be a mistake if people rejected all the claims made for modernization, or assumed that they necessarily bring further monotony each time. Forms of automation are constantly changing, and some at the moment undoubtedly bring better, rather than more inhuman, conditions to those whose work they change. And the benefit may spread to the whole of life. The imaginative experiments being made in Sweden and elsewhere[10] at the moment in redesigning assembly-line work are thus significant far outside the area of work itself.

People vary greatly in the degree to which they want interest and stimulation. There may even be systematic psychological differences between introverts and extroverts in these needs. As we have seen, some people – mostly the less intelligent – like repetitive work.[11] Even for others it may have some function – for instance a defence against self-consciousness in the melancholy, or a source of satisfaction for the obsessive. We all need some degree of regularity and repetition.

The problem is for each person to find or invent the form of work, with the degree of repetition or originality, that suits his character. At the moment, in our society, this is made difficult by the fact that uninteresting jobs are in such plentiful supply, and carry with them often such attractive money rewards. If such jobs affect the whole of a person's life – if their effects cannot be contained within the confines of work, under present conditions and hours – then other rewards would seem to be more appropriate; either very much shorter hours or, better still, where it is possible, the re-designing of the job.

Until recently the logic of our economy has precluded such changes, since they could not be shown in all cases to be profitable. However, particularly since the coming of much lighter industries such as electronics, forms of work have been devised in mass-production, for instance the Philips work--structuring experiments in Holland,[12] which do offer more interesting work without being less productive. In Sweden, car firms have been forced to make such changes because – as with certain types of domestic labour here earlier in the century – nobody Swedish could be persuaded to do the job of old-fashioned car-assembling at any price whatever.

But can these ideas and these new developments be dealt with and understood in the old philosophical concepts – 'alienation',

'self-estrangement' and the like. The argument of the present
book has been that other concepts have to be found, because the
nineteenth century ones now being revived threaten to distort the
evidence they represent; they bring to it values deriving from the
experience of a previous generation with a different set of
relationships between work and leisure, and deriving also from
the experience of a particular group – the philsophical observers
of industrialization, who did not themselves for the most part
work with their hands.

Such concepts are rooted in assumptions about nature,
redemption, and the true being or essence of man, inextricably.
They imply general theories of the role of work in the life of 'man'
which are metaphysical in origin, and which reflect the values
and education of those who coined them – men who read, wrote
and talked for their work, and who did not work with their hands
and when they did so, did not depend on their manual work for
their living.

Yet such concepts are used extensively today, and have formed
the foundation in particular for an influential and – from an
empiricle point of view valuable – modern study. In *Alienation
and Freedom* Robert Blauner interpreted the results of surveys of
people's attitudes to their work in a number of different
industries; and made particular use of a comparative investiga-
tion of sixteen American industries carried out after the Second
World War. From these he drew a remarkable and graphic conclusion. The incidence in modern industry of 'alienation', defined
in terms of four 'sub-dimensions', – 'powerlessness, meaningless-
ness, isolation and self-estrangement' – was found to describe an
'inverted U-shaped curve' as technology advanced.

In the early period, dominated by craft industry alienation is at
its lowest and the worker's freedom at its maximum. Freedom
declines and ... the alienation curve continues upwards to its
highest point in the assembly-line industries of the twentieth
century ... Thus in the extreme situation a depersonalized
worker, estranged from himself and larger collectives, goes
through the motions of work in the regimented milieu of the

conveyor belt for the sole purpose of earning his bread. . . .

But with automated industry the alienation curve begins to decline from its previous height as employees gain a new dignity from responsibility and a sense of individual function – thus the inverted U.

'Alienation' was the not the same as 'dissatisfaction', for an 'alienated' worker could be satisfied in his work;[13] in fact it was not necessarily anything a worker actually felt, although Blauner's evidence about it seemed to be mainly evidence about what working people felt. There was considerable doubt about whether people's position on these four 'sub-dimensions', were in fact correlated[14] or even whether the 'sub-dimensions' – derived from an earlier five-fold scheme of Melvin Seeman's[15] – belonged to logically compatible conceptual systems.[16] But 'alienation' was assumed to be 'negatively valued'[17]

There was a footnote qualification that technology might not continue to advance in this or any other single way.[18] And this was a wise qualification as subsequent studies have suggested.[19] But 'the inverted U-shaped curve of alienation' has nevertheless been accepted as a significant pattern of industrial evolution in the modern world. A reader is likely to assume since 'alienation' sounds an ugly thing, that something very general and very wrong with human work – something which according to this theory, the industrial revolution had greatly intensified – had in recent years been getting much better. And this is how the 'inverted U-shaped curve' of alienation has generally been interpreted; and how it has found its way into much theory and discussion of contemporary working life.

This book questions the value not of the evidence given in that study but of such concepts for its interpretation today. If men's ideas of their central interests in life are to be criticized and changed, it can only be by understanding their own concepts, by offering them further evidence and by persuasion; not be reviving philosophical assumptions about what they ought to think and feel from another generation in a different situation, and applying them to the present without revision.

A concept of 'alienation' defined in terms of a subjection of work to the rest of life, has been used again today, in an age when the proportions of work and leisure hours are very different from those that prevailed when it originated; and when the 'freedom' and 'productive activity' whose absence gave the sting to 'alienation' are more possible for many people in leisure than at work. Meanwhile the idea that these constitute some kind of 'human essence' – an idea that rested on an early nineteenth-century philosophical assumption – has been incorporated as a concealed value, underlying supposedly descriptive concepts, in much contemporary writing about society. Work is 'essential' to men. And so is play. So is love. Neither has any primacy independent of people's individual decisions to give emphasis to one rather than the other at any particular time in their own lives.

19
Conclusions

It was particularly in the early nineteenth centuries that work acquired its extraordinary importance in the theories of philosophers and writers about society. Rousseau had praised craftsmanship as a way of life, yet he had shown an equal concern for other aspects of human life besides work. It was these that his successor Schiller developed, especially the idea of play rather than work as the 'essential' and defining element in human nature.

But after Schiller, instead of abandoning the quest for an 'essential' element in human nature, philosophers increasingly took work as their natural concern. With Marx 'free conscious productive activity' was presented as the defining characteristic or 'species-essence' of 'man'. A factory worker who laboured in order to live was thus 'alienated' from his true humanity.

From such a philosophy much of the reforming concern for the improvement of industrial labour has subsequently drawn its inspiration; perhaps without it nothing would have been done.

But other roots are needed for theory today closer to human nature as it is and to the language in which men think and feel, if people at work are to be mutually comprehensible.

In search of such alternative roots, this book considered how industrial work is experienced by some of the people who actually do it today. It also looked for what could be known about the experience of those who first encountered machinery, and of men in pre-industrial, and in some so-called 'primitive', societies.

In broad terms, about the period of the 'industrial revolution' it seems that a change took place in the consciousness of many working people : that 'more work and more money' became either a chosen or an imposed alternative to doing nothing. The same change can be found in many parts of the world that are beginning to industrialize today. A British firm accused of underpaying its African labourers recently pleaded that if they were paid more than a living wage they simply stayed away from work until they needed to earn some more. Similar behaviour among working people may be traceable as early as ancient Greece, and it can be found in most 'simple' societies. It could almost be said to be the normal pre-industrial attitude to work wherever there is freedom for it. It was no doubt the attitude of many weavers under the 'putting out' system, whose week's work would be completed over midnight candles in the days and nights just before it was called for; it is the way many people who can still do so – some students, some writers – work today.

Industrialization, with earlier changes in agriculture and the diffusion of money exchange into every part of life in the industrializing countries, succeeded slowly against opposition in creating comparatively regular hours of work. In the case of Britain, very long though less regular hours already existed at the industrial revolution, as a result of previous 'rationalities' – the destruction of church festivals, and the pauperization and conversion into labourers of many of the peasants and small farmers whose land had been enclosed. Industrialization, with the development of leisure industries and the consumer market, gave system to these hours, and made them eventually 'chosen'. Although they were cut by trade union action and by legislation through the nineteenth century, they remained comparatively stable after the inter-war depression, despite the temporary increases created by the Second World War; so that as late as the 1960s people went on taking up falls in the official working week largely as overtime, rather than as further leisure; and actual hours worked did not fall appreciably between about 1938 and 1966. Only since then has there been the beginning of a change, and it is too early to know whether it is a permanent one, and how far 'moon-lighting' counteracts it; but at least in the matter of holidays people are now beginning to choose leisure rather than money, at a little above forty hours a working week on average in Britain, and a little less in America, when they have the choice.

It is sometimes said that in the course of these developments industrialization and mechanization created or greatly intensified an 'instrumental' attitude to work by taking the meaning out of labour; that before the industrial revolution, work was done either for its own sake because of the intrinsic interest of the tasks it required, or for the sake of some obligation to the community which industrialization destroyed, substituting a mere 'cash nexus' where previously there had been enjoyment and satisfaction in labour.

Of a total change in attitudes to work brought about by mechanization alone, this book was able to find little convincing evidence. In the first place, satisfaction with work – even with work that could seem extraordinarily unattractive to commentators from a distance – could be found existing side by side with dislike even in factory industry today; indeed it may well be that the peculiar nature of satisfaction with work can only be understood when both the enjoyment and the dislike are considered together; that it is a complex taste, of the kind Adrian Stokes identified in an essay once as particularly satisfying for adults for reasons which he traced back speculatively to the fusion of 'good' and 'bad', 'sweet' and 'sour', in the formation of the 'whole object' in early childhood, a fusion of which complex tastes such as bitter beer, strong meat – and perhaps, it might be added, hard work – may conceivably be reminders. Highly complex attitudes to work – dislike, and also satisfaction despite or even in some way because of the intrinsic hardness of the tasks – can be found in different areas of industry and agriculture both before and after the industrial revolution. There is little evidence that this study could discover of an absolute change in attitudes to work simply because it was mechanized.

The awareness of reward for work in terms of money or consumption, for a man or for his family, and the execution of work with the conscious or even exclusive wish for reward, did not appear to be a new invention of the industrial revolution. Work done for its own sake, enjoyed for its own intrinsic satisfaction, seemed less widespread in any past that there was evidence of, than in the imaginations of those philosophers who wrote about work in the nineteenth century; though they themselves may have been among the small minority of human beings who perhaps did experience such work regularly and almost exclusively, and they may well have assumed it was more widely diffused than it really was

Thirdly, both before and after the industrial revolution, many people seemed to be more interested in the social aspects of working life, in the kindness, cruelty or justice of those they dealt with at work, in family life and in elements of 'play' both in and out of work, than in the intrinsic nature of the tasks involved in their labour.

There was evidence that the curtailment of much of this social life and play in work, in the early period of industrialization at least, together with severe restrictions on freedom of time and on spontaneous working rhythms, and the destruction of the poetry and community life which surrounded some pre-industrial work, may have been highly traumatic. The hints that songs in particular leave behind are at least consistent with this possibility.

Meanwhile they suggest strongly that certain changes happening concurrently with industrialization – but not themselves specifically involving the mechanization of the trades involved – were acutely painful for those who experienced them – more so in some cases perhaps than the mechanization itself. Examples included the reduction of skilled headweavers to the out-workers' life described in *Jone O'Grinfilt Junior* or *The Oldham Weaver*; the lives of sailors on the mid-nineteenth-century clipper ships and whaling ships, or those of the bothy labourers on the Aberdeenshire farms. These, like the conditions of the Spitalfields weavers, were all instances where other things than mechanization were directly responsible for the conditions involved, but where the conditions apparently became more appalling, at the same time as – and to some extent because of – the industrialization of the rest of the economy.

Finally, two forms of manual work in contemporary society were examined, and some of the sociological and psychological theories that seek to assess the relative place of work and leisure in contemporary life were discussed in the light of the preceding evidence. The question of how contemporary work may in detail actually be improved needs another study.[1] In outline, these are the provisional conclusions the present book suggests.

If it is a task of this civiliaztion to improve the quality and interest of the work that it offers – particularly the manual labour on whose deprivations much of its prosperity is based – this is important not merely for the direct effects such reforms may have on work, but for the improvements that may be expected to follow in the possibilities of leisure and the rest of life as well. Such reform is not likely to be possible everywhere, and not everywhere as valuable as the nineteenth-century philosophers thought; the idea of shortening working hours and the idea of introducing 'leisure-like' elements into work are probably more relevant to some trades than any attempt to improve the intrinsic nature of the work. Some tasks may be simply unimprovable. But others can be transformed, as recent experimenters have shown.

Such ideas may have a hard time before they are widely accepted, a harder time even that the nineteenth-century theoritsts thought. For not only do they go against the logic of much modern economics; they also confront a lack of interest on the part of many of those most closely involved – people who work with their hands – in any serious possibility of improvement in the quality of their work. And this probably has deeper roots than industrialization. The reformers are to be seen not so much as revivers of a recently lost world of work that everyone enjoyed before industrialization, but as a minority with highly original views, not likely to seem 'natural' to the vast majority of people without a considerable shift in consciousness.

Yet such shifts do occur. Ideas for replacing assembly line labour similar to some that were considered 'unrealistic' when published a few years ago[2] are now accepted as eminently practical in Swede, campaigned for by trade unions in America and more recently in Britain, and most recently of all have been advocated for the European Economic Community as a whole by its Commission.[3]

If the ideal of intrinsically interesting and absorbing work has belonged mainly to a limited group of artists, writers and craftsmen who have had regularly what most people have had rarely – the choice of earning their living in interesting ways, or of not having to earn it at all – it is not without wider foundations in common experience. Craftsmanship has been associated with the making of household objects, as well as with art, games and play, in nearly all simple societies, and it may well have been one of the main sources of satisfaction in work for the minorities who were engaged in it in earlier periods of European history. If its nineteenth-century enthusiasts over-estimated the relative significance it has had for working people, compared with a provision for the necessities of life, and if it may have been incapable of inspiring many personal sacrifices of money and productivity in our present society, that is not to say that it will be irrelevant in a less needy future. The desire to make things that are valued and useful – and in some cases things that are beautiful – is among the feelings that many modern people pick out when describing their work even in the most repetitive technologies. The idea of providing more interesting and satisfying work, difficult as it may be to imagine it and to incorporate it in any political and economic programme at the moment, need not be conceived in a vacuum; the conditions of satisfying work are not unknown, and there are small, but real, signs of response already to the idea that they should be extended, to be within reach of anyone who wants them. Perhaps a hundred years or so of failure are not very long in the time-scale of an idea like this.

Notes

Introduction

[1] Simone Weil, *L'enracinement* (Paris 1949), English translation by A. F. Wills, *The Need for Roots* (Routledge, London 1952), pp. 91–2.
[2] Herbert Marcuse, *Eros and Civilization* (Boston 1955); *One Dimensional Man* (New York 1964).

Chapter 1

[1] Jean-Jacques Rousseau, *Discours sur cette question proposée par l'Académie de Dijon: Quelle est L'Origine de L'Inégalité parmi les hommes et si elle est autorisée par la loi naturelle?* (Paris 1754), in Rousseau, *Du Contrat Social, Discours*, etc., (Editions Garnier, Paris 1962), p. 100. Cf. 'If ever I could have written even the quarter of what I saw and felt . . . with what clarity I should have revealed all the contradictions of the social system, with what force I would have demonstrated that man is naturally good and that it is through their institutions alone that men become bad.' Rousseau, *Lettres à M. de Malesherbes*, ed. G. Rudler (London 1928) p. 33.
[2] Rousseau, *Discours*, p. 73.
[3] *Ibid.*, p. 76.
[4] Translations in the text, unless otherwise noted, are by the present author. 'Il n'y a peut-être. . .pas un vaisseau en mer dont le naufrage ne fût une bonne nouvelle pour quelque négociant. . .pasun peuple qui ne réjouisse des désastres de ses voisins.' *Ibid.*, p. 101.
[5] Hors de la société l'homme isolé, ne devant rien à personne, a droit, de vivre comme il lui plaît; mais dans la société, où il vit nécéssairement aux dépens des autres, il leur doit en travail le prix de son entretien; cela est sans exception. Travailler est donc un

devoir indispensable à l'homme social.' Rousseau, *Émile* ed. F. et P. Richard (Paris 1964), p. 226.

[6] L'enfant vivant au campagne, aura pris quelque notion des travaux campagnards. Il est de tout âge, surtout du sien, de vouloir eréer, imiter, produire, donner des signes de puissance et d'activité. Il n'aura pas vu deux fois labourer un jardin. . .qu'il voudra jardiner à son tour.' *Ibid.*, p. 226.

[7] Chacun respecte le travail de autres afin que le sien soit en sûreté,' *Ibid.*, p. 91.

[8] Le fer doit être à ses yeux d'un beaucoup plus grand prix que l'or et le verre que le diamant. De même il honore beaucoup plus un cordonnier, un maçon, qu'un l'Empereur, un Le Blanc et tous les jouailleurs de l'Europe.' *Ibid.*, p. 215. Cf. Thomas More, *Utopia*, for an earlier expression of these ideas.

[9] J'aime mieux qu'il soit cordonnier que poète; j'aime mieux qu'il pave les grands chemins que peindre des fleurs de porcelaine.' *Émile*, p. 250.

[10] 'Un métier, un vrai métier, un art purement méchanique où les mains travaillent plus que la tête, et qui ne mène pas à la fortune, mais avec lequel on peu se passer.' *Ibid.*, p, 229.

[11] 'De toutes les conditions la plus indépendant de la fortune et des hommes, est celle del l'artesan. L'artesan ne dépend que de son travail, il est aussi libre que le labourer est esclave; car celui-ci tient à son champ, dont la recolte est à la discretion d'autres.' *Ibid.*, p. 226.

[12] 'Enfin je n'aimerais pas ces stupides professions, dont les ouvriers, sans industrie et presque automates, n'exercent jamais leurs mains qu'au même travail. Les tisserands, les faiseurs de bas, les scieurs de pierre, à quoi sert d'employer à ces metiers un homme de sens? C'est une machine qui en mène une autre.' *Ibid.*, pp. 233–4.

[13] 'Il y a deux sortes d'homme dont les corps sont dans un exercice continuel, et qui sûrement songent aussi peu les uns que les autres à cultiver leur âme, savoir, les paysans et les sauvages. Les premiers sont rustres, grossiers, mal-adroits; les autres, connus par leur grand sens, le sont encore pas la subtilité de leur esprit; généralement il n'y a rien de plus lourd qu'un paysan, rien de plus fin qu'un sauvage. D'ou vient cette difference? C'est que le premier, faisant toujours ce qu'on lui commande, ou ce qu'il a vu faire à son père, ou ce qu'il a fait lui-même dès sa jeunesse, ne va jamais que par routine; et dans sa vie presque automate, occupé sans cesse des

mêmes travaux, l'habitude et l'obéissance lui tiennent bien de raison.' *Ibid.*, p. 118.

[14] 'Un enfant, de dix à douze ans ... je le vois bouillant, vif, animé, sans souci rongeant; ... tout entier à son être actuel, et jouissant d'une plenitude de vie qui semble vouloir s'étendre hors de lui.

L'heure sonne, quel changement! A l'instant son oeil se ternit, sa gaieté s'efface, adieu la joie, adieu les folâtres jeux! Un homme sévère et faché le prend par la main, lui dit gravement *'Allons, Monsieur'* et l'emmène.' *Ibid.*, p. 176.

[15] 'Il ne sait ce que c'est que routine, usage, habitude; ce qu'il fit hier n'influe point sur ce qu'il fait aujourd'hui; il ne suit jamais de formule, ne cède pas à l'autorité ni à l'example.' *Ibid.*, pp. 177–8.

[16] Je ne veux pas qu'on entre...dans un cabinet de physique expérimentale. Tout cet appareil d'instruments et de machines me deplaît. L'air scientifique tue la science.' *Ibid.*, p. 198.

[17] 'Les hommes ne sont point faits pour être entassés en fourmillières, mais épars sur la terre qu'il doivent cultiver. Plus ils se rassemblent, plus ils se corrompent.' *Ibid.*, p. 37.

[18] 'Il y a deux sortes de dépendance: celle des choses et de la nature; celle des hommes et de la société. La dépendance des choses ne nuit pas à la liberté et n'engendre point de vices. La dépendance des hommes étant désordonnée, les engendre et c'est par elle que le maître et l'esclave se dépravent mutuellement ... Maintenez l'enfant dans la seule dépendance des choses ... N'accordez rien à ses désirs par ce qu'il le demande, mais parce qu'il en a besoin ... Ce sont nos passions qui nous rendent faibles parce qu'il faudrait, pour les contenter, plus de forces que nous en donne la nature. Diminuez donc les désirs.' *Ibid.*, pp. 70, 182.

Chapter 2

[1] Quoted in Barnes, *Goethe's Knowledge of French Literature* (Oxford 1937), p. 56.

[2] Thus Hölderin, most strikingly of all, in his *Hyperion*, pictures modern society as a battlefield where the separate individuals lie about as severed limbs, their blood dripping into the sand.

[3] He had a tutor, Abel, who was an enthusiastic proponent of English empiricism; cf. E. M. Wilkinson and L. A. Willoughby (translators and editors), *Schiller's Aesthetic Education of Man in a*

Series of Letters, Oxford 1967; see also the same authors' The 'Whole Man' in Schiller's Theory of Culture and Society: On the Virtue of a Plurality of Models' in S. S. Prawer, R. Hinton Thomas and L. Forster (eds), *Essays in German Language, Culture and Society* (London 1969), pp. 177–210.

4 See, e.g., Francis D. Klingender, *Art and the Industrial Revolution* (ed. A. Elton, (revised edition London 1968), pp. 18–42 and J. Warburg, *The Industrial Muse* (London 1958), pp. 1–2, 7–8.

5 Cf. Victoria Rippere, 'Schiller and Alienation: A problem in the transformation of his aesthetic and philosophic thought' (Doctoral Thesis, University College, London 1972).

6 'Die Griechen beschämen uns . . . zugleich voll Form und voll Fülle, zugleich philosophierend und bildend, zugleich zart und energisch, sehen wir sie die Jugend der Phantasie mit der Mannlichkeit der Vernunft in einer herrlichen Menschheit vereinigen. . . Jenem die alles vereinende Natur, diesem der alles trennende Verstand seine Formen erteilten.' Schiller, *Briefe über der Aesthetischen Erziehüng des Menschen* (Stuttgart, 1967), pp. 18–19, 20 (My translation.).

7 Der Nutzen ist das Grosse Idol der Zeit, dem alle Krafte frönen und alle Talente huldigen sollen. Auf dieser groben Waage hat das geistige Verdienst der Kunst kein Gewicht, und, aller Aufmunterung beraubt, verschwindet sie von dem lärmenden Markt des Jahrhunderts. Selbst der philosophische Untersuchungsgeist entreisst der Einbildungskraft eine Provinz nach der andern, und die Grenzen der Kunst verengen sich, je mehr der Wissenschaft ihre Schranken erweitert.' *Ibid.*, pp. 7–8.

8 *Ibid.*, p. 22.

9 . . . der Genuss wurde von der Arbeit, das Mittel vom Zweck, die Anstrengung von der Belohnung gescheiden. Ewig nur an ein einzelnes kleines Bruchstück des Ganzen gefesselt, bildet sich der Mensch selbst nur als Bruchstück; aus ewig nur das eintönige Geräusch des Rades, das er umtreibt, im Ohre, entwickelt er nie die Harmonie seines Natur auszuprägen, wird er bloss zu einem Abdruck seines Geschäfts, siener Wissenschaft.' *Ibid.*, p. 21.

10 'Die losgebundene Gesellschaft, anstatt aufwärts in das organische Leben zu eilen, fällt in das Elementareich zurück.' *Ibid.*, pp. 16–17.

11 '. . . selbstsüchtig und gewalltätig, vielmehr auf Zerstörung als auf Erhaltung der Gesellschaft zielt. Schiller.' *Ibid.*, p. 11.

12 'Diese Zerrüttung, welche Kunst und Gelehrsamkeit in dem

innern Menschen anfingen, machte der neue Geist der Regierung vollkommen und allgemein. Es war freilich nicht zu erwarten, dass die einfache Organisation der ersten Republiken die Einfalt der ersten Sitten und Verhältnisse überlebte; aber anstatt zu einem höhern animalischen Leben zu steigen, sank sie zu einer gemeinen und groben Mechanik herab. Jene Polypennatur der griechischen Staaten, wo jedes Individuum eines unabhängigen Lebens genoss und, wenn es Not tat, zum Ganzen werden konnte, machte jetzt einem kunstreichen Uhrwerke Platz, wo aus der Zusammenstückelung unendlich vieler aber lebloser Teile, ein mechanisches Leben im Ganzen sich bildet.' *Ibid.*, pp. 20–1.

¹³ *Ibid.*, p. 46.

¹⁴ *Ibid.*, pp. 42–8, 60–1.

¹⁵ 'Und in welchem Verhältnis stünden wir also zu dem vergangenen und kommenden Weltalter, wenn die Ausbildung der menschlichen Natur ein solches Opfer notwendig machte? Wie wären die Knechte der Menschheit gewesen, wir hätten einige Jahrtausende lang die Sklavenarbeit für sie getrieben und unserer verstümmelten Natur die beschämenden Spuren dieser Dienstbarkeit eingedrückt ... Kann aber wohl der Mensch dazu bestimmt sein, über irgendeines Zwecke sich selbst zu versäumen?'

¹⁶ 'Der Mensch soll mit der Schönheit nur spielen, und er soll nur mit der Schönheit spielen. Denn ... der Mensch spielt nur, wo er in voller Bedeutung des Worts Mensch ist, und er ist nur ganze Mensch, wo er spielt.' *Ibid.*, p. 59.

¹⁷ 'Wenn der Löwen kein Hunger nagt und kein Raubtier zum Kampf herausfordert, so erschafft sich die müssige Stärke selbst einen Gegenstand; mit mutvollen Gebrüll erfüllt er die hallende Wüste, und in zwecklosen Aufwand geniesst sich üppige Kraft. Mit frohem Leben schwärmt das Insekt in dem Sonnenstrahl; auch ist es sicherlich nicht der Schrei der Begierde, den wir in dem melodischen Schlag des Singvogels hören. Unleugbar ist in diesen Bewegungen Freiheit.' *Ibid.*, pp. 109–10.

¹⁸ 'Jetzt sucht sich der alte Germanier glänzendere Tierfolle, prächtigere Geweihe, zierlichere Trinkhörner aus, und der Kaledonier wählt die nettesten Muscheln für seine Feste. Selbst die Waffen dürfen jetzt nicht mehr bloss Gegenstände des Schreckens, sondern auch des Wohlgefallens sein, und das kunstreiche Wahrgehänge will nicht weniger bemerkt sein als des Schwertes tötende

Schneide. Nicht zufrieden, einen ästhetischen ▊berfluss in das Notwendige zu bringen, reisst sich der freie Spieltrieb endlich ganz von den Messeln der Notdurft los, und das Schöne wird für sich allein ein Objekt seines Strebens. Er *schmuckt* sich. Die freie Lust wird in die Zahl seiner Bedürfnisse aufgenommen, und das Unnötige ist bald der beste Teil seiner Freuden.' *Ibid.*, p. 112.

19 *Ibid.*, p. 82.

20 *Ibid.*, p. 117.

21 *Ibid.*, p. 116.

Chapter 3

1 Letter of 16 April 1795; J. Hoffmeister (ed.), *Briefe von und an Hegel,* (Hamburg 1952), vol. 1, p. 25.

2 Memoir 1839; quoted in W. Kaufmann, *Hegel: Reinterpretation Text and Commentary* (New York 1965), p. 36.

3 Diary, 1796; J. Hoffmeister, *Dokumentezu Hegels Entwicklung* (Stuttgart 1936), p. 223, quoted and translated by W. Kaufmann, *Hegel*, p. 305.

4 Kaufmann, *Hegel*, p. 306.

5 Cf. Karl Löwith, *From Hegel to Nietzsche* (New York 1964).

6 Hegel, *Jenenser Realphilosophie*, herausgegeben von J. Hoffmeister (Leipzig, I, 1932; II, 1931).

7 Jacques d'Hondt, *Hégel Secret* (Paris 1968).

8 Hegel, *Realphilosophie*, vol. 1, p. 236.

9 'Indem er die Natur durch mancherlei Maschinen bearbeitet lässt, so hebt er die Notwendigkeit seines Arbeitens nicht auf, sondern schiebt es nur hinauf, entfernt es von der Natur, und richtet sich nicht lebendig auf sie als eine lebendige; sondern es enflieht diese negative Lebendigkeit, und das Arbeiten, das ihn übrig bleibt, wird selbst *maschinenmässiger.* Er vermindert sie nur fürs Ganze, aber nicht für den Einzelnes, sondern vergrössert sie vielmehr, denn je maschinenmässiger die Arbeit wird, desto weniger Wert hat (sie), und desto mehr muss er auf diese Weise arbeiten.' *Ibid.*, pp. 236–7. (ed. E. Cannon) (1950), vol. 2, pp. 267–8.

10 Adam Smith *An Inquiry into the Nature and Causes of the Wealth of Nations* (ed. E. Cannon) (1950), vol. 2, pp. 267–8.

11 Compare E. G. West, 'The Political Economy of Alienation', *Oxford Economic Papers*, vol. 21, No. 1 (March 1969), p. 13.

12 Hegel, *Realphilosophie*, vol. 1, p. 240.

[13] H. Marcuse, *Reason and Revolution: Hegel and the Rise of Social Theory* 2nd ed. (New York, 1954), p. 79.

[14] Hegel, *Realphilosophie*, vol. 2, p. 215.

[15] e.g., *ibid.*, vol. 2, p. 259.

[16] 'Da seine Arbeit diese Abstrakte ist, so verhält er sich als abstraktes ich oder nach der Weise der Dingheit, nicht als umfassender, inhaltreicher umsichtiger Geist, der einen grossen Umfang beherrscht und über ihn Meister ist.' *Ibid.*, p. 215.

[17] '... ebenso (wird er) ... mechanischer, abgestumpfter, geistloser. Das Geistiges, dies erfüllte selbstbewusste Leben, wird ein leeres Tun.' *Ibid.*, vol. 1, p. 237.

[18] For the concepts *Entfremdung* and *Entäusserung* see, for example, *Jenenser Realphilosophie*, vol. 2, p. 245, and *Die Phänomenologie des Geistes* in Hegel, *Werke* (Berlin 1832), vol. 2, p. 15, and the division of the Phenomenology entitled *Der sich entfremdete Geist: die Bildung*.

[19] Cf. Hegel (trans. Jean Hyppolite), *La Phénoménologie de L'Esprit* (Paris 1947): Introduction.

[20] Hegel, *Werke*, vol. 2, 146.

[21] 'Die Arbeit ... hingegen behesste Begierde, aufgehaltenes Verschwinden, oder sie *bildet*. Das arbeitende Bewusstsein kommt also hierdurch zur Anschauung des selbständigen Seins.' *Ibid.*, pp. 147–8.

Chapter 4

[1] H. Marcuse, *Reason and Revolution: Hegel and the Rise of Social Theory* 2nd ed (New York 1954).

[2] Cf. Paul Asfeld, *La Pensée Religieuse du Jeune Hegel: Liberté et Aliénation* (Louvain 1953), chapter 2. As one modern writer has pointed out, Calvin uses the word 'aliénation' of the soul's distance from God. (L. Feuer, 'What is Alienation? The Career of a Concept', *New Politics*, Spring 1962, p. 117.) But if there is a 'source' here, the idea of a Calvinist origin for the concept should not be overstressed. *Aliénation, Enfremdung* or *Entäusserung* in the languages of Europe are concepts that do not have the slightly outlandish sound that 'alienation' has in English; and there is no question of their being coined at any time in recent history. They seem to have been in fairly constant use to describe any form of selling or renunciation— especially of land and rights, under feudal law—and also any separation, of friends from each other as much as of men from God

or of a man from his senses. Thus a single writer, in sixteenth-century France—Amynot—can be found using *aliénation* in all three senses: speaking in legal terms of *puissance de rendre et aliéner*; in terms of relationships, of two people who *partirent l'un d'avec l'autre, encore plus aliénez qu'*. . .*auparavant*: and of a man's mind or senses *aliéné par quelque griefre maladie* (quoted in Littré, *Dictionnaire de La Langue Française*). German has generally distinguished the act of taking from someone else or of separating—*Entgremdung*—from the act of renouncing or giving up—*Entäusserung*—though the two words are not consistently distinct. Again the concept carries in German no necessarily religious or psychological meaning in itself, for while the word *entfrembdet* is used in the sixteenth-century German version of Ephesians—where man is '*entflrembdet von dem Leben das aus Gott ist*'—Luther also uses it in the simple sense of man's taking from God what is God's property: 'Das wir Gottes Namen heiligen, ihm seine ihre, Güter und alle Ding von uns entfrembdet wiedergeben' (cf. Grimm, *Deutsches Wörterbuch*). Thus while it is possible that Hegel found the concept of alienation in specifically theological writings, the religious overtones in his use of it need not be tied to any one particular Christian doctrine, while in the *Jenenser Realphilosophie*, the concept occurs in s purely political context, an account of the formation of the general will (Hegel, *Realphilosophie*, vol. 2, p. 245).

3 Cf. P. Demetz, *Marx, Engels and the Poets* (Chicago 1965), p. 63.

4 Francis D. Klingender, *Art and the Industrial Revolution* (ed. by A. Elton, revised edn London 1968), pp. 3–42.

5 H. Marcuse, *Eros and Civilisat on* (Boston 1955).

6 Jacques Ellul, *La Technique ou L'enjeu du Siecle* (Paris 1954) (English edn 1965).

7 Wolfgang Fischer, conversation.

8 Cf E. P. Thompson *The Making of the English Working Class* (Penguin ed. 1968), p. 211.

9 Wolfgang Fischer, conversation.

10 A. Smith, *The Wealth of Nations* (ed. E. Cannon, 1961), p. 8.

11 Hegel, *Jenenser Realphilosophie* 1803–4 (herausgegeben von J. Hoffmeister, (Leipzig 1932), p. 239.

12 Wolfgang Fischer, conversation.

13 *Das Kapital*, p. 537; *Capital* vol. 1, p. 462.

14 Marx *Kapital*, vol. 3, p. 147; cf. *Capital*, vol. 3, p. 431.

15 Letter to David Hume, 4 August 1766.

16 Karl Löwith, *From Hegel to Nietzsche* (New York 1964), p. 431 note 18.

17 Keith Thomas, 'Work and Leisure in Pre-Industrial Society', *Past and Present* No. 29 (1964), p. 56; cf. F. D. Klingender, *Art and the Industrial Revolution* (edited by A. Elton, revised edn 1968), p. 56.

18 Peter Burke, discussion on K. Thomas in *Past and Present*, No. 29 (1964), p. 65.

19 K. Thomas in *Past and Present*, No. 29 (1964).

20 Quoted in Karl Löwith, *From Hegel to Nietzsche*, p. 274.

21 Klingender, *Art and the Industrial Revolution*, pp. 58–60.

22 Cf. Isaiah Berlin, Preface to H. G. Schenk, *The Mind of the European Romantics* (Constable 1966).

23 Quoted in Karl Löwith, *From Hegel to Nietzsche* (New York 1964,) p. 288.

24 Löwith, *From Hegel to Nietzsche*, p. 288. Another modern commentator has echoed this thought, recalling Aristotle's epitaph on his predecessors: that while the Athenians knew what to do in peace 'the Spartans remained secure as long as they were at war; they collapsed as soon as they acquired an empire. They did not know how to use the leisure that peace brought.' Aristotle, *Politics*, vol. 2, 1271b, quoted in Sebastian de Grazia, *Of Time, Work and Leisure* (New York 1962), p. 9.

Chapter Five

1 *Exherpte aus Paris* (referred to here as EH), in *Marx-Engels Gesamtausgabe* (Berlin 1932) (MEGA), ed. V. Adoratskij, Abteilung I, band 3, pp. 411–583, and *Ökoniscje-Philosophische Manuskripte aus dem Jahre 1844* (■PM), in MEGA, pp. 33–172 and 389–596. English versions of both works exist in Lloyd D. Easton and Kurt H. Guddat (E & G) (editors and translators), *Writings of the Young Marx on Philosophy and Society* (New York 1967). This particualr passage ■PM MEGA 1/3, p. 156 cf. E & G, p. 321. The English versions given here are broadly those of the translators referred to, with slight variations: some for the sake of consistency within this book— for instance 'estrangement' for *Entfremdung* and 'supersession' for *Aufhebung*—and some for the sake of greater literalness. References are given both to a German and to an English edition and when interpretations are disputed, the German text is quoted below.

2 'Maschinerie und Grosse Industrie', in K. Marx, *Kapital* ed.

H. J. Lieber and S. Kautsky (Stuttgart 1962), 3 vols (henceforward referred to as K. 1, 2, 3), vol. 1, pp. 423–592.

The English versions here are from *Capital*, vol. I (referred to as C. 1) translated by Moore and Aveling, edited by Engels, London, 1887 and from vols 2 and 3, (C. 2 and C. 3) translated by Untermann Chicago, vol. 2, 1919, based on the 2nd German edition, and vol. 3, 1909, based on the 1st German edition.

³ K. Marx, *Grundrisse der Kritik der Politischer Ökonomoie (Rohentwurf) 1857–58, Anhang 1850–59* (Berlin 1953), selection translated in D. McLellan, *Marx's Grundrisse* (Macmillan (1971). Cf. *Marx's Notes on Machines* (trans. B. Brewster, 1968), from *Grundrisse*, pp. 582–94, with introduction by A. Barnett.

⁴ McLellan, *Marx's Grundrisse* (1971) Introduction.

⁵ Critique of Hegel's Philosophy of the State, 1843; cf. E & G, *Writings*, p. 176.

⁶ From *Zur Judenfrage: Bruno Bauer: Die Föhigkeit der heutigen Juden und Christen, frei zu werden* (1843), MEGA 1/1, pp. 605–6; cf, E & G, p. 248.

⁷ EH MEGA 1/3, p. 536, cf., E & G, *Writings*, p. 271.

⁸ EH MEGA 1/3, pp. 544–5; cf, E & G, pp. 277–80.

⁹ EH MEGA 1/3, pp. 544–5; cf, E & G, pp. 277–80.

¹⁰ EH MEGA 1/3, pp. 544–5; cf, E & G, pp. 277–80.

¹¹ PM MEGA 1/3, p. 89; cf, E & G, p. 295.

¹² *Das Kapital* (Stuttgart 1962), vol. I, p. 779; cf. *Capital* (1887), vol. I, p. 661.

¹³ K. I., pp. 514–5, C. I., vol. 1, pp. 442–3.

¹⁴ K. I. p. 540, C. I, p. 465.

¹⁵ Cf. E. P. Thompson *The Making of the English Working Class* (Penguin Edition, 1968), p. 288.

¹⁶ *Die Deutsche Ideologie*, in MEGA 1/5, p. 22; cf. E & G, *Writings*, p. 424.

¹⁷ Marx, *Grundrisse*.

¹⁸ '. . .die „Ruhe" erscheint als der adäquate Zustand, als indetisch mit „Freiheit" und „Gluck". . .Dass das Individuum. . .das Bedürfnis einer normalen Portion von Arbeit hat, und von Aufhebung der Ruhe, scheint A. Smith ganz fernzuliegen . . . Dass (diese) ■berwindung von Hindernisse an sich Betatigung der Freiheit . . . und dass ferner die äusseren Zwecke den Schein bloss äusserer Naturnotwendigkeit abgestreift erhalten und als Zwecke die das Individuum selbst erst setzt, gesetzt werden—also als

Selbstverwirklichung, Vergegenständlichung des Subjekts, daher reale Freiheit deren Aktion eben die Arbeit, ahnt A. Smith ebensowenig.' *Ibid.*, p. 515. Cf. McLellan, *Marx's Grundrisse, p. 124*, for a less cumbersome but slightly less literal translation.

[19] 'Wirklich freie Arbeiten, z.B. Komponieren, ist grade zugleich verdammtester Ernst, intensitivste Anstrengung.' Marx *Grundrisse*, p. 515; cf. McLellan, *Marx's Grundrisse*, p. 124.

[20] One modern commentator advances two quotations taken out of context that might purport to suggest this. Cf. R. Tucker, *Philosophy and Myth in Karl Marx*, Cambridge University Press (1961), p. 199, and *The Marxian Revolutionary Idea* (Allen & Unwin (1970), pp. 28–9. He implies that Marx is talking about men's activity after the revolution when he uses the word '*almost artistic*'—'*halbkünstlerisch*'—of labour. But Marx's use of this term refers to the work of makers of machinery not after the communist revolution but in the early days of industrialization: to men who impeded industrial expansion by the '*halbkünstlerisch*' nature of their activity. Secondly, he implies that for Marx a feeling of being a member of an orchestra is to be taken as in itself some kind of improvement in a factory worker's condition after the revolution. But this is not true. Marx's orchestral metaphor is thrown away in a discussion of the role of supervision in any form of mass production—not specifically a post-revolutionary one—and of its particular necessity in 'antagonistic' forms of production such as capitalism.

The actual quotation is from *Das Kapital*, vol. 3 (1962), p. 147; cf. *Capital*, vol. 3, (1909), p. 431.

If the orchestral image has any significance it applies at least as much, or more, to pre-revolutionary industry. It has been suggested that Stalin was a Marxist. The idea that Marx was a Stalinist is more unusual.

[21] 'Die Arbeit der materiellen Produktion kann diesen Charakter nur erhalten dadurch als.

1) ihr gesellschaftlicher Charakter gesetzt ist

2) dass sie wissenschaftliches Charakters, zugleich allgemeine Arbeit ist, nicht Anstrengung des Menschen als bestimmt dressierte Naturkraft, sondern als Subjekt das in dem Produktionsprozess nicht in bloss natürlicher naturwüchsiger Form, sondern als alle Naturkräfte regelnde Tätigkeit erscheint.' Marx, *Grundrisse*, p. 515; cf. McLellan, *Marx's Grundrisse*, p. 124.

[22] Marx, *Kapital* vol. 3, pp. 671–2; cf. *Capital*, vol. 3, pp. 954–5.

[23] Marx, *Grundrisse*, p. 599; cf. for this view also E. Mandel, *New Left Review*, No. 72 (March-April 1972), p. 107.

[24] Marx, *Kapital*, vol. I, p. 490, *Capital*, vol. I, p. 422.

[25] Marx, *Kapital* vol. I, p. 490; cf. *Capital*, vol. I, p. 423.

[26] Cf. V. I. Lenin, *Pravda* (April 1918); quoted in G. Friedmann, *Industrial Society* (1955), pp. 422–4. Cf. Charles S. Maier, 'Between Taylorism and Technology: European Ideologies and the Vision of Industrial Production in the 1920's', *Journal of Contemporary History*, vol. 5, no. 2 (1970), pp. 27–61.

[27] Blauner, *Alienation and Freedom*, p. 15.

Chapter 6

[1] *The Collected Works of William Morris, with an introduction by his daughter May Morris*, especially vol. 22, (Longmans Green 1914) and vol. 23, 1915; May Morriss, *William Morris, Artist, Writer, Socialist*, (Basil Blackwell 1936); Eugene D. Lemire (ed) *The Unpublished Lectures of William Morris*, (Detroit, Wayne State University Press, 1969). A complete list of Morris' platform appearances and of all the lectures, with the history of their publication, is given in Lemire's book, pp. 234–90 and pp. 291–322.
Compare also the biographies cited below by J. W. MacKail and E. P. Thompson; Philip Henderson's edition of the letters, and Morris works in the Nonesuch edition selected by G. G. D. Cole.

[2] Philip Henderson (ed) *The Letters of William Morris to his Family and Friends*, (Longmans Green 1950) (Letter to Mrs William Morris of 18 March 1884) p. 195.

[3] E. P. Thompson: *William Morris: Romantic to Revolutionary* (Lawrence and Wishart 1955).

[4] William Morris: 'How I became a Socialist' in *Justice*, 16 June 1894 reprinted in William Morris: *Stories in Prose, Stories in Verse, Shorter Poems, Lectures and Essays*, ed by G. D. H. Cole, (Nonesuch Press 1948 edition) p. 656.

[5] William Morris: Letter of 5 September 1883 to Andreas Scheu published in *The Socialist Review*, March 1929 and in *Letters* ed. Henderson p. 185.

[6] Letter to Stead, Editor of *The Pall Mall Gazette* 2 Feb 1886; quoted by May Morris: 'Note on my father's favourite reading books' in May Morris (ed) *The Collected Works of William Morris*, vol. 22

(Longmans Green 1915) p. xi. Also published in *Letters* ed. Henderson (p. 247) with the grouping given differently.

[7] 'How I Became a Socialist' in *Nonesuch*, Morris p. 657.

[8] See for example Raymond Williams, *Culture and Society 1780–1950*, (Chatto and Windus 1958).

[9] Williams, *Culture and Society*, p. 71.

[10] See particularly chapter 5 above.

[11] The Works of Thomas Carlyle, vol. 2, p. 233–5, cited in Williams, *Culture and Society*, pp. 72–3

[12] Carlyle, *Past and Present*, book 3, chapter 4, chapter 11; cited in Thompson, *Morris*, pp. 62 and 752.

[13] Peter Demetz, *Marx, Engels and the Poets*, (first German edition 1959) London and Chicago, 1967, pp. 34–6.

[14] Thomas Carlyle, *Past and Present*, book 3, chapter 9, cited in Thompson, *Morris*, p. 60.

[15] John Ruskin, 'The Squirrel Cage: English Servitude (1874) Letter 44 in *Fors Clavigera* from *The Works of John Ruskin*, (1874), pp. 172–7.

[16] Ruskin, 'The Whitethorn Blossom' Letter 5 (1871) in *Fors Clavigera*, (1874).

[17] Ruskin, *Praeterita*, (1886), p. 4.

[18] Ruskin 'The Mystery of Life and its Arts' (1868) in *Sesame and Lilies* (1871), pp. 156–7.

[19] John Ruskin 'Modern Manufacture and Design' in *The Two Paths*, (1878), pp. 104–5.

[20] John Ruskin, 'The Nature of Gothic', chap. 6 of *The Stones of Venice*, vol. 2, London, 1853, pp. 160, 171.

[21] *Stones of Venice*, vol. 2. p. 172.

[22] *Ibid.*, p. 161.

[23] *Ibid.*, p. 163.

[24] *Ibid.*, p. 169.

[25] 'Fontainebleau', from *Praeterita*, vol. 2 (1888) in John D. Rosenberg (ed) *The Genius of John Ruskin*, (Allen and Unwin 1964), p. 525.

[26] J. W. MacKail *The Life of William Morris*, (Longmans Green 1899), p. 46, quoting Canon Dixon, Morris' (and Gerard Manley Hopkins') friend.

[27] The man whom Shaw portrayed as John Tanner in his 'Don Juan', and who, Shaw says, when a young man, took his friend Disraeli a copy of *Das Kapital*, with the excited suggestion that he should found social policies on it.

[28] Walthamstow MSS, cited in Thompson, *Morris*, p. 67; he refers

the passage to *Capital* vol. 1 chap. 14, section 5, as a free translation from the French version.

29 Morris, *Letters* ed. Henderson (24 July 1884 to Robert Thompson) pp. 204–5.

30 See for example Morris' editorial in *Supplement* to *The Commonweal*, vol. 1, no. 4, p. 37, May 1885.

31 *Letters* (24 July 1884 to Robert Thompson) p. 207.

32 Morris in *The Commonweal*, vol. 3 No. 97 (19 Nobember 1887) pp. 369–70.

33 *Letters* ed. Henderson (1 January 1885 to Robert Thompson) pp. 228–9.

34 Cf. John Ruskin *The Storm Cloud of the Nineteenth Century*, Lecture 1, (1884), quoted in Rosenberg ed. *Ruskin*, p. 448.

35 *Letters* ed. Henderson (11 February 1878 to Jenny) p. 111 (23 February 1881 to his wife) p. 144 and (26 November 1884 to William Allingham) p. 216.

36 *Ibid.*, p. 174, 181, 194 and 198.

37 *Ibid.*, p. 190, 217.

38 *Ibid.*, (24 July 1884 to Robert Thompson) p. 206.

39 *Ibid.*, p. 228.

40 *Ibid.*, p. 307, p. 228.

41 William Morris 'Art and Labour' (1884) in Eugene D. Lemire (ed). *The Unpublished Lectures of William Morris*, Wayne State University Press (Detroit 1969), p. 118.

42 Thompson, *Morris*, p. 752.

43 *Letters* ed. Henderson (24 December 1884 to Mrs. Burne-Jones) p. 223.

44 Morris, (Nonesuch ed): pp. 517–37 'The Lesser Arts'. Morris' first lecture, delivered 12 April 1877 to the Trades Guild of Learning, London, published as a pamphlet 'The Decorative Arts: Their Relation to Modern Life and Progress' 1878 and republished in Morris, *Hopes and Fears for Art*, (Ellis and White 1882) Morris *Nonesuch* ed pp. 603–23 'Useful Work Versus Useless Toil': Lecture of 16 January 1884, published as a pamphlet 1885 and in Morris, *Signs of Change*, (Reeves and Turner 1888), pp. 151–73.

Morris Nonesuch ed. pp. 646–54 'A Factory as it Might Be' in *Justice* No. 18, (1884) published by the Twentieth Century Press, 1907; Morris, (Nonesuch ed.) pp. 588–602 *The Aims of Art*, (1887): a pamphlet published at The Commercial office reprinted in Morris, *Signs of Change*.

⁴⁵ Morris (Nonesuch ed.) p. 654.
⁴⁶ Morris (Nonesuch ed.) p. 649.
⁴⁷ Morris (Nonesuch ed.) p. 649.
⁴⁸ 'The Aims of Art', Morris, (Nonesuch ed.) p. 594.
⁴⁹ 'A Factory As It Might Be', Morris, (Nonesuch ed.) pp. 649–50.
⁵⁰ Morris, (Nonesuch ed.) p. 650.
⁵¹ Morris, (Nonesuch ed.) p. 650.
⁵² Morris, (Nonesuch ed.), p. 651.
⁵³ 'Useful Work Versus Useless Toil' Morris, (Nonesuch ed.) pp. 603–5.
⁵⁴ 'A Factory As It Might Be', Morris, (Nonesuch ed.) p. 648.
⁵⁵ Morris, (Nonesuch ed.) p. 653–4.
⁵⁶ 'How I Became A Socialist' Morris, (Nonesuch ed.) p. 659.

Chapter 7

¹ Quoted in William Morris: *On Art and Socialism*, selected with an introduction by Holbrook Jackson, (John Lehmann 1947), p. 11..
² Cf. A. J. Youngson, *Possibilities of Economic Progress*, (Cambridge University Press 1959), pp. 7ff.
³ G. Friedmann, *Industrial Society, The Emergence of the Human Problems of Automation*, (Paris 1947) New York, 1955, pp. 84ff.
⁴ Blauner, *Alienation and Freedom*, p. 2.
⁵ William Morris, *The Aims of Art*, in Morris, (Nonesuch ed.) p. 588.

Chapter 8

¹ Quoted by A. L. Lloyd in notes to *Jack of All Trades* (Caedmon Records, Lochrae Corporation, New York, 1961).
² Introduction to *English Folksongs of the Southern Appalachian Mountains*, (Oxford University Press 1932), quoted in Maud Karpeles, *Cecil Sharp, His Life and Work*, Routledge, 1967), p. 169.
³ Sharp, quoted in Karpeles, *Cecil Sharp*, p. 149.
⁴ Letter to Mrs Storrow, quoted in Karpeles, *Ibid.*, p. 153.
⁵ Cf. John Clare, *Selected Poems and Prose*, ed. Eric Robinson, and Geoffrey Summerfield, (Oxford U. Press 1967) p. 66.
⁶ Crabbe, *The Village*, (1783) London 1812, p. 5.
⁷ *Ibid.*, p. 9.
⁸ Stephen Duck, 'The Thresher's Labour' in *Poems of Several Subjects*, 7th ed., 1730. (Reprinted Swan Press, Chelsea, 1930).

[9] E. P. Thompson 'Time, Work and Industrial Discipline' in *Past and Present* No. 38, (1967) p. 62–3.

[10] Mary Collier: now a washerwoman at Petersfield in Hampshire, *The Woman's Labour: an Epistle to Mr Stepehn Duck; in Answer to his late Poem called the Thresher's Labour* (1739) quoted by E. P. Thompson in *Past and Present*, No. 38 p. 79.

[11] E. J. Hobsbawn, *Industry and Empire*, (Weidenfeld and Nicolson, 1968), p. 15.

[12] E. P. Thompson, and Eileen Yeo (eds) *The Unknown Mayhew*[9] *Selections from the Morning Chronicle 1849–1850* (Merlin Press 1971), pp. 112–15.

[13] E. P. Thompson in *Past and Present* (38) p. 70ff.

[14] Cf. R. W. Malcolmson, *Popular Recreations in English Society, 1700–1850*, (Cambridge University Press 1973).

[15] The Rev. J. Clayton, *Friendly Advice to the Poor*, Manchester 1755, quoted by Thompson in *Past and Present* (38) p. 76.

[16] Thompson in *Past and Present* (38) p. 91.

[17] Tom Burns, 'Public Good and Communication Control' in J. A. Halloran and M. Gurevitch (eds) *Broadcaster/Researcher Co-operation in Mass Communication Research*, (Leicester University Press 1971), pp. 138–9.

[18] George Sturt, *The Wheelwright's Shop*, (Cambridge University Press 1923), 1963 edition p. 16.

[19] Cf. Wright, *Habits and Customs*, pp. 112–6 and E. P. Thompson in *Past and Present*, (38) pp. 73–4. For the Docks see chap. 15 below.

[20] See chapter 18 below.

[21] Sturt, *Wheelwright's Shop*, p. 6.

[22] W. Cooke Taylor, *Notes on a Tour of the Manufacturing Districts of Lancashire*, 1842, p. 261, cited in R. Pike *Human Documents of the Industrial Revolution*. (George Allen and Unwin 1968) p. 204.

[23] William Wordsworth, *Poetical Works*, vol. 2 ed. E. de Selincourt, 2nd edn. (Oxford University Press 1952), p. 83, *Michael* lines 109–128; *Poetical Works*, 5, ed. E. de Selincourt and H. Darbishire, 2nd Edn (Oxford University Press 1949), p. 26, *The Excursion* Book 1, lines 513–34. I am grateful to Edward Thompson for pointing to the relevance of both these poems to the argument.

[24] E. P. Thompson, *English Working Class*, (Penguin 1968), p. 378.

[25] E. P. Thompson, *English Working Class*, p. 298.

[26] Cf. Frances Collier, *The Family Economy of the Working Classes in the Cotton Industry 1784–1833*, edited by F. S. Fitton, (Manchester

University Press 1964) pp. 6–7. At no period does it appear that high prices were common for the weaving of fustians, checks and smallwares, and it is doubtful whether those engaged upon the calicoes and coarse cloths, manufactured after the water-frame was introduced, ever received the high wages paid to the weaver of muslins and cambrics.'

[27] George Sturt, *The Wheelwright's Shop*, (Cambridge University Press 1923) cf. F. R. Leavis and Denys Thompson, *Culture and Environment, The Training of Critical Awareness*, (Chatto & Windus 1933), p. 87, 97; and F. R. and Q. D. Leavis, *Lectures in America*, (Chatto & Windus 1969), pp. 11–12, 20–21. Cf. also Alfred Williams description of Chiseldon foundry in

[28] Sturt, *The Wheelwright's Shop*, p. 17.

[29] Sturt, *The Wheelwright's Shop*, p. 12.

[30] Raymond Williams, *Culture and Society 1780–1950*, (Chatto and Windus 1958), pp. 259, 260, cf. Richard Wollheim 'The English Dream' in *The Spectator*, 10 March 1961, p. 334 and Paul Filmer 'The Literary Imagination and the Explanation of Socio-Cultural Change in Modern Britain' in *Archives Européenes de Sociologie*, vol. 10 (1969), pp. 271–91.

[31] Cf. P. Laslett Sturt *The World We Have Lost* London 1961.

[32] Williams, *Culture and Society* pp. 259–60. Cf. Sturt, *The Wheelwright's Shop*, p. 206 note to p. 55. 'I think people used to be happier then. They weren't so stuck up. There wasn't so much difference between classes, but 'twas more like a family'. This was the aunt's recollection in the 1880's of the celebration when a new waggon was finished in the 1820s.

[33] J. Fielden, *The Curse of the Factory System*, Halifax n.d. (1836). Cf. also Mrs Gaskell *North and South* and Mary Barton (1811).

[34] P. Gaskell, *Prospects of Industry*, (1835); cf. P. Gaskell, (Surgeon) *Artisans and Machinery*: *The Moral and Physical Conditions of Manufacturing Populations considered with reference to Mechanical Substitutes for Human Labour* (1836).

[35] Cf. Frances Collier *The Family Economy of the Working Classes in the Cotton Industry 1784–1833* edited by F. S. Fitton, (Manchester University Press 1964) p. 17.

[36] Neil Smelser, *Social Change in the Industrial Revolution*, (Chicago 1959).

[37] Herbert G. Gutman 'Work, Culture and Society' in *American Historical Review*, June 1973, pp. 531–87: a study of men and women

new to factory life in two periods of United States history, the years before 1843, and 1893–1917.

[38] Christopher Hill, Comments on Keith Thomas, 'Work and Leisure in Pre-Industrial Society', in *Past and Present*, No. 29 (1964), p. 63.

[39] E. P. Thompson, 'Time, Work-Discipline and Industrial Capitalism' in *Past and Present*, No. 38 (1967), pp. 81–86.

[40] E. J. Hobsbawn, *Industry and Empire*, pp. 66–7.

[41] Collier, ed. Fitton, *The Family Economy*, Appendix A, pp. 56, 55 'Indentures at Styal'.

[42] Cited by A. L. Lloyd in *Folksong in England*, (Lawrence and Wishart 1968) pp. 326–7.

[43] C. P. Snow, *The Two Cultures*, Reith Lectures, (BBC 1957).

[44] F. R. Leavis, 'Pluralism, Compassion and Social Hope', Lecture to the University of York (1970) in *The Human World*, No. 2, February 1971, pp. 30–1, reprinted in *Nor Shall my Sword, Essays in Pluralism, Compassion and Social Hope*, (Chatto and Windus 1972).

Chapter 9

[1] R. M. Hartwell: 'The Standard of Living Controversy', in R. M. Hartwell (ed) '*The Industrial Revolution*', (Basil Blackwell 1970) p. 170.

[2] R. Blauner, *Alienation and Freedom*, (Chicago 1964).

[3] Tom Burns: 'Public Good and Communication Control' in J. D. Halloran and M. Gurevitch (eds) *Broacaster/Researcher Co-operation in Mass Communication Research*: (Leicester University, Centre for Mass Communication Research, 1971), p. 135. For a shorter version of this, see Tom Burns, 'A Meaning in Everyday Life' in *New Society*, 25 May 1967.

[4] For example Risely Parish Register *Bedfordshire Parish Registers* 26 in the Bedfordshire Record Office, quoted by P. E. Razzell; 'Statistics and English Historical Sociology' in R. M. Hartwell ed. *The Industrial Revolution*, p. 120.

[5] Collier, *The Family Economy*, p. 6–7.

[6] Peter Matthias, *The First Industrial Nation*, (Methuen 1969) pp. 123, 122.

[7] See chapter 18 below.

[8] E. P. Thompson, letter to the author.

[9] E. J. Hobsbawn, Industry and Empire, pp. 14, 24.

[10] R. Baxter, *A Christian Directory*, (1673), and *The Law Book of the Crowley Ironworks* (1700) ed. M. W. Flinn, Surtees Society 167, 1957,

and British Museum Additional Manuscripts 34555, quoted in E. P. Thompson, 'Time, Work-Discipline and Industrial Capitalism' in *Past and Present* (38), 1967, pp. 87, 82–3.

[11] G. Sturt, *The Wheelwright's Shop*, pp. 17, 16.

[12] Bernard Mandeville, *The Fable of the Bees*, (3rd ed. vol. 1, 1724, vol. 2, 1729), cf. Mandeville *The Fable of the Bees* (ed.) F. B. Kaye (Oxford University Press 1924).

[13] Mandeville, *A Vindication of the Book*, in *The Fable*, p. 444.

[14] *The True Meaning of the Fable of the Bees*, (1726).

[15] Mandeville, *The Fable*, 1, p. 357.

[16] Cf. A. Hayek, in *Proceedings of the British Academy*, vol. 52, 1966, pp. 123–41.

Chapter 10

[1] John Bayley, *The Characters of Love*, (Chatto and Windus 1960). The source is E. P. Brenton, *The Naval History of Great Britain 1783–1822*, (1823–5).) Asked whether he thought the song was sung ironically, John Bayley writes in a letter: 'Captain Brenton had commanded a seventy-four (the 'Ajax' I think) and one of his anecdotes is of a party of sailors singing this song 'Hearts of Oak' which the marine band was playing on board. Brenton says in his naïve way how touching it was to hear the tars trolling out the ditty —we know from another page how 70 per cent of his ship's company had been pressed, and I put two and two together, assuming the gallant captain hadn't, and that he was very likely right in assuming his gallant tars hadn't either. But it is always possible that they *had*, and sang the song in the spirit of trench humour (Hush, here comes a whizzbang etc). But from what one reads of the strange life on those ships, their petitions etc. I don't think so. They seem to have intensely valued any kind of 'higher sentiment'—patriotism, wooden walls of old England etc. as much as or *more than* the lubberly civilians, and this I find remarkable, because it is so unlike today or yesterday.'

[2] Cf. R. Dubin, 'Industrial Workers' Worlds. A Study of the Central Life Interest of Industrial Workers', in *Social Problems* 3, 1956, pp. 131–42.

[3] Friedrich Engels, *The Condition of the Working Class in England in 1844* edited and translated by W. M. Henderson & W. H. Chaloner, (Basil Blackwell 1958), pp. 133–4.

[4] (Thomas Wright): *Some Habits and Customs of the Working Classes*, by 'A Journeyman Engineer' (1867). Other working men's autobiographies of this period include Samuel Bamford: *Passages in the Life of a Radical*, (Heywood 1841), and *Early Days*, (Simpkin Marshall 1849); Alexander Somerville, *The Autobiography of a Working Man* (1848); James Myles, *Chapters in the Life of a Dundee Factory Boy, written by himself* (1850); C. M. Smith *The Working Man's Way in the World, being the Autobiography of a Journeyman Printer* (W. & N .Cash, n.d. *1853*); William Lovett, *Life and Struggles in Pursuit of Bread, Knowledge and Freedom*, (Turner 1876) William Thom, *Rhymes and Recollections of a Hand-Loom Weaver*, (Paisley 1880); James Burn, *The Autobiography of a Beggar Boy* (1882); 'An Old Potter', *When I Was a Child* (with an introduction by R. S. Watson, Methuen 1903); Tom Mann, *Memoirs*, (Labour Publishing Co. 1923), T. Barclay, *Memoirs and Medleys, Autobiography of a Bottle Washer*, (Edgar Backins 1934); and another book, not an autobiography but a tract against drinking, John Dunlop, *The Philosophy of Artificial and Compulsory Drinking Usages in Great Britain and Ireland*, 6th edition (1839), which reveals much about the life of the period.
I am grateful to Edward and Dorothy Thompson for making several of these known to me and for showing me copies from their own collection.

[5] Wright, *Habits and Customs*, pp. 83–4.

[6] *Ibid., p. 111*.

[7] *Parliamentary Papers* 1833, vol. 20, D. i, p. 35 quoted in E. Royston Pike, *Human Documents of the Industrial Revolution*, (Allen and Unwin 1966), p. 244; which also quotes the texts referred to in notes 8 (p. 225), 13 (pp. 253–5), and 14 (p. 275–86) below.

[8] *Parliamentary Papers* 1833, vol. 20, 76–7.

[9] Michael Argyle, *The Social Psychology of Work*, (1972), chapter 6.

[10] Marx, *Das Kapital*, 1, p. 543, *Capital*, 1, p. 468.

[11] Engels, *Condition*, p. 127.

[12] *Ibid.*, p. 127.

[13] Richard Ayton, *A Voyage round Great Br. tain undertaken in the Summer of 1813* (1814), vol. 2, pp. 155–60; *Parliamentary Papers* 1842, *vol. 16*, 24, 196.

[14] *Parliamentary Papers* 1843, vol 15, p. 949; *Parliamentary Papers* 1843, vol. 15, Q.65.

15 Mayhew, '1851, or the Adventure of Mr and Mrs Sandboys, who came to see the Great Exhibition'. Quoted C. T. Harvie, Graham Martin and Aaron Sharf, *Industrialisation and Culture 1830–1914*, (Open University Press 1970).

16 Angus McIntyre mentions in a letter, for example, the contrast between the rapidity with which the Mines Act of 1843 went through Parliament, and the two long battles on the Factory Acts; though, as he adds, this was no doubt partly due to a special sense of the intolerability of employing women and children underground.

17 Frank Darvall, *Popular Disturbances and Public Order in Regency England*, (1934) reprinted with a new introduction by Angus McIntyre, (Oxford 1969), chaps. 12–16; E. P. Thompson, *The Making of the English Working Class*, (Penguin 1968) p. 211; E. J. Hobsbawm, 'The Machine Breakers' in *Past and Present*, No. 1, Feb. 1952 p. 67, reprinted in *Labouring Men: Studies in the History of Labour*, (Weidenfeld and Nicolson 1964); E. J. Hobsbawm and G. Rudé: *Captain Swing*. (Lawrence and Wishart 1969).

18 'Like heaven, the drifters steam after sail! a fisherman in Charles Parker, Ewan MacColl and Peggy Seeger *Singing the Fishing*, (BBC Radio 16 August 1960) and Philip Donnellan, *Shoals of Herring*, (BBC TV 1972).

19 *Black Dwarf*, 30 September 1818, quoted in E. P. Thompson, *The Making of the English Working Class*, pp. 218–21.

20 'I think much of the evidence shows at least in the Midlands hosiery and lace industries, that the poor products of the machines were hated as much as, and probably more than, the machines themselves', Angus MacIntyre, letter. Cf. eg. William Felkin, *History of the Machine-Wrought Hosiery and Lace Manufacturies* (1867) new edn., ed. with introduction by S. D. Chapman, 1967, pp. 41–62, cited in Darvall, ed. MacIntyre, *Popular Disturbances*, p. x.

21 Augus MacIntyre, in Darvalled MacIntryre, *Popular Disturbances*, p. xi.

22 Hobsbawm, *Labouring Men*, pp. 7–10.

23 Darvall ed. MacIntyre, *Popular Disturbances*, xi pp. 118, 204ff.

24 Thomas Cooper, *Some Information Respecting America*, (1794) pp. 77–8 quoted by E. P. Thompson *The Making of the English Working Class*, p. 379.

25 For a stress on this interpretation of Blake's poems, see e.g. J. Bronowski: *William Blake and the Age of Revolution*, (Routledge 1972),

Chapter 11

[1] A. L. Lloyd, *Folksong in England*, (Lawrence and Wishart 1967) p. 523.

[2] Cf. *Ibid.*, p. 319.

[3]. *Ibid*, pp. 320–1.

'A characteristic early instance of the erotic imagery of the industrial age. First printed on a broadside by Swindells of Manchester in 1804, and subsequently re-issued over and over again by Shelmordine (1818) and other northwestern printers.'

[4] Lloyd, *Folksong*, p. 319.

[5] From Peggy Seeger & Ewan MacColl ed. *The Singing Island*, (1960) where the original pronunciation is given.

[6] Collected and sung by Ewan MacColl; printed in Alasdair Clayre, ed. *A Hundred Folksongs and New Songs*, (Wolfe 1968).

[7] 'Call the Horse, Marrow', from Lloyd, *Folksong*, p. 336. When John Berger and Nuala O'Faolain made a documentary film about the mines at Bakewell in Derbyshire—'*Zola's Germinal*, BBC Open University 1973—they showed it to the miners first and asked if they agreed with the picture it presented. The miners said they did, except for one thing: it showed nothing of the enjoyment they had in their work. Again, in Philip Donnellan's documentary *Death of a Miner*, BBC TV, one younger member of the Elliott family says that their father was always joking about his work. A. L. Lloyd comments in a letter, however, that miners' tales, as opposed to songs, may give more evidence of another feeling: fear.

[8] 'The Recruited Collier', collected by A. L. Lloyd from Jim Huxtable of Workington, and printed in his collection, *Come All Ye Bold Miners*, (Lawrence and Wishart) cf. Clayre *A Hundred Folksongs*, p. 22.

[9] 'Jone O'Grinfilt Junior' from John Harland (ed) *Ballads and Songs of Lancashire* (1865), pp. 223–7. Cf. A. L. Lloyd, *Folksong*, and Seeger and MacColl *The Singing Island* for variants. Samuel Bamford (*Walks* p. 169) says the original *Jone O'Grinfilt* was the most popular song in Lancashire. Harland writes that this particular version was taken down from the singing of an old hand-loom weaver at Droylsden. It was written just after the battle of Waterloo when times were bad and hand-loom weavers' wages fell from about £3 to a guinea or 25s a week. He adds incidentally 'i.e. for three or four days work; for then weavers could seldom be induced to 'buckle to' on Monday, Tuesday, or often Wednesday; these days being devoted to recreations procured with high wages'.

[10] 'Poverty Knock', Recorded by A. E. Green in 1965 from an old Batley Weaver, Tom Daniel, quoted in Lloyd *Folksong* p. 328. 'Guttle' means eat.

The weavers of the south eastern United States can match such images of monotony:

> 'Weaver's life is like an engine
> Comin' down that mountain steep'

sang Jimmy Tarleton with Tom Darby in a *Weaver's Blues*:

> 'And at night we cannot sleep'

he goes on, and:

> 'Very oft we'll take the headache
> When our looms are runnin' bad
> When we frown and snatch the lever . . .'

[11] *Letters to Young Persons on Progress in Pudsey*, (Stanningley 1887), p. 30, quoted by E. P. Thompson, *The Making of the English Working Class* p. 318.

[12] 'Jute Mill Song', by Mrs Mary Brooksbank of Dundee. Printed in Seeger & MacColl, *Singing Island*, and Clayre *A Hundred Folksongs*. p. 150.

[13] Robert Blauner, *Alienation and Freedom*, (Chicago 1964).

[14] 'Drumdelgie' sung by Davy Stewart of Dundee, verses 1, 2, 3, *The Folk Songs of Britain*, vol. 3, 'Jack of All Trades' (Caedmon Records, Lochrae Corporation, New York 1961).

[15] 'Off to Sea Once More' sung by Ted Howard, collected by A. L. Lloyd, printed in Seeger & MacColl eds, *Singing Island*.

[16] 'The Bonnie Ship The Diamond', collected by A. L. Lloyd. Sung by Tich Cowdray, in Liverpool, 1937. Printed in Seeger & MacColl eds, *Singing Island*, pp. 58–9, verses 1–4.

[17] From 'Jim The Carter Lad', sung by Jack Goodfellow, Rennington, Northumberland; recorded by Peter Kennedy, 'Jack of All Trades', *The Folk Songs of Britain*, vol. 3, (Caedmon Records, Lochrae Corporation, New York, 1961).

[18] 'The Merry Haymakers', from the singing of Bob and Ron Copper of Rottingdean, Sussex, recorded by Peter Kennedy; 'Jack of All Trades', (Caedmon Records, Lochrae Corporation, New York 1961).

[19] A. L. Lloyd comments in a letter:

> The factors that determined the persistence
> of idyllic country songs among certain rural
> communities are complex . . . As Kodaly found

in twentieth century Hungary . . . the more
prosperous villagers might well consider deep
folk song altogether too 'ignorant' for them,
and they'd fancy something reflecting a finer,
perhaps less realistic outlook. Between poor
and prosperous, a whole spectrum of colouring
would exist, as far as songs were concerned.
Somewhere along that spectrum, the idyllic
songs of the *Haymakers* kind occupy a space,
perhaps notably among the more
book-affected singers of the fatter Southern
counties.

[20] For the question of clock time *cf.*, E. P. Thompson 'Time, Work and Industrial Discipline', in *Past and Present*, (1967), no. 38, pp. 56–97 and chapter 9 above.

Chapter 12

[1] Tolstoy, *Anna Karenina*, translated by Rosemary Edmunds, (Penguin 1954), pp. 271, 272, 273, 276, 297, 344, 345.

Chapter 13

[1] S. de Grazia, *Of Time, Work and Leisure*, (New York, Twentieth Century Fund 1962) chapter 1.

[2] St Benedict, *Rule for Monasteries*, translated from the Latin by Leonard J. Doyle, (Collegeville, Minnesota n.d. p. 68).

[3] Thomas More, *Utopia*, in H. Morley (ed.) *Ideal Commonwealths* (1889) p. 155.

[4] Keith Thomas 'Work and Leisure in Pre-Industrial Society', in *Past and Present*, 29 (1964) p. 54 cf also W. G. Hoskins 'The Midland Peasant'

[5] cf. Georges Rudé '*The Crowd in the French Revolution*' quoted by Tom Burns, 'A Meaning in Everyday Life' in *New Society*, 25 May 1967.

[6] Joan Thirsk in *Past and Present*, 29, p. 63.

[7] Francis D. Klingender, *Art and the Industrial Revolution* (1947) edited by A. Elton, revised edition London 1968, p. 56; Andrée Andrieux et Jean Lignon *L'Ouvrier d'Aujourd'hui*, (Paris 1960), p. 56.

[8] Keith Thomas in *Past and Present*, 29, p. 55.

[9] John Larner, 'The Artist and the Intellectuals in Fourteenth Century Italy', in *History*, vol. 54, 1969, pp. 22–3.

10 M. I. Finley 'Aristotle and Economic Analysis', in *Past and Present*, No. 47, May 1970, pp. 24, 22.

11 *Ibid.* p. 25.

12 Klingender, *Art and the Industrial Revolution*, p. 55.

13 G. Glotz, *Ancient Greece at Work* (Paris 1920) London, 1926, pp. 266–7.

14 Xenophon *Cyropaedia* VIII 2, 4, 5 cited in Alison Burford, *Craftsmen in Greek and Roman Society*, (Thames and Hudson 1972) pp. 61, 96.

15 Finley, in *Past and Present*, 47, p. 14.

16 Glotz, *Ancient Greece at Work*, p. 338; Burford, *Craftsmen* pp. 138–9, notes from *Inscriptiones Graecae* I², 374 that among the six groups of masons who fluted the columns of the Erechtheion those that included free men were paid less over the 36–7 day period than the slave or metic groups, who were however paid at the same rate for a day's work. Slaves who worked independently had to pay over a portion of their earnings to their masters (p. 45); their maintenance therefore was not necessarily cheaper than that of free men (p. 59). It is possible that even though 'wages were never high', free men had a margin within which they did not need to work all the time. Dr Burford infers that they supplemented their pay with other work, but the evidence appears to be incomplete.

17 Burford, *Craftsmen*, p. 79, cf. Ruskin, *The Stones of Venice*, vol. 2 (1853) p. 159.

18 Burford, *Craftsmen*, p. 43; Glotz, *Ancient Greece at Work*, pp. 316–20.

19 R. P. Fortune; G. Morechand; E. E. Evans-Pritchard; A. R. Radcliffe-Brown; quoted in Willard Trask, *The Unwritten Song*, (Jonathan Cape 1969) vol. 1, pp. xiv, xiii, xvi.

20 L. T. Hobhouse, G. C. Wheeler & M. Ginsberg, *The Material Culture and Social Inst'tutions of the Simpler Peoples* (1915, reprinted 1965).

21 Trask, *Unwritten Song*, vol. 1, pp. 108–9.

22 Trask, *Unwritten Song*, vol. 1, p. 55.

23 C. M. Bowra, *Primitive Song*, (Weidenfeld and Nicolson 1962) p. 108.

24 Bowra, *Primitive Song*, p. 124.

25 A. L. Lloyd, *Work, Magic & Folksong*, (BBC Radio) Broacdast for the Open University, 1971.

26 Lloyd, *Work, Magic and Folksong*.

27 Quoted in Bowra, *Pr m tive Song*, p. 45.

[28] Trask, *Unwritten Song*, Vol. 1, p. 12.

[29] Bowra, *Primitive Song*, pp. 44–5.

[30] Trask, *Unwritten Song*, vol. 1, p. 200.

[31] Charles Darwin, *A Naturalist's Voyage round the World in HMS Beagle* (1839) (Oxford University Press 1930), p. 218.

[32] Adriano Tilgher, *Work: What it has meant to men through the ages* (*Homo Faber*), (Harrap 1931) pp. 19–21.

Chapter 14

[1] Cf. Alasdair Clayre, *A Gentle Easy-Flowing River*, Documentary with songs, (BBC Radio 1965). The names of people speaking are fictitious.

Chapter 15

[1] Some of the words quoted here were included in Alasdair Clayre, *Spring is here, now we can go out together*, (BBC radio 1967), The names of people speaking continue to be fictitious.

Chapter 16

[1] H. L. Wilensky 'Work, Careers and Social Integration' *International Social Science Journal* 1960, vol 12, pp. 543–60, especially p. 544.

[2] S. R. Parker, *The Future of Work and Leisure*, (MacGibbon & Kee 1971).

[3] Cf. Jeremy Tunstall, *The Fishermen*, (MacGibbon & Kee 1962).

[4] Cf. Roger Mansfield, 'Need Satisfaction and Need Importance In and Out of Work', *Studies in Personnel Psychology*, October 1972, vol. 4, no. 2, pp. 21–7. This study deals with managers, who, according to Parker's scheme might in any case be expected to display the pattern that Mansfield finds. Such results cannot necessarily be generalized to people in other forms of work.

[5] Cf. A. J. Youngson *Possibilities of Economic Progress* (Cambridge University Press 1959), pp. 7ff.

Chapter 17.

[1] Alasdair Clayre, *Factory*, Documentary with songs, with David Kennard, musical director Peggy Seeger, produced by Charles Parker, (BBC Radio 1965). All names are fictitious.

Chapter 18

[1] E. Hobsbawm, *The Age of Revolution* (Weidenfeld and Nicolson

1962), ch. 2, cf. E. P. Thompson, *The Making of the English Working Class*, pp. 210–11.

2 Cf. J. C. Flugel *L'appétit vient en mangeant: Some Reflections on the Self-sustaining Tendencies*, British Journal of Psychology 38 pp. 171–90; W. Baldamus, *Efficiency and Effort*, (Tavistock Publications) 1961, pp. 59–62; A. N. Turner and A. L. Miclette 'Sources of Satisfaction in Repetitive Work', *Occupational Psychology*, 36, (1962) pp. 215–31.

3 Among surveys which list evidence about the characteristics frequently found in 'satisfying' forms of work, are S. R. Parker, R. K. Brown, J. Child and M. A. Smith, *The Sociology of Industry* (Allen & Unwin 1967), especially chap. 13; Michael Argyle, *The Social Psychology of Work*, (1972) and, less recently, F. Herzberg, S. Mausner, R. Peterson and D. Capwell, *Job Attitudes, Review of Research and Opinion*, (Pittsburg 1957).

4 From Alasdair Clayre, *Spring is Here, Now we can go out together*, Documentary with songs, (BBC Radio 1967).

5 Argyle, *Social Psychology of Work*, ch. 1.

6 Robert Blauner, *Alienation and Freedom*, (Chicago 1964) p. 30, p. 203.

7 John H. Goldthorpe, David Lockwood, Frank Bechhofer and Jennifer Platt, *The Affluent Worker: (1) Industrial Attitudes and Behaviour*, (Cambridge University Press 1968; and *The Affluent Worker (3) in the Class Structure*, (Cambridge University Press) 1969.

8 Goldthorpe and others, *Industrial Attitudes*, p. 182.

9 From Alasdair Clayre, *Work and Change: 2 'Mass Production'* (BBC radio 1969).

10 David Wilson, 'Saab's Experiment Pays Off' in The *Observer*, 15 October 1972.

11 Cf. Turner and Miclette in *Occupational Psychology* 36, pp. 215–23.

12 Andrew Leigh, *Human Beings Matter*, The *Observer*, 4 May 1969; cf. J. van der Does de Willebois, editor, *Work-Structuring, 1963–8* N. V. Philips (Gloeilampenfabrieken, Holland 1969).

13 Blauner, *Alienation and Freedom*, p. 29.

14 Daniel Vidal 'Un Cas de Faux Concept: La Notion d'Aliénation' in *Sociologie du Travail*, 11 (1969) especially pp. 67–9; cf. Daniel Vidal, 'L'Aliénation: structure du nonsens', in *Sociologie du Travail*, 9, (1967) 2, pp. 185–90, and cf. D. D. Dean, 'Alienation: Its Meaning and Measurement' in *American Sociological Review*, 26, October 1961.

15 M. Seeman 'On the Meaning of Alienation' in *American Sociological Review*, 26 (1959) pp. 783–91. For a defence by Seeman of his own concept see M. Seeman 'Quatre Problèmes concernant l'Aliénation:

vers un "nouveau" débat' in *Sociologie du Travail*, 9 (1967) No. 2,
pp. 202–9.

[16] Steven Lukes 'Alienation and Anomie' in P. Laslett and W. G.
Runciman (eds): *Philosophy, Politics and Society, Third Series*, (Basil
Blackwell 1969).

[17] Blauner, *Alienation and Freedom*, p. 15 n.

[18] Blauner, *Alienation and Freedom*, p. 182 n.

[19] Gerald I. Susman 'Process Design, Automation and Worker
Alienation' in *Industrial Relations* (Berkeley) vol. 3 (1) Feb. 1972,
pp. 34–45.

Chapter 19

[1] Alasdair Clayre, *Modern Times* (forthcoming).

[2] Alasdair Clayre' 'Imagination and Labour' in *New University*,
Summer 1961, reprinted in *Works Mamagement*, April 1962.

[3] 'Brussels call to end assembly line work throughout the EEC'
The Times, 21 April 1973, p. 3.